CW00969504

The Militancy of British Miners

BY THE SAME AUTHOR
Power in Trade Unions (Longmans, 1954)
Trade Union Leadership (Longmans, 1957)
Trade Unions and the Government (Longmans, 1960)
Militant Trade Unionism (Merlin Press, 1966)
International Bibliography of Trade Unionism (Merlin Press and Maspero, 1968)
The Sociology of Industrial Relations (Longmans, 1971)
Social Analysis: A Marxist Critique and Alternative (Longman, 1975)

The Militancy
of
British Miners

V. L. ALLEN

THE MOOR PRESS

Published by
The Moor Press,
Bank House,
Baildon Green,
Shipley, BD17 5JA.

First published 1981

ISBN 0 907698 00 X Cased
ISBN 0 907698 01 8 Paper

Printed and bound by The Scolar Press Limited
Ilkley, West Yorkshire.

*In recognition of the vision, the
commitment and the selfless endeavour of
Sammy Taylor, Jock Kane, Bill McLean, Dai
Francis and Jack Dunn who have now either sadly
departed or retired. Their achievements cannot be
forgotten or erased for they are being lived out
through the experiences of men and women.*

CONTENTS

ILLUSTRATIONS

ACKNOWLEDGEMENTS

The photographs in this book are published through the courtesy of people and institutions. Some of the photographs are valuable historical records of mining conditions. None, however, depicts the worst conditions for, in the main, these were not photographed. It was very difficult for photographs to be taken in and around pits without the consent of employers or managers, who, understandably, wanted to show things in their best light.

I wish to thank the following for permission to reproduce their photographs: Photo. Science Museum, London, for permission to reproduce the photographs of two paintings by Gilbert Dakin on pages 3 and 91; Mrs. R.J. Short for permission to reproduce three of her late husband's photographs on pages 21, 35, 93; Cliff Williams, author of *The Derbyshire Miners 1880-1980: A Pictorial History*, for photograhs on pages, 28, 31, 27, 43, 46, 49, 52, 72, 73, 96, 97, 98, 147, 149, 150, 151, 262; Mrs. F. Horsley, Derbyshire, pages 45, 47, 51; Bertien van Manen, Amsterdam, pages 16, 33, 80, 81, 82, 83, 261; The South Wales Miners' Library, Swansea, pages 7, 120; Roy J. Sabine, Barnsley, page 196; Photocraft, Dunfermline, page 193; National Coal Board, Yorkshire Area, page 138; National Coal Board, Western Area, page 54; National Coal Board, North Derbyshire Area, page 99; National Coal Board, Archives Centre, Mansfield, pages 76, 77, 78 (these photographs originally appeared in the "Annual Report of the Miners Welfare Committee,"1938); National Union of Mineworkers, Scottish Area, pages 123, 129, 227. "Miners" by Wilfred Owen has been selected from *The Collected Poems of Wilfred Owen;* edited by C. Day Lewis.

xiv

BIBLIOGRAPHY

There are few footnote references in this book for two reasons. First, the data in much of the book does not have a precise, recognizable source to which reference can be given for it results from more than two decades of experience with miners, their families and their Union. Some of this data belongs to specific historical events and cannot be replicated or verified. In such cases, my ability as a research worker has to be taken on trust. Other data can only be verified by going into the coalfields, down the pits, into the miners' homes and into their Union offices. I have recorded what I have seen and heard.

Secondly, I have tried to avoid footnote references because they tend to interrupt the narrative flow and make the book more difficult to read. For this reason there may be occasional instances where readers think I should have provided references but where I have decided otherwise. In the main, however, where I have used quotations I have given sources.

The information I have acquired through experience is backed by published and unpublished material from the National Union of Mineworkers and from published material from the National Coal Board. The statistics have been drawn from the Annual Reports of the Union, the National Coal Board, the Chief Inspector of Mines and Quarries and from the Department of Employment Gazette.

There is a slowly growing literature about the coal industry and mining trade unionism to which readers can refer if they wish to broaden their knowledge and deepen their understanding.

There are useful bibliographies in *The British Coalmining Industry 1870-1946* by M.W. Kirby, 1977, pages 209-214; *The British Coalmining Industry* by A.R. Griffin, 1977, pages 210-216 and *Wages Policy in the British Coalmining Industry* by L.J. Handy, 1981, pages 304-307. These bibliographies contain references to the official and semi-official Government reports which have been issued about coalmining and to articles on relevant subjects which have appeared in academic journals.

Those who want a comprehensive bibliography of mining trade unionism can find it in the pages of the *Bulletin* of the Society for the Study of Labour History which, since its first issue in 1960, has published detailed up-to-date lists of works on the subject. This *Bulletin*, along with its sister publication *Llafur*, the Journal of the Society for the Study of Welsh Labour History, and publications of the Scottish Labour History Society, contain articles, references and reviews about mining trade unionism. In *Llafur*, Spring, 1979, there is a bibliography of the coal industry in Wales. *History Workshop*, a twice yearly journal for socialist historians also occasionally carries articles about mining trade unionism.

The following is a short list of accessible books which are useful as either background or follow-up reading. There is as yet no comprehensive history of the coal mining industry which reaches contemporary times. *The British Coalmining Industry 1870-1946*, by M.W. Kirby, 1977, is both readable and informative. *The British Coalmining Industry. Retrospect and prospect* by A.R. Griffin, 1977, covers a wide historial period necessarily superficially but with useful information and references. A picture of the economic history of coalmining since nationalization can be obtained from *Wages Policy in the British Coalmining Industry* by L.J. Handy, 1981. This book was originally a doctoral thesis and is not easily read. It can best serve as a source book. Another useful work for background data about the coal industry is *Pay and Productivity Bargaining* by R.G. Searle-Barnes, 1969. This book is primarily about the Nottinghamshire Coalfield.

Information about the actual working conditions in coalmining is less readily available. Malcolm Pitt gives a first-hand description of coal-getting in the first part of his book *The World on our Backs. The Kent Miners and the 1972 Strike*, 1979. Pitt is a working miner in the Kent coalfield. And although *Coal is our Life* by N. Dennis, F. Henriques and C. Slaughter, 1956, is dated it remains a graphic description of mining conditions. The miners' environment in Northern France in the 1880s as it is described in *Germinal* by Emil Zola and in South Wales in the inter-war years as in *Cymardy* and *We live* by Lewis Jones, 1939, is mainly of historical interest but these novels provide insights into coalmining which non-fiction generally lacks and should be read. A readable history of health and safety in mining is contained in *The Evolution of Health and Safety in Mines* by Sir Andrew Bryan, 1975, a former Chief Inspector of Mines and Quarries. This evolution occured against a long catalogue of deaths caused by disasters which are described in *Great Pit Disasters: Great Britain 1700 to the present day* by Helen and Baron F. Duckham, 1973. Difficulties associated with the negotiation of wages, piecework and day-wage systems and the application of wages agreements, including the National Power Loading Agreement are described by L.J. Handy and R.G. Searle-Barnes in their books mentioned above.

The function of the household in coal mining, the position of the women in the household and their part in the process of collective action by miners have been barely recorded, inadequately researched and only superficially analyzed. Until the emergence of the Women's Liberation Movement in the 1970s households and women were either largley ignored as being of little consequence or misinterpreted. *Coal is our Life* by Dennis, Henriques and Slaughter, 1956, contains sections on leisure and the family but, reflecting the prevailing views of the time, it failed to analyze them as production relations. During the last decade increasing attention has been given by social scientists to households and women but it remains difficult to direct readers to specific texts. *Hidden from History* by Sheila Rowbotham, 1973, and *Beyond the Fragments. Feminism and the making of Socialism* by Sheila Rowbotham, Lynne Segal and Hilary Wainwright, 1979, make substantial basic reading. Another such book is *One hand Tied Behind Us. The Rise of the Women's Suffrage Movement* by Jill Liddington and Jill Norris, 1978. *Dutiful Daughters*, edited by Jean McCrindle and Sheila Rowbotham, 1977, relates the essential life histories of a group of women, including Janet Daly, the mother of Lawrence Daly, General Secretary of the N.U.M. Women were employed as surface workers, in particular coalfields, long after they were excluded from undergrond work. An account of these "pit brow lassies," as they were called, has now been given by Angela V. John in *By the Sweat of their brow: Women Workers at Victorian Coal Mines*, 1980. They are also shown in *Victorian Working Women. Portraits from Life* by Michael Hiley, 1979. Women surface workers are not, however, a Victorian phenomenon. The last such women left the pits in 1972.

Those who wish to learn something about the lives of miners' leaders should read the autobiographies of Arthur Horner, *Incorrigible Rebel*, 1960, Abe Moffat, *My Life with the Miners*, 1965, and Will Paynter, *My Generation*, 1972. These comprise one political spectrum. There are no books by any of the right wing leaders of the National Union of Mineworkers. Earlier miners' leaders such as Thomas Burt, Robert Smillie, Peter Lee and Herbert Smith have been written about but in a not very informative way. Autobiographies, often written with the assistance of journalists, are not the best means for interpreting and conveying the tasks and problems of union leadership. There is no work of analysis about union leadership. In order to learn about the way management sees the situation then read *Ten Year Stint* by Lord Robens, 1972. This is a highly personal account of the 1960s by the former Chairman of the National Coal Board.

Mining trade unionism has been better served by writers than have the structure and conditions of the coal industry. There are now national and regional histories. Readers should consult the four volumes of the official history of the Miners' Federation of Great Britain by Robin Page Arnot, covering the period from its formation in 1889 until 1947 by which year the National Union of Mineworkers had been formed and the coal industry had been nationalized. The volumes are: *The Miners, 1889-1910*, 1945; *The Miners: Years of Struggle, 1910-1930*, 1953; *The Miners in Crisis and War, from 1930 onwards*, 1961 and *The Miners. One Union, One Industry*, 1979. These books concentrate on institutions and are largely descriptive. The earlier ones are the best. There is no history as yet of the National Union of Mineworkers since the nation-alization of the coal industry in 1947.

There are regional histories for Northumberland and Durham, Yorkshire, Scotland, Lancashire and Cheshire, Nottinghamshire, South Wales and Derbyshire. Derbyshire has been well served with by far the most comprehensive, though much too large history, *The Derbyshire Miners* by J.E. Williams, 1962 and a fascinating centenary pictorial history by Cliff Williams, 1980. A similar, though less systematic pictorial representation of some aspects of the Yorkshire miners' history is to be found in *The Yorkshire Miners in Camera* by Robert G. Neville, 1975. Although Robin Page Arnot has written two volumes of the history of the South Wales Miners' Federation covering the period from 1898 to 1926 and published in 1967 and 1975, they have been superceded by *The Fed. A history of the South Wales Miners in the twentieth century* by Hywel Francis and David Smith, 1980. *The Fed* examines miners in their changing economic and political environment with great understanding. Most of the new works deal with earlier periods, such as the *Independent Collier,* a collection of essays edited by Royden Harrison, 1978 and *Militant Miners* edited by Ian McDougall, 1981. The *Independent Collier* contains essays covering a variety of mining situations in the nine-teenth century. *Militant Miners* consists of the recollections of John McArthur, a Scottish miners' leader from the 1920s to the 1960s, and the letters of David Proudfoot to G. Allen Hutt, The first section is a high quality example of oral history.

There are, of course, many miners who are a part of the contem-porary history of the National Union of Mineworkers and whose oral recollections also need to be recorded. Many of the same people possess the records of branches which are essential for contemporary history writing. It is important, I believe, that miners should not regard history as something which is presented to them in books but should locate it in their own experiences, contribute wherever possible to recording it and see themselves as historians. In this way we shall achieve a history of the miners which effectively blends together the experiences of people with those of their union into social, economic and political processes.

MINERS

There was whispering in my hearth,
  A sigh of the coal,
Grown wistful of a former earth
  It might recall.

I listened for a tale of leaves
  And smothered ferns;
Frond-forests; and the low, sly lives
  Before the fawns.

My fire might show steam-phantoms simmer
  From Time's old cauldron,
Before the birds made nests in summer,
  Or men had children.

But the coals were murmuring of their mine,
  And moans down there
Of boys that slept wry sleep, and men
  Writhing for air.

And I saw white bones in the cinder-shard.
  Bones without number;
For many hearts with coal are charred
  And few remember.

I thought of some who worked dark pits
  Of war, and died
Digging the rock where Death reputes
  Peace lies indeed.

Comforted years will sit soft-chaired
  In rooms of amber;
The years will stretch their hands, well-cheered
  By our lives' ember.

The centuries will burn rich loads
  With which we groaned,
Whose warmth shall lull their dreaming lids
  While songs are crooned.
But they will not dream of us poor lads
  Lost in the ground.

Wilfred Owen, 1918

CHAPTER 1

COAL

The place of coal in the history of the world in general and Britain in particular is unquestionably assured. The industrial revolution in the eighteenth and nineteenth centuries was based on coal. The technological changes which gave capitalism its dynamism, which made it a viable economic and social system, occurred because coal was available in plentiful supplies. It did not have to be invented. Nor did its use have to be discovered. Coal was dug from outcrops possibly before Roman Britain. In medieval times there were out-croppings and shallow drift mines. The production of coal increased as it gradually displaced wood and by the 17th century there were extensive workings, particularly in the North East of England from whence coal was exported by sea to London. Thus when steam power was invented there was already a basis for a coal industry to supply the fuel to displace charcoal and to enable technological developments to proceed and spread.

The coal industry expanded almost continuously from the middle of the eighteenth century until after the First World War. The expansion depended upon overcoming technological barriers to make deep-mining possible and on improving transport facilities to get inland coal to markets. It was not until the railway network was laid after the second half of the nineteenth century that inland coalfields were able to be opened up on the scale of the coastal Durham and Northumberland ones.

Coal was historically vital in all respects for Britain. It was an indigenous fuel, available in large quantities. It was technologically relatively simple to exploit as a source of power. It was an export commodity. When the First World War broke out it constituted 10 per cent of the value of Britain's export trade. It was a major employer of labour. One and a quarter million workers were employed in coal mining in 1920, amounting to about 10 per cent of the total male labour force. British capitalism developed and, on its own terms, flourished through plentiful supplies of cheap coal.

Coal, however, does not exist simply as an historical pheno-menon. There were politicians, industrialists and trade unionists during the 1960s who believed that that was its place. They were proved wrong by the international fuel crisis of the 1970s. Now only economic blindness will prevent the effective exploitation of coal for the development of British industry. Unfortunately, as I write, there are signs of such blindness amongst politicians.

The factors which made coal a vital commodity in British industry also relate to its future. Coal is the earth's most plentiful energy resource. It has been estimated that 90 per cent of the world's

1

reserves of fossil fuel comprises coal. Britain, in particular, is well endowed with this hydro-carbon energy source. Although we have worked coal seams intensively for more than 100 years there are reserves for at least another 100 years with the present methods of exploitation. If the methods are improved to enable thin seams to be exploited and to gain access to hitherto inaccessible seams then there should be enough coal for hundreds of years more. Its quality as an indigenous fuel is as vital now as it ever was, though for different reasons.

If coal remains as an indispensible commodity for the future of the British economy then what about those who produce it, the coal miners? Are they not equally indispensible? If they are then how should they be treated? The answer is provided by the history of coal mining. The indispensibility of coal never resulted in preferential treatment being given to miners. Their status was low and their rewards minimal. They obtained improvements in their treatment only through industrial and political struggle. Miners long ago learned that there was no correlation between the importance of the commodity they produced and the rewards given to producers. This is a general feature of free market economies. So long as British capitalism survives, then, coal miners will have to struggle for their sustenance.

From a painting by Gilbert Dakin, a miner from Yorkshire, who spent most of his working life at Warsop Main Colliery in Derbyshire. This painting was completed between 1934 and 1936.

CHAPTER 2

IDENTIFICATION

Images

Coal mining evokes popular images of hard, unrefined men, distinct and separate from other workers, hewing in mysterious dungeons of coal; of dirty, strange men, in some ways frightening and for this reason repellent, yet attractive because they are masculine and sensuous. The fascination they generate is based largely on apprehension but it acknowledges a grudging respect for survival against physical odds. The images, of course, have some basis in fact but they owe much to folklore, as well as imagination, and are protected from scrutiny by the fact that the reality of mining is hidden, except to those who descend pit shafts. Even the social lives of miners tend to be insulated through geographical isolation, though there is less of this nowadays than hitherto.

The power of miners, however, does not lurk behind images; it is real, there for everyone to see and experience, resting on the importance of coal as a source of energy. This power may fluctuate as the relevance of coal in the economy fluctuates and it may be misrepresented but only so long as coal is supplied. When supplies cease because miners stop extracting coal the effects are obviously, painfully visible and become a part of real-life experience.

There is a contradiction here for when miners strike those who suffer from it, and even those who do not, look to their images for explanations. They contrast the real with the imagined, not with ordinary men with wives and children, motivated by simple aspirations but struggling vainly in harsh, unrelenting conditions to achieve these. This is no one's fault for how can people without experience of mining ever know its pressures, the violence it commits on people. And if they do not know these how can they understand what produces cohesion, determination and militancy or, indeed, what does not produce these characteristics.

The problem is that in the main people really know only their own situations which they approach with greater perception and understanding than those of others, though people may misinterpret even their own activities. We are always far more glib about other people than we are about ourselves. We scrutinize and rationalize what we are doing as individuals or groups and use a completely different set of values to judge others. How do we overcome this schizophrenic approach so that we can understand other people's behaviour as we understand our own?

The issue is one which in the first place concerns social scientists and authors who provide and publish information and analyses about different social situations. If what they write and publish lacks

4

understanding then this will be communicated to the readers. The false images or fantasies about other people will not be destroyed. There are real obstacles in the way of obtaining information and processing it in a manner which relates to the experience of people. They are especially formidable in matters concerning the working class, particularly socially insulated groups in it such as miners.

One difficulty is that most social investigators and authors tend to be middle class intellectuals with views and attitudes which are a barrier to communication. They do not talk the same language as the people they are studying and their attitudes and emphases differ. But what is perhaps more important is that because they are middle class or intellectuals they are not given the opportunity to communicate. This question of communication, of course, is not confined to people from different social classes for it exists when men are investigating women, white persons are studying blacks and adults are questioning children. Whenever there are marked differences of experience there are likely to be problems of communication.

These are not, however, insuperable. It is possible to gain insights into the situation of others so as to avoid major misinterpretation at least, by identifying with others in a close and sympathetic manner. This identification has to be seen and believed. It has, therefore, to be serious and consistent. It cannot be put on for the occasion. It is a most difficult social research problem because it is rarely recognized as such. Social scientists just breeze into situations as if they have a prescribed right of entry. This is their first and major mistake. If they do not attempt to overcome it then nothing worthwhile can come from their work.

Commitment

For the last 20 years I have identified myself with the causes of miners in an increasingly complex manner. I know what identification involves and how it encompasses one's political commitment as well as social attitudes and common interests and how it is articulated in one's whole analytical approach to social questions. But this book is not a product of my identification. My object has been to work with miners and never, until recently, to write a book about them. The book is a by-product of my experiences with miners. Perhaps it is better for penetrating the imagery and exposing the reality of mining for that.

During my contact with British miners I have seen how they responded to changes in the material conditions of extracting coal either by adjustment to them or by resistance. This process was not a mechanical, automatic one for throughout the miners were influenced in their assessment of the changes by competing, alternative ideas and explanations about them. When they

5

acquiesced in the changes it was largely because the prevailing explanations which urged them to do so were dominant. When they resisted they were influenced by a campaign to convince them that they should not be passive recipients of change but should try to control their own destinies. There was a perpetual interaction between ideas about mining conditions and experiences of it.

I have witnessed this process of struggle to alter the consciousness of miners to the point where they acted to initiate their own cure and I have recorded its progress and setbacks. My position in relation to British miners has been in some ways unique. I have not had a formal relationship with the National Union of Mineworkers. Mine has been informal, stemming from friendships and close political affinities. I always felt, and still feel, that it was a privilege to be drawn into a close circle of tough, committed, intellectual miners, as one of them. It was a demanding commitment, sometimes an emotionally exhausting one, but it added a dimension to my existence which has been, and still is positive, purposeful and rewarding.

It was Ernest Jones, the then president of the National Union of Mineworkers, who introduced me to the N.U.M.'s new general secretary, Will Paynter, in 1959. We became friends and I saw much of him at his office in Euston Road, London, and at conferences. I knew many union leaders but Paynter was the first one I had met who combined leadership qualities with a humility and sympathy in his personal relationships. It was impossible not to admire him from the outset.

Through Will Paynter I attended the Annual Conferences of the N.U.M. from 1960 and became involved in discussions about the mining industry, the N.U.M. and the Government, with officials and miners who identified themselves with him. These were always informal, social, rather small affairs and through them I developed close relationships which encouraged and facilitated open exchanges. There was one particular occasion during the 1963 meeting of the T.U.C. when Paynter, Bill Whitehead, the president of the South Wales Area, Bert Wynn, the secretary of the Derbyshire Area and I, met in a Brighton public house and had a most depressing conversation about the absence of any spirit of protest in the N.U.M. The Union was compliant in its relations with the N.C.B. and appeared set on a course of contraction without exercising any influence over its direction or pace. It played no part in the wider movement.

Will Paynter was contained by a National Executive Committee which disagreed with him on almost all issues. He was frequently compelled as a spokesman for the Union to speak to policies with which he disagreed. His natural inclination was to criticize and rebel but his commitment to union solidarity forced him to act as the agent for consensus. He had no opportunity at that T.U.C. to use his exceptional talents. It was as if he was an observer just as I was,

6

Will Paynter, General Secretary of the N.U.M., 1959-68 at the South Wales Miners'
Gala, 1964. Paynter was previously President of the South Wales Area, N.U.M.,
1951-59.

with no access to the decision-making councils and no opportunity to influence opinion from the rostrum. He was excluded from membership of the T.U.C. General Council because of his membership of the Communist Party, although the N.U.M. nominated him until he refused to be set up to be turned down. Paynter did become a member of the General Council between the 1960 and 1961 Congresses when he replaced a sitting member who had died but he was displaced by the 1961 Congress because the main unions refused to support him for political reasons. As he stated in his autobiography, *My Generation,* "I got on by accident but was put off by design." Both Bill Whitehead and Bert Wynn who sat with us were talented union leaders who, though they had scope for some initiative in their respective Areas, were frustrated at national level. The significance of the T.U.C. in 1963 was that it was a convenient place to meet and talk. That evening nothing we did or said penetrated the mood of gloom and pessimism so we decided to meet again informally but with a purpose, and to invite others.

We met again at the Derbyshire miners' convalescent home in Skegness on 11th October, 1963 at the invitation of Bert Wynn. Alex Moffat, the president of the Scottish Area, had been invited but he refused to attend. The only additional person was John Hughes from Ruskin College who was present in the same advisory role as myself. There we drafted a pamphlet called *A Plan for the Miners* which set out policies for the next decade over a range of issues facing the mining industry and miners. When the draft was completed we held a fairly large representative weekend meeting at the end of November, 1963, at Wortley Hall, near Sheffield to prepare it for publication. Our discussions there were dominated by unresolved criticisms of the draft but as it was important to extend the debate to a wider circle of miners the pamphlet was published in time to become the focus of official union attention at the 1964 Annual Conference of the N.U.M.

My personal contacts with Paynter and Whitehead continued and developed whilst the wider discussions were taking place. I went to West Africa in the Spring of 1964, however, before the pamphlet was published and stayed there for one year. When I returned I attended two further meetings convened by Bert Wynn but with changed compositions. With the pamphlet completed and with no other specific objective before us we became merely a discussion group and lost whatever cohesion we had.

A Forum

A different grouping emerged in 1967 which had a largely new and more representative membership. The Scottish Area became effectively committed for the first time. Yorkshire, Kent and Lancashire miners joined in. Rank and file members participated along with full-time officials. This new group became a forum for exchanging ideas between Areas as well as between ordinary miners and full-time officials. It comprised members from all of the traditional militant Areas as well as militant members from other Areas. By the 1970s it had become an established but informal means for propagating ideas amongst miners. Because it did not arise out of the Union's constitutional provisions for policy-making its meetings were viewed by some as being clandestine, even subversive. The forum was not viewed in this way by its members. It avoided publicity but it was always openly held. Its membership sometimes changed at the periphery so that its activities became known to an increasing number of miners.

The forum quickly became involved in discussions, analyses and arguments about the manner in which miners and their Union had accepted the contraction of the mining industry and the consequential deterioration of relative wages and conditions without collective protest. What had become of the traditional militancy of the miners? Why had they behaved so much out of character? Why did they not strike against pit closures with the same alacrity as they had hitherto struck over wages and conditions of work in their individual pits? It was believed that conditions in the pits generated a militant attitude so why was it not being expressed? Might it have been because the experience of contraction depressed the miners or influenced the organization of the union? Perhaps the views of the miners were not being communicated through the union hierarchy because its organization was not democratic.

The forum's objective was to alter the way of life of miners by reminding them of what was possible. It was not its purpose to create strike situations. It would give a false impression, however, if I slipped into the conventional attitude towards strikes by playing down their significance and denigrating them. It was believed that if the miners were prepared to strike for improvements it would be a substantial indication that they were recovering from the demoralization which the contraction of coal mining had spread. In this sense strike action was seen as being a positive achievement. Strikes in our society are maligned. Even union leaders are apologetic about them. They do, of course, have negative aspects for they penalize and punish, and often the strikers themselves are the sufferers. But many other experiences, such as pit closures, unemployment, low wages also penalize and punish but they do not evoke the same kind of conventional hostility. The stigma rests on strike action because it challenges the rights of property. If the stigma is ignored strike action can be seen as an activity possessing dignity for it merges pride with defiance and evokes a sensation of solidarity. Its characteristics are reflected by the cliche "we are getting off our knees." Workers who strike do not perceive of themselves as supp-

9

licants or servants or hands but as people with rights and the power to obtain them. In terms of the values of a free society that should be a positive, praiseworthy characteristic.

The immediate intention of the forum was to create a debate amongst miners about their wages and conditions of work; to generate a critical faculty so that they would ask questions about who or what was responsible for their situation and reject fatalistic interpretations. It wanted miners to query explanations, to be disrespectful of ideas. In some measure it succeeded and great debates were conducted in the pits and in the Union.

The Wider Context

The attitudes of miners began to change in the wake of these debates but there was obviously not a direct one to one relationship between them. Many events occurred in Britain from the late 1960s which reflected an alteration in the consciousness of trade unionists in general and miners were a part of the events. Even if there had been no catalyst in their own ranks they could not have insulated themselves from the general movement. Trade unionists began to react to the Government's interventions in industrial relations. They put aside the constraining ethic which caused them to separate industrial from political action and which inhibited them from using their collective power for political purposes. Always in their history, with a brief exception in 1919 to 1920, unions had used the conventional political decision-making process to influence Government policy. They had retreated from situations where their actions, as in 1926, might have had constitutional implications. Yet when the Labour Government introduced its White Paper 'In Place of Strife' in 1968 with proposals to use legislation to control unofficial strike action a movement of collective protest developed during which hundreds of thousands of trade unionists showed their hostility by striking. The Government was compelled to drop its proposals.

The alteration in attitudes generated during this episode was emphasized and intensified by the trade union movement's campaign against the introduction and application of the Conservative Government's Industrial Relations Act between 1970 and 1974, culminating in an unprecedented successful negation of the Act. The miners formed a part of this campaign. Other momentous events in the trade union calendar occurred during the term of office of the Conservative Government which took office in 1970. The Upper Clyde Shipbuilders' dispute when shipyard workers occupied the yards and operated them in defiance of a decision to close them altered the Government's industrial 'lame duck' policy through which it refused to support ailing firms and left them to the fate of the market mechanism. After the U.C.S. dispute there were hundreds of 'work-ins' and 'sit-ins' to assert the right to work and question the rights of capital. The miners' strike in 1972 which destroyed the effectiveness of the Government's n-1 incomes policy and the 1974 miners' strike which ended Phase III of the Government's incomes policy and, indirectly, the life of the Government itself, have to be seen in this wider context. It is inconceivable that these strikes would have occurred in their precise form if the general climate had not been encouraging.

The Cost of Protest

The composition of the forum has changed largely through the death or retirement of its members. It possesses its third chairman. It still has a solid core of founding members from Kent, South Wales, Scotland and Yorkshire providing continuity between activities in different situations. These members have experienced the cost of protest. It is, of course, commonplace for activities and explanations which are critical of capitalism to be derided as propaganda, jargon, even subversion. This derision is transmitted through political speeches and comments in the press, radio and television. It is sometimes crude and stark whereas at other times it is subtle, almost unnoticed and presented with great expertise. For people in minority oppositional groups derision is a fact of life. They become accustomed to being stereotyped. Such people survive because of their intense belief in the validity of their protests. Some of the miners of whom I write possessed this quality in almost messianic proportions. They were aware, however, that if protest is rooted in the conditions of people's lives and reflects real grievances no amount of derision and intrigue can stifle it completely and for ever.

The protests which miners have engaged in since 1967 have been rooted in the reality of mining coal. It is, as I try to show, a harsh, uncompromising reality which makes few concessions to wage labour. Yet miners have always been ambivalent about it, wooed by the consensus-making forces in society to accept their lot while being jolted by the impact of experience. My association with miners brought me into close contact with that ambivalence and the processes which brought it about.

The book is intended primarily for miners. It is a continuation of the explanation and argument which have been conducted for the last 14 years in the pits of Britain. Its purpose is to help miners better understand their own reality. But it is also aimed for a wider public, for those people who on occasions have suffered from the impact of miner's protests and who, in consequence, have expressed opinions about miners aspirations but without any knowledge of the conditions which gave rise to them. It is important that people in general should be better informed about the causes of militancy, not in order to be able to contain it more effectively but to recognize its validity, its force and its inevitability. For those who do not need to be convinced about this factor the miners' experiences show the tenuousness of political conciousness and how readily it can be contained by the manipulation of procedures. Political awareness is a very fragile thing and it has to be handled with constant care and attention.

CHAPTER 3

UNCERTAINTY

Surviving under Private Ownership

British coal miners have always experienced the consequences of pit closures. It has been a common feature of mining activity to close pits in the older coalfields and in the older sections of newer coalfields as they exhausted their reserves or for some other reasons lost their profitability. In the main, until nationalization, the closures were fragmentary, occurring in an *ad hoc* manner, a normal consequence of capitalist activity in an industry where geological conditions determine profitability more than anything else. For the same reason new pits were sunk, or old ones were extended into new or deeper coal seams.

This fragmentary character of pit closures appeared against a background of expansion until 1913, the peak production year of all time. The coal industry had been an expanding, dominating one since the invention of steam power. Coalfields had become bigger and more numerous until, in the year before the outbreak of the First World War, 287,430 tons of coal were produced by 1,127,900 miners from 3024 pits, Afterwards the industry declined, first, until 1920, in the number of pits being worked and the output from them, and then in manpower as well. The decline in the interwar years was accelerated and intensified by cyclical trade depressions. The giant industry with just more than one and a quarter million miners in 1920 lost more than a third of these and almost half of its pits by the beginning of the Second World War.

Random, unsystematic pit closures were a consequence, in large part, of the intense competition between numerous colliery owners of varying sizes, struggling to survive by any means, dog eating dog, remorselessly refusing to act rationally even in their own interests and declining advice from Governments to pursue amalgamation policies. In 1924, for instance, there were as many as 1,400 colliery companies owning 2,481 pits. Three hundred and twenty three of these pits produced 84 per cent of the total output leaving many owners in positions of economic insecurity.

Uncertainty entered the lives of miners in different ways. Once for all pit closures was one way. Another was partial and temporary closure resulting in indecently high unemployment levels. The coal industry was hit particularly hard in the inter-war years. Almost one quarter of all insured mineworkers were wholly unemployed in 1934. This was an average figure. In Wales the miners' unemployment rate was 35 per cent. Some miners there barely entered a pit yard in twenty years. Even the coalfields with the lowest level of unemployment still had almost 10 per cent on the dole.

A Miners' Row, 150 years old, at Newcraighall, Scotland.

Behind these figures lay a multiplicity of personal problems, of deprivation and family tragedy, unrecorded except in the minds of men and women, and in the memoirs of a few, like Arthur Horner, Will Paynter and Abe Moffatt who from their positions as miners' leaders had the facility to write and the notoriety to be read. It is difficult, however, to describe the violence of poverty for it is degrading, humiliating and debilitating. What the poor cannot articulate the historians, with few exceptions, cannot record. Like women, the poor are hidden from history.

There was uncertainty in the very process of mining coal, reflected in the high accident and disease rates. The rate of human depreciation was high. Its incidence was certain but rarely anticipated. Men who worked in the mines were prepared by that very fact to risk the uncertainties relating to their health to obtain a wage. The denial of a regular, consistent right to work was a denial of the means of subsistence upon which families depended for their existence. This was seen to be more important than the continued health of individual miners.

Yet for miners in the inter-war years uncertainty relating to work was as much an integral part of their social situation as that relating to their health. The probability of unemployment was so high that no miner could be sure that he was insulated from it. Those whose labour power was not required at all in the mining industry had to seek other work and in most cases it was in other areas. The geographical isolation of many collieries meant that there were few alternative job opportunities for miners. Where there was alternative work it was usually effected by the same cynical alternations in trade as mining. In North Staffordshire miners could alternate between the coal industry and the pottery industry but in the inter-war years both were depressed. In North and South Wales the steel industry existed as a source of alternative employment, but the steel industry could not utilize its own labour force. In Scotland the steel and shipbuilding industries were depressed along with mining.

Miners were involved then in a multiplicity of decisions centred on themselves and their immediate families about their present and their future lives. Given the prevalence of uncertainty about continuing in a job every miner was forced to ask himself questions about staying or moving but then had answers imposed on him by the industrial and social context of his life. Some miners were forced to move by the sheer necessity of survival but others were forced to stay for the same reasons. They were in a painful contradiction, without reasonable alternative courses of action. How could miners move if there were no jobs to move to, no houses cheap enough to live in and no money to pay for the transportation of their families and belongings. But equally how could they stay at home if there was no work, no possibility of it in the foreseeable future and no

A Miners' Row, New Sharlston, Yorkshire.

escape from the blanket of despair that descended on unemployed people.

It was a problem for any miner to achieve self-respect, to maintain an integrity, to have a belief in the future, under such conditions of harsh, uncompromising reality. Surviving meant making ends meet today and leaving tomorrow to look after itself. Such people could not afford the luxury of planning beyond a week. Living for today became a way of life.

Discrimination

There were miners who were exceptions but they faced additional uncertainties. The miners were collectively weak, especially after the General Strike and miners' lockout in 1926. Unemployment was a great weakener of trade unions but defeat in conflict in a situation of unemployment was worse. The united power of the Miners' Federation of Great Britain was broken in 1926 and county unions had to struggle divided and isolated. Employers freely victimized active trade unionists; they issued blacklists and circularized them between coalfields. Communist miners were especially vulnerable. They were never sure of their jobs but they did maintain their integrity.

After 1926 Jock Kane, who later became a miners' leader, tramped from Scotland to Yorkshire before he could get a job. Many blacklisted miners went to the newish Kent coalfield under assumed names in order to get work. Both Abe and Alex Moffat, successive presidents of the Scottish miners, were dismissed as checkweighers by the Fife Coal Company in 1929 because they engaged in strike action.

Abe Moffat was never employed by the Fife Coal Company again. Will Paynter also became a checkweighman in 1929 at the Cymer colliery in South Wales. His tenure came to an end in January 1931 due to his part in a three week strike there. Paynter was taken to court by the colliery company for breaching the 1860 Checkweighman's Act which stipulated that a checkweighman must not interfere with the management of a colliery. Organizing a strike was, of course, regarded as such interference. Paynter was unemployed for most of the 1930s. The fate of Jock Kane, Abe Moffat, Alex Moffat and Will Paynter was that of thousands of other miners after 1926.

The attempts by the coalowners to protect their markets and to preserve their profits, immediately and inevitably affected labour costs for, in the mining industry, these constituted two-thirds of the total costs of production. There were constant pressures to reduce wages, to increase working hours, to intensify effort and to neglect working conditions. Life for miners with work in the 1930s was very little better than for those who were without it. When a miner

17

turned up at the pit he never could be sure that things would be the same as they were when he was there last.

The exercise of the owners' power to manipulate and exploit the labour power of miners led them to attack the miners' unions which were the only means the miners had of countering and containing oppressive uncertainties. Coal owners did this continually from the beginnings of coal mining and hampered and delayed the creation of durable mining unions for at least a century. In coalfields west of the Pennines it was almost the end of the nineteenth century before they were fully established. From then the miners' unions, established on a county basis and federated in the Miners' Federation of Great Britain, resisted the pressures of employers. They used different methods to achieve their ends reflecting degrees of collaboration with the coalowners. There were national strikes in 1912, 1920, 1921 and 1926. After the defeat of 1926, however, the power of employers was greatly enhanced. District agreements were imposed and the county unions were separated and isolated from each other. The coal-owners were able to pick the county unions off from each other for special undermining, destructive attention.

The most blatantly arrogant and hostile attempt to undermine trade unionism was the creation of company unions, formed by employers for their own interests, financed by them and staffed by their nominees. Company or yellow-dog unions were common in American trade union history but less so in Britain. Here they have usually been confined to banks, insurance companies and managerial grades in private industry. After the 1926 lock-out, however, coal-owners set up the Nottinghamshire and District Miners' Industrial Union with the connivance of a Nottingham miners' leader, George Spencer. It was a sign of their confidence and arrogance. They could, they believed, do anything. Coal owners elsewhere encouraged Spencerism, as it was called. It spread to South Wales, where it had many branches, Northumberland, Durham and Scotland where it made a brief appearance at the Lochgelly Iron and Coal Company in Fife in the winter of 1929.

The campaign against company unionism created dissention in some coalfields, resulted in violence and caused a number of miners to be sent to prison. It lasted a decade before the coal-owners were compelled to recognise only the county unions affiliated to the Miners' Federation of Great Britain. The culmination came in 1936 when a dispute over union recognition occurred in Harworth Colliery in Nottingham.

When the Harworth miners were on strike they were harrassed by the police, some were evicted from their homes, their leaders were arrested. Their chairman, Mick Kane, whose brother Jock figures prominently in the main events in this book, was arrested with 16 others and, after the end of the strike which lasted for 6 months, was sentenced to 2 years' imprisonment with hard labour. Ten of the others went to prison for shorter terms.

The Harworth dispute focussed attention on company unionism. South Wales miners organized sit-in strikes while the South Wales Federation pressed the M.F.G.B. for national action. But the Nottingham coal-owners who had had a tame union for 10 years did not give in easily. One of them, a Captain Muschamp, advocated the "German idea," which was the Nazi manner of dealing with unions. Pressure from the membership culminated in a national ballot for strike action in which four fifths of the M.F.G.B. membership voted in favour. Under the threat of a national strike, with pressure from Parliament, the issue was settled in May, 1937 through an amalgamation between the Nottingham Miners' Association and the Nottingham and District Industrial Union. At the same time the Spencer union was eliminated from the South Wales coalfield. From 1937 the British miners were able to concentrate on consolidating and amalgamating their own unions.

Company unionism left its impact. Will Paynter commented in his memoirs that the "menace of company unionism was stamped out but the strife it caused within communities lasted many years." One particular consequence was non-unionism. Even where coalowners did not actively encourage Spencerism to spread they were not sympathetic to trade unionism. Even to admit membership of a trade union was sufficient in some cases to invite victimization. Non-unionism was specially prevalent in the Powell Duffryn Combine which owned many pits in the centre of the South Wales coalfield. In Durham its extent could be gauged by the sharp increase in recruitment to the union in 1937. The Durham Miners' Association increased its membership by 35 between 1935 and 1936 but by 2,500 in the following year. In Scotland it was estimated that 30 per cent of the miners were still non-unionists by 1938. This problem for the unions was slowly eradicated though in some coalfields not until after Nationalization.

Despite the strife which company unionism created, perpetuated by the long collective memory of miners, and the extent of nonunionism indicating a 'plague on both houses' attitude, the county unions, even the collaborative ones such as in Scotland, had a close social and industrial identity with miners and their families. In order to undermine the county unions the coal-owners had to destroy this social involvement in the lives of miners in general and they failed. Will Paynter describes some of his work as a miners' agent in the South Wales Rhymney valley in his autobiography *My Generation*. The South Wales Miners' Federation, he wrote, "was a lot more than a trade union; it was a social institution providing through its local leaders an all-round service of advice and assistance to the mining community on most of the problems that could arise between the cradle and the grave . . . The leaders of the local miners' lodges were very much more than representatives dealing with problems of wages and conditions of employment in the mines. They were acknowledged social leaders called upon to help and advise in all kinds of domestic and social problems . . . I can, in a limited way, testify to the truth of this from my own experience as a miners' agent . . . I was a sort of professional letter-writer especially in the village where I lived. Harrassed wives who had fallen behind in hire-purchase instalments on some household goods, or had accumulated arrears of rent or any other kind of debt, would require letters to be sent appealing for a stay of action by the firms involved. Many times have I appeared in the local court to testify as to the character of a man or child who had fallen foul of the law . . ." (p.110). Other officials of the county unions were involved in some degree in community work.

Consequences of War

The characteristics of high unemployment: low and irregular earnings, poverty and social dislocation which dominated the lives of miners in the inter-war years were altered by the impact of the Second World War and its economic consequences. From 1940 until 1946 the market for coal moved out of reverse as the demand for coal exceeded the industry's capacity to supply it. The industry, however, was in no fit state to cope with the demands made of it. It had been neglected, rundown, every bit of profit had been extracted from it. There had been little new investment of any kind in the industry in the interwar years. New reserves could not, of course, be tapped quickly or easily. Extra output could only be obtained by exploiting existing resources more intensively and this meant working miners harder. Unfortunately for the Government, production fell in the first years of the war. Many miners quickly escaped from the industry by volunteering for the armed forces; others were conscripted. By 1941 the mining labour force had declined and with it fell total production. To counter this the Government intervened, employed Emergency Powers and assumed control of coal production.

The consequences of the war situation for miners were contradictory. Their real wages rose absolutely and in relation to other groups of workers. They had no fear of losing their jobs. Indeed after the Essential Work Order was applied in May 1941 miners had guaranteed work and guaranteed wages. They had stability of employment but instability in employment. As far as possible, without actual re-organisation and rationalization, production was concentrated in the most efficient pits. The possibility of miners having to move between pits increased. Some also had to travel increasingly long distances to work, as for example in Lanarkshire where some miners had to travel 20 miles to their pits. On the other

20

Coal picking at Darfield Main Colliery, Yorkshire, in the 1930s.

hand, the ability of miners to move voluntarily from one pit to another because, say, of dissatisfaction with working conditions, was severely curtailed by the Essential Work Order. By the same regulations the disciplinary powers of colliery managers was increased and overall, over-riding authority was placed with Government officials. The inevitable war-time emphasis on short-term production gains caused a deterioration in working conditions as managers infringed work practices designed to make work easier. Managers tried to prevent early lousing, made men clear up faces before they left them, compelled them to undertake extra work when a member of a team was absent and generally made small but irritating demands on the workers which sometimes caused a loss of earnings.

Two developments occurred during the war which in a sense transcended the unpleasantness and irritations of everyday life in the pits. The two were related in that they arose out of the same environmental conditions. One was the creation of a single union for mineworkers. The other was the introduction of Government control of coal production leading up to Nationalization. Both of these factors interacted with the lives of miners but slowly and not always obviously.

One Union for Miners

There had frequently been discussions amongst miners about the desirability of amalgamating the county unions into a single entity but the conditions had not favoured its fulfilment. The county unions were autonomous, like little kingdoms, deeply conscious of their identity, jealous of their traditions and suspicious of each other. When the amalgamation took place in 1944 there were 36 county unions. There had been many more. Just before the amalgamation six county unions in Scotland had merged to form the National Union of Scottish Mineworkers. Most of the coalfield based unions were formed in the second half of the nineteenth century. The earliest, the South Yorkshire Miners' Association was formed in 1858, followed by the Northumberland Miners' Mutual Confident Association and the South Staffordshire and East Worcester Amalgamated Miners in 1863, the North Staffordshire Miners' Federation and the Durham Miners' Association in 1869, the Fife and Kinross Miners in 1870 and the Cumberland Miners' Association in 1872. The South Wales Federation was not formed until 1898. There had been many unsuccessful attempts to form unions before these permanent organizations were established. They had emerged out of conditions of intense struggle and bitterness and of recrimination by coal owners. In some instances even the counties were divided and district unions were formed.

Although the coalfields were physically isolated and the workers in them tended to be insular and chauvinistic, it was not inevitable that trade unionism in mining should have been organized on a county basis. The unions were formed after the establishment of the railway system and after the coal markets had become national in scope. The coalfields possessed many divisive factors, including competitiveness, but the unifying ones were strong. The pattern of county unions was, in fact, preferred by coal-owners as the least threatening form. On two occasions the owners imposed their will to support the pattern. The first was in the period 1868-1875 and the second was in 1926.

The Amalgamated Association of Miners

A loose alliance of county and district unions was created in 1863 in the form of the Miners' National Union under the leadership of Alexander Macdonald, primarily to promote Macdonald's parliamentary programme. The autonomy of the county unions was unchallenged within it. In effect Macdonald's union was a parliamentary pressure group. The county unions associated with Macdonald, outside of Scotland, were all located on the east of the Pennines with leaderships which favoured close collaboration with the coal-owners. On the west of the Pennines through Lancashire to South Wales and the Forest of Dean, the miners were organized, from 1869, in a centralized union called the Amalgamated Association of Miners. The leaders of this union, especially its General Secretary, Thomas Halliday, wanted to develop arbitration procedures but where these were refused they pursued a policy of supporting district strikes. It was not a collaborative union. The Amalgamated Association of Miners was the largest union in Britain by 1874 with 106,000 members. Because of its centralized constitution and its intention to embrace all miners it was a threat to the autonomy of the county unions. Because of its militant policy it challenged the collaborative leaderships of Macdonald, John Normansell of the South Yorkshire Miners, Thomas Burt of the Northumberland Miners' Mutual Confident Society and William Crawford of the Durham Miners, who in consequence, connived with the coal-owners West of the Pennines to destroy the union.

The coal-owners refused to accept arbitration or to establish joint committees with the Amalgamated union and they forced it into an almost unbroken series of strikes and lockouts producing starvation conditions for mining families and an eventual unbearable financial situation for the union. The struggle was especially intense and bloody in South Wales where there was a three months' lockout in 1873 and a five months' strike in 1875. The centralized union was insolvent by the summer of 1875 and was forced into a merger with the Miners' National Union.

The fates of the two unions were symbolised by the lives of their leaders. Macdonald and Burt became Members of Parliament while

Normansell and Crawford achieved local conventional respectability. Thomas Halliday, on the other hand, when the Amalgamated Association of Miners ceased to exist, moved to Cardiff where he lived by selling oil and odds and ends around the collieries. Halliday witnessed the virtual demise of mining trade unionism in South Wales for two decades.

Development and Decline of County Unions

The disappearance of the Amalgamated Association of Miners allowed the county unions to develop and consolidate their positions. The county union pattern was imposed over the whole of the British coalfields. Mining trade unionism West of the Pennines arose out of the wreckage in bits and pieces, not even in county union form. Thirteen separate district unions were eventually formed in South Wales after 1875 with most of them appearing just before the creation of the South Wales Miners' Federation in 1898. There were also thirteen unions in Lancashire until the Lancashire and Cheshire Miners' Federation was formed in 1897. In the Midlands a number of unions, some of which had been districts of the Amalgamated Association, established the Midland Counties Federation of Miners round about 1886. Until near the end of the nineteenth century there were strong, large county unions in Northumberland, Durham and Yorkshire whereas in Scotland, Lancashire, the Midlands, South Wales and Somerset trade unionism was fractured into numerous small, local, district unions. This situation in some areas was rationalized through the formation of the Miners Federation of Great Britain in 1898.

Once the very idea of a centralized national union was killed off and the county unions were fully established miners began to see virtues in them and legitimized their existence. The county unions, however, had to operate in an environment which had both centralizing tendencies and divisive factors which were iniquitous and oppressive and in order to survive as credible organizations they had to adapt themselves. The physical isolation of the coalfields was gradually eroded by compelling unifying factors. So despite institutional separateness the miners in different coalfields were compelled to act together for common aims. There was a national strike for a minimum wage in 1912. After the first world war there were accelerated demands for nationalization. Through the impact of the war they negotiated national rather than local agreements. It started with the Miners' Federation applying for a wage increase in August 1917 for all mineworkers to meet the increase in the cost of living. The Government war-time control of the industry raised national issues. A National Wages Board was established in 1921 which fixed minimum wages. There were two national strikes, one in 1920 and the other in 1921. There was an unmistakeable trend away from district autonomy.

The 1926 General Strike was the second major offensive by coal-owners to divide the county unions from each other and so make it easier to influence and control them. If the unifying pressures had continued without interruption it is possible that the Miners' Federation of Great Britain would have become a national union in practice though not in form by the end of the 1920s with greater collective power at its disposal. The coal-owners' imposition of district agreements after their victory in 1926 prevented this possibility. The formation of company unions in the aftermath of the strike made unity even more difficult.

The experience of company unionism accelerated the need for a single union but it was not until it ended that even discussions about amalgamations could take place. The rifts caused by Spencerism were not removed after 1938 but they were sufficiently repaired to enable discussions to take place. The county unions which had suffered from Spencerism behaved with greater confidence. The South Wales Miners' Federation negotiated a new pay structure which, for the first time, stipulated a rate for the job thoughout the coalfield and became a model for post-nationalization agreements. The county unions experienced a confidence they had lacked since before 1926. They were assisted by the changing economic situation. Trade improved, armaments production expanded and the demand for coal rose. When the Miners' Federation of Great Britain met in 1939 it demanded that all workers in and around the coal mines must belong to it. The South Wales miners, by now under the leadership of Arthur Horner, went on to negotiate a closed shop agreement with check-off arrangements.

The second world war created conditions which facilitated both amalgamation between all the 36 county unions and the transition to nationalization. The chief officers of the M.F.G.B. were increasingly drawn into negotiations with Government Ministers over measures to deal with the coal crisis and the problems these created. They were particularly concerned with the recruitment of miners, absenteeism and strikes. With every step that the Government took towards controlling coal production the significance of the county unions declined despite attempts by the coalowners to maintain the principle of district agreements. A new National Conciliation Scheme was introduced in May, 1943. A National Board was formed which comprised a Joint National Negotiating Committee with miners and mine-owners equally represented, and a National Reference Tribunal to deal with those national questions over which the Negotiating Committee could not agree. The situation was as Sam Watson, the leader of the Durham miners, described it to an M.F.G.B. Conference in 1943: "Has not the war experience taught us, on wages, on holidays, on compensation or rehabilitation . . . that you have only been able to get satisfaction from a national angle and on a national basis . . ." Moreover, on the sheer practical level of deciding who to meet with when particular problems arose, the Government Ministers and senior civil servants always preferred national representatives and placed on them the responsibility for communicating decisions to county unions and sorting out differences between them.

The Miners' Federation of Great Britain, then, acted as a national union after 1940 even though formally it was not one. It seemed logical to give it an organizational framework which made it formally what it was appearing to be in reality. The first step was taken in 1942. A sub-committee of the M.F.G.B. Executive Committee formulated proposals "to merge all the districts and sectional miners' unions into one national organization covering all mineworkers employed in or around the collieries of Great Britain." Many months of negotiation and compromise followed during which the real sources of county union attitudes were tapped. The dilemma of those with the responsibility of devising a constitution was, as Arthur Horner described it at the 1943 Annual Conference of the M.F.G.B., that "we have to take into account not only the general interests of the men, which would drive me to one all out Mineworkers' Union involving the liquidation of the District Unions, but we have to be realists and take into account the vested interests of the Districts . . ."

The result was a constitution which, in Horner's view was 'emasculated.' It had the pretentions of a national union but its practice was to remain largely unchanged. The county unions were to become Areas of the National union; the county union officials were to become Area officials. The Areas were to retain the responsibility for collecting dues with the obligation to remit part of these to the centre. They were to continue, therefore, to control their accumulated funds, with the possibility of building on them. The Areas continued to maintain their county union ways of formulating policy and of administering it. All that was achieved, in effect, was the centralization of the industrial activities of the county unions, leaving everything else alone. All of this fell short of the aspirations of the advocates of a centralized union but when the National Union of Mineworkers was formed in 1944 at least it provided an institutional framework for an effective centralized union to grow within it. It was unlikely that the divisive organizational uncertainties implicit in the Miners' Federation of Great Britain would recur.

Government Control and Nationalization

The coal crisis which the lack of planning and foresight created made Government intervention in the control of the coal industry inevitable. From June, 1942, a system of dual control existed in the industry. The Government assumed the responsibility for the operation of the mines while the coal-owners retained their ownership and financial control. The production of coal was regulated by Regional Boards under the authority of a National Coal Board. There were trade union representatives on each of the Boards. The county unions and the M.F.G.B. collaborated fully with the Government in its attempt to run the industry. The experience was, indeed, a preamble for nationalization after the war.

Nationalization of the coal industry had been seen as a panacea for the troubles of the industry since the late 19th century. The representatives of the Scottish county unions had convinced the Trades Union Congress of 1892 to advocate nationalization. Two years later the M.F.G.B. resolved that "in the opinion of this Conference the best interests of the nation will be served by the nationalization of the mines of the country." Keir Hardie presented a Bill to nationalize the mines and minerals of Great Britain in 1893. Thereafter the issue was kept alive and appeared on the agendas of the M.F.G.B., the T.U.C and the International Miners' Federation. A Bill was drafted by the M.F.G.B. in 1913, which excluded compensation for royalties, but it failed to be discussed in the House of Commons.

The issue was raised again in the aftermath of the First World War when the M.F.G.B. voted by 615,164 to 105,082 in 1919 to strike for four demands, including nationalization. The strike notices were postponed after the Government had agreed to set up a Royal Commission to inquire into the coal industry under the chairmanship of Mr. Justice Sankey. The notices were withdrawn after the Government had intimated its acceptance of the interim Sankey recommendation to end the private ownership of the mines. All four final reports of the Sankey Commission recommended the State ownership of all seams of coal and endorsed the principle of State control of mining. Before the end of 1919 the Government had reversed its policy. The Sankey Commission had been used successfully to defuse the strike threat. The miners, by a small majority, voted to strike for nationalization in March 1920 but the Special Trades Union Congress convened shortly afterwards decided emphatically against a strike. The issue was shelved then until the Second World War.

Arthur Horner commented in 1943 that when the question of Government control was raised the miners asked for nationalization. They were not given it because the Labour Party was committed to the National Government and wanted to avoid controversial questions and, of course, because the dominant party in the National Government was Conservative. During a debate on the coal situation in the House of Commons in October 1943 the Prime Minister, Mr. Winston Churchill, made clear the National Government's attitude towards the nationalization of the mines. He said "we

Vesting Day, 1st January, 1947, at Bolsover Colliery in Derbyshire

should not be justified in embarking upon it without a General Election . . ." Well, in 1945, there was a General Election in which the Labour Party was given a mandate to nationalize the mines with a substantial majority.

The Labour Government introduced the Coal Industry Nationalization Act in 1946. It transferred all the rights, assets and liabilities of the industry to a National Coal Board and provided for the payment of compensation to the former coal-owners. The vesting day was on 1st January, 1947. It was a great day for miners. Through nationalization the miners saw a real possibility of planning the resources of the industry to provide job security as well as improved wages and working conditions in a manner consistent with increasing efficiency. Indeed nationalization stood as the antithesis of all the conditions which free competition had created and which ordinary miners suffered. So for most miners the 1st January, 1947, was the beginning of a new era in which the mines belonged to the nation and, in consequence, to the miners themselves. Uncertainty was, it was believed, at an end.

CHAPTER 4

CONTRACTION

The Dominance of Coal Owners

The uncertainty which dominated the lives of miners in the years up
to the nationalization of the coal industry stemmed directly and
immediately from the capitalist nature of British society. The coal
owners did virtually as they liked with their mines, constrained only
by geological conditions and the collective reactions of miners.
They strutted about the coal scene intent on making profit, with
local authorities, Government politicians, the police and the armed
forces in their wake, supporting and preserving the conditions
which made the maximization of profit possible. The fictionalised
character, Lord Cwmardy, in Lewis Jones's classic account of mining
conditions in South Wales, *Cwmardy*, exercising virtually absolute
control over the valleys in which his pits lay was not a caricature but
a portrayal of coal-owners in reality, of Lord Rhondda, who employed
Lewis Jones, of Lord Merthyr of Senghenydd, the name of the
South Wales colliery where 439 miners lost their lives in October,
1913, of Lord Lambton of Durham, of Lord Aberconway and the
Markham family in Derbyshire, of the Duke of Hamilton and the
Earl of Dalkeith in the Scottish coalfields and of Major Barber,
chairman of Barber, Walker and Co. which owned the Harworth
colliery in Nottinghamshire and the village itself, except, it is said,
for the bit of land on which stood the local Co-op, and of coal-
owners in general who used men as commodities and women simply
as the means to reproduce, sustain, nurture men as commodities.

The reality and substance of producing coal for private profit
within a market situation consisted of coal-owners making decisions
in response to changes in the markets for coal, producing more of all
types or less of all types; producing more of one type and less of
another; cutting costs directly by reducing wages or indirectly by
increasing productivity. Labour costs in mining were always high in
relation to total costs - in the 1920s they averaged about 72 per cent
and in the 1930s they were around 67 per cent. In some areas such as
Scotland and South Wales where seams were narrow and conditions
difficult they were higher than these figures. So whenever there was
a problem of costs the first item to be scrutinized was labour power.
Could its price be reduced; could more effort be extracted from it;
could it be used more effectively there rather than here, in that face
but not this face, in that pit rather than this pit; or would it be
cheaper to pay in this way rather than that, to discipline more or
less. Or might not the answer lie in employing less men and more
machines or simply less men. Uncertainty for miners was normal.

Control over cost flexibility which the coal owners insisted was

Miners returning to the pit bottom at Clay Cross Number 2 pit in 1910. Only the young boy is able to walk upright.

theirs implied no interference by workers, either individually or collectively. This meant that they continually opposed the county unions and the Miners' Federation of Great Britain, tried to undermine their authority with ordinary miners, to win the collaboration of their leaders, to beat them down with physical force, to establish alternative organizations of their own making. Even at the level of trade unionism there was no certainty.

The Content of Nationalization

The miners saw the solution to uncertainty in the formation of a single, national union, strong against outside pressures and resistant to any undermining forces within it, operating within a publicly-owned industry which planned the use of its resources for the service of society. When the National Union of Mineworkers was formed and the coal industry was nationalized miners saw before them an era of basic stability.

Matters did not turn out as most miners expected. Capitalism is a pervasive phenomenon; it is virtually an all or nothing phenomenon. The only way to escape the upsetting pressures of markets is to eliminate the markets themselves and to use planning techniques to distribute resources rather than free market ones.

Nationalization ended the competition between coal-owners for greater shares of coal markets but it did not touch the coal markets themselves. It removed competition in the production of coal but left the use of coal, and, therefore, the primary determinant of the production of coal, to be determined by market forces. The coal industry, in consequence, continued to be shaped by market forces over which the administrators of its unified organization exercised no control. There were no means within the industry of insulating coal from the ravages of fluctuations in the level of trade generally, of displacement by other sources of energy. The coal industry under nationalization was as sensitive, responsive and malleable to market fluctuations as it had been under private ownership.

It was bound to be like this because of the way in which the Labour Government, which introduced nationalization, considered it should be applied. That Government saw nationalization simply as a means to plan resources within particular investment-deprived industries and not as a basis for planning resources between industries. It left each industry it nationalized safely and securely within the control of capitalist market structures, to be shaped, moulded, destined to serve these as certainly as if there had been private ownership.

For miners this meant that the basic cause of uncertainty remained unchanged. The industry continued on a course which was not related in any way to the destinies of its human constituents. Nationalization brought improvements in conditions of employment

Miners at Sharlston colliery, Yorkshire, on their way to the pit bottom.

but in terms of the uncertainty experienced by miners the contribution was more about explanations than anything else.

What made the immediate and short term experience of nationalization so different from private ownership in the interwar years was that its economic context was so different. From the inception of nationalization until 1957 the industry was expanding. There appeared to be an almost insatiable demand for coal. The requirements of post-war industrial reconstruction made demands on the coal industry it could not meet. The output of deep-mined coal rose from 184.4 million tons in 1947 to 210.6 million tons in 1952 but this was still nearly 14 million tons less than the total demand. The difference between production and demand was bridged by coal imports and the consumption of stocks. The consequence for miners was that there were too few of them. Miners who were displaced because of pit closures were readily relocated in other pits. There was no fear of unemployment for miners.

But if miners had been rejected by their industry they would still have had jobs for in the whole of the period of expansion, and for almost a decade afterwards, there was full employment in the British economy as a whole. Light manufacturing industries were located in mining areas. It so happened that these tended to utilize women's labour power more than men's but it did not matter much for miners could, if they wished, move over to the steel industry in South Wales, the textile industry in Lancashire, the pottery industry in North Staffordshire, the ship-building and engineering industries in Scotland, Northumberland and Durham. Elsewhere, in Yorkshire, the Midlands and Nottingham established industries were diverse and alternative job opportunities multiple.

Optimism

There was a great optimism in the coal industry during this phase. The "Plan for Coal," published in 1950, reflected the management's optimism. It estimated that coal production would rise by 18 per cent by 1965, that is to a level of between 230 and 250 million tons. It proposed to sink 20 new collieries and to go ahead with 250 major reconstructions entailing an investment of £635 millions. This Plan was revised in 1956. The major investment schemes had been slower to materialize than had been anticipated. The extension of the Fife coalfield at Glenrothes, for example, had encountered unexpected geological difficulties. There had been problems of labour recruitment, especially in the productive coalfields of Yorkshire, Nottingham, and the Midlands where industry was diversified and many alternative job opportunities existed. It had not been possible, moreover, for the industry to finance its expansion from its own resources on the scale stipulated in the 1950 Plan largely because of the pricing policy it had to follow and the burden of

34

Before the spread of diesel trains. The railways in Scotland, for example, consumed 2.33 million tons of coal, representing 11.25 per cent of total consumption in Scotland in 1947.

compensation payments. The general reconstruction plans were broadly unchanged in "Investing in Coal," published in 1956, but the sharp rise in prices meant that more capital had to be raised in order to carry the 1950 Plan through. It was calculated that the domestic demand would rise to 230 million tons by 1962 and that exports would then be between 25 and 35 million tons.

This optimism was not confined to Britain. It was estimated in 1956 that there would be a continuing shortage of coal in European countries. The member countries of The European Coal and Steel Community entered into large forward contracts for American coal in anticipation of shortages. Governments began to take steps to economize in the use of coal in anticipation of future shortages.

Right from the time that the Government assumed control over coal production in 1942 the Government, the management and the unions acted from the presumption that the industry should be made more efficient. This, in the first instance, involved doing what the private coal owners had been unable to do, namely, rationalizing, amalgamating and generally improving the efficiency of existing resources. Under the 1930 Coal Mines Act a Coal Mines Reorganization Commission had been established with statutory powers. Its purpose was to encourage large-scale undertakings or amalgamations where these would 'result in lowering the cost of production or disposal of coal,' and where they would not be 'financially injurious to any of the undertakings proposed to be amalgamated.' The terms of any amalgamation had to be 'fair and equitable to all persons affected thereby.' Where these conditions could be satisfied the Commission had the powers to compel firms to amalgamate.

These conditions in total, of course, could never be satisfied. In any event the coal-owners were not in favour of accelerating amalgamations and neither the Commission nor the Cabinet members of the National Government could force them to act against their will. The Government attempted to remove some of the defects of the 1930 Act in a new Bill in 1936 but the Mining Association campaigned successfully to force its withdrawal. Another attempt was made in 1938 and again the political machine of the coal-owners went into action, this time not wholly successfully but enough to make the Coal Act of that year difficult to enforce. Every scheme for compulsory amalgamation had to be examined by a select committee of the House of Commons, thus giving the owners the chance to maintain their political opposition. The war intervened, however, and the 1938 Act was never applied.

The coal-owners were supported by the Miners Federation of Great Britain in their opposition to compulsory amalgamation in the 1930s because it was believed they would increase unemployment amongst miners. The miners had supported compulsion in the 1920s

A railway siding.

but had altered their view as the trade depression from 1929 took its toll of them. Voluntary amalgamations involving Powell Duffryn in South Wales and the Fife Coal Company in Scotland increased localised unemployment. From the miners' point of view the less of these they had the better for them.

The miners altered their view again from the middle years of the war. This change was reinforced by the Reid Committee report in March 1945 which showed that increased efficiency could not be obtained unless the industry was "merged into units of such sizes as would provide the maximum advantages of planned production."* Once the industry was nationalized, with the coal-owners out of the way, there were no institutional obstacles to the full implementation of the Reid Report, except those which might come from union opposition, but with a rising demand for coal, full employment in general, public ownership and a Labour Government these did not occur.

Contraction through Rationalization

The National Coal Board was able to set about its initial task with what might be described as a ready-made setting. It eliminated small, inefficient pits and endeavoured to concentrate production in a relatively small number of large pits in each major coalfield. There were many pit closures. The N.C.B. took over 980 mines in 1947 but by 1957 there were only 822 and many more were scheduled to close in pursuit of concentration and efficiency. Many of the pits which were closed in this period were in Scotland. Indeed the N.C.B. intended that about 80 per cent of the Scottish Division's production would come from new collieries and major reconstructions such as Bilston Glen, Killoch, Seafield, Rothes and Monktonhall. The Lanarkshire coalfield was almost obliterated. A similar process of concentration was planned in the other coalfields, although the incidence of closures was not intended to be so intense. Eighty per cent of the production in the Yorkshire coalfield was aimed, by 1965, to come from reconstructed collieries. Pits in all coalfields whose reserves were wholly or virtually exhausted, or which had high production costs or poor quality coal were faced with closure. Not all such pits, however, were closed before 1957 because of the high demand for coal.

The experience of miners in this phase of expansion was much the same underground as it had been before. They worked on piece-work systems with their built-in supervisory mechanisms and were subjected to cost-reducing pressures as they had been under private ownership. Life at the face seemed to change very little, as if it could hardly be changed anyway. Individual miners continued to

---

* *Coal Mining.* Report of the Technical Advisory Committee, 1945, Cmd. 6610, H.M.S.O., p. 138.

Domestic coal consumers in Liverpool before the Clean Air Act of 1956.

be subjected to uncertainty in the interest of efficiency. But it was not accompanied by the frightening prospect of long-term unemployment. Individual miners in inefficient pits were transferred to new pits, sometimes within daily travelling distance of their homes, sometimes to other coalfields involving moving house, leaving a network of family relationships, creating new friendships, even, in the case of Scottish and Welsh miners, of leaving behind cultures.

The consequences for individuals of working in a cost conscious environment were the same no matter what reasons were given for it. The National Coal Board was not strictly pursuing profitability in the expansionist phase but this did not make uncertainty more palatable to those affected by it. The miners at Southfield, Stane, Calderhead and Fortissat collieries in Shotts, Lanarkshire, were not comforted in 1949 by the thought that their collieries were threatened by endeavours to rationalize production. Nor were the face workers at Devon colliery in Alloa placated in 1959 because they knew that the closure of their pit would release much needed labour for nearby Glenochil pit. The reasons for uncertainty, however, were important for miners collectively; for they then took into account general, national factors such as the need to re-equip and expand industry after the war, the acute national and international shortage of fuel which played an immediate and direct part in determining the outcome of the struggle of miners for subsistence.

Pit closures for a decade after 1947 were selective and concentrated in particular areas. Most miners were untouched by them. This situation changed when the demand for coal began to fall after 1957. From that year until 1963 a phase of contraction began which was severe by any earlier standards but which was not regarded as being inevitable, permanent and irreversible. The attitude persisted that if only a Labour Government could be elected to pursue an expansionist policy, if only there could be a general improvement in trade to lift the coal industry out of what was seen as a trade depression, then the industry could return to its initial post-war prosperity.

There were some misleading signs at the time which led to optimism. A moderate depression in industry occurred late in 1957 causing a reduction in the demand for coal in Britain and throughout Western Europe. Some measures taken earlier to economize in the use of coal began to have an effect on the demand for coal at about the same time. It was not simply the National Union of Mineworkers which was misled. When the N.C.B. published its *Revised Plan for Coal* in 1959 it did not envisage a severe contraction in the industry. It estimated that the total demand for coal in 1965 would be between 200 and 215 million tons a year compared with the earlier estimate of between 230 and 250 million tons. It did not anticipate a major displacement of coal by oil.

Dramatic Contraction after 1957

The N.C.B.'s plans played no part in the events after 1957. As the demand for coal fell it closed pits accordingly and by 1963 there were 264 pits less than there had been six years earlier. The number of miners fell by nearly thirty per cent. The older, low productivity areas felt the brunt most of all. In that six year period Scotland lost 39 per cent of its pits while South Wales, Northumberland and Durham lost round about 30 per cent. Lancashire, North Wales and the West Midlands were also heavy sufferers. Yorkshire by comparison had less than 6 per cent of its pits closed.

Amongst the closures were some dramatic reminders that the process of contraction might not be of the kind to be halted by a different Government. Rothes, a brand new colliery in Fifeshire, a show-piece opened by the Queen in 1957, planned to produce 5000 tons a day from almost 2,500 miners, was closed in 1962. The glossy brochure handed out by the Scottish Division of the N.C.B. projected a life-span of 100 years dipping into reserves of 120 million tons yet the pit was closed before it had reached full production. Then there was Glenochil colliery in the Alloa district of Scotland, opened in 1956, with its own new township of Tallibody half a mile away, with an expected life of 40 years which was terminated at the age of 6 years with the same sweeping blow at the Scottish coalfield which destroyed Rothes. Bill Whitehead, speaking at the N.U.M. Annual Conference in 1964, gave similar, though less dramatic, illustrations from the South Wales coalfield. He said "What are some of the assets which are increasing in value yet being written off? Llanharan Colliery in South Wales. The Board spent millions of pounds. There were 150 years of coal there, they said . . . The colliery has been closed completely . . . Take Getly Colliery in the Rhondda . . . two years before they closed it, they spent a very, very substantial sum of money on an overhead ropeway, a very valuable asset and completely unused now. Llanbradach Colliery - new winders, new everything went in. Hoptin, you know about it. Well over a million pounds to my knowledge. Closed. They are not assets any more . . ."

Other areas doubtless had similar experiences for such was the character of contraction at that time.

The doubts which were germinated by such closures as the Rothes and Glenochil ones, were transformed into complete awareness after the return of the Labour Government in 1964 for then the administrative axe was swung wide and wildly across the low-productivity coalfields of Britain. Illusions about the causes of contraction and about the future of the coal industry were dispelled by a massacre of the pits. The impact of closure was so great that the coal industry was visibly disappearing, seemingly to nothing. By 1968 only 317 collieries remained open. There had, remember, been almost a thousand of them at the time of nationalization.

Between 1964 and 1968 the number of collieries fell by 40 per cent and the labour force was cut by almost the same percentage. There were in 1968 half as many miners as there had been when the demand for coal began to fall in 1957. The coal industry was pushed ignominiously from its majestic place at the centre of Britain's industrial life. The older coalfields were devastated most of all. Lancashire, North Wales and Durham were the worst hit, followed by Scotland and South Wales.

Although the operation carried out by the N.C.B. appeared to make little economic sense to miners at the time because new pits as well as old ones, efficient as well as inefficient ones and large ones as well as small ones were all being closed, it had a logic about it for production was being concentrated in the relatively new thick-seamed coalfields in which advanced mechanization could be applied. For this reason output did not decline as rapidly as manpower and the number of pits. Moreover, whilst the contraction was taking place coal production was subjected to an unprecedented degree of mechanization. Most pits in 1968 could produce more coal with fewer men than in 1957. Put differently, the output of 1957 could have been maintained in 1968 with fewer pits and less men. The complete picture of the contraction of the coal industry must include then a description of the process of mechanization.

Miners at work in Clay Cross pit in Derbyshire before the First World War.

CHAPTER 5

MECHANIZATION

Mechanization as a Cost

Miners in the 1960s were caught in a pincer movement between pit closures and mechanization. Oil displaced coal as a source of power and, as the market for coal declined, pits were closed and miners lost their jobs. The National Coal Board tried to resist the market decline by improving the efficiency of coal production, lowering costs and thereby coal prices. The struggle to make coal more competitive involved an extension of the mechanization of production. Machines were used to do the tasks which had traditionally been done by hand and in doing so they both displaced labour power and altered its use. In general labour power was rationalized. The two arms of the pincer then reinforced each other's pressure to cut down on jobs.

It did not matter much to the men who lost their jobs what the causes were. A job lost is a job lost and no amount of explanation which breaks down the causes can make the impact easier to bear. The position was different for those who remained at work. Miners worked with the threat of losing their jobs hanging continually over their heads. The impact of pit closures was so unpredictable that working miners never knew which pits were next on the list.

Miners also had to contend with the direct effects of mechanization, which were immediate, intense and which had unpleasant and disruptive consequences.

There is a logic and plausibility in using machines for extracting coal. The conditions underground are so arduous, dangerous and generally exacting that it would be thought that any one with even the slightest sense of humanity would encourage the exposure of machines rather than people to them. Yet the mechanization of coal production had been slow and protracted. Humanitarian issues have never figured in the calculations of coal owners. Coal has been produced for profit and for most of the history of coal mining it has been more profitable to exploit labour power than machines in the process because it has been more plentiful and, therefore, cheaper than capital.

Capital, however, has always had to be used in the development of deep mining. Shafts had to be sunk and roadways cut underground. Machines had to be used to get men into the pits and both men and coal out of them. As coal faces moved away from the pit-bottom miners have had to be conveyed for at least part of the journey in order to maximise their time at coal faces. Man-riding facilities consisting of open, draughty, narrow, wooden seated carriages were introduced. But the items requiring capital were always kept

44

A coal-getter at Denby colliery, hand loading large lumps of coal into his tub stall. The fork was used for filling so that the small coal was left behind. Miners found using a shovel for loading tubs were often fined.

A young pony driver taking a train of coal to the pit bottom.

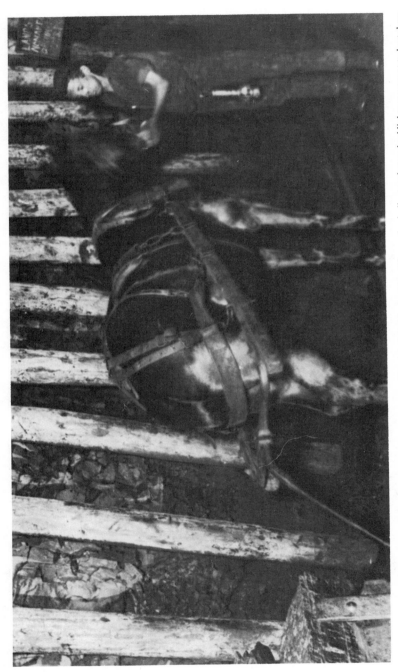

A pony driver leading his pony along the timbered road-way at Denby pit in Derbyshire. The notice indicates that naked lights were not to be taken beyond that point. Ponies, in the main, ceased to be used in pits in the early 1970s.

to a minimum. This was so even where safety was concerned. Legislation had to be passed to force employers to sink ventilation shafts. Roadways were made only with sufficient space to convey coal so that miners had to walk to faces along roadways which had low ceilings and uneven tracks and were too narrow for easy, comfortable, even safe walking.

Coal mining is an unnatural activity. It cannot take place unless air is introduced and circulated through the workings. It requires precautions to be taken against explosions and to control the flow of water. These factors require an outlay of capital. Machines have had to be installed to pump water away. But as with shafts and man-riding facilities the amount of capital has been determined by cost considerations. Never has the welfare of the workers been a primary consideration except when it has been conclusively shown that an increase in the welfare would reduce costs or increase productivity. Thus after nationalization pit head baths and surface canteens were installed but not underground eating and toilet facilities.

The point is that for the greater part of the history of coal mining capital had to be forced out of the coal owners by unavoidable production problems, by government legislation and by trade union pressure. The process was slow with the result that generations of miners have worked in a largely unchanged environment. Women and children were forced out of underground work by legislation in 1842. They had often been employed in carrying coal along with adult male barrowmen. Their places were taken by asses and ponies in the second half of the nineteenth century, though in some coal-fields ponies had been used in the late eighteenth century first to haul sledges then to pull barrows on rails. Whether pit ponies could be used at all depended upon the size of the roadways. In some fields, for example the East Midlands, the roadways were the same height as the seams, and they could be as narrow as 18 inches. Only humans could operate in that type of work environment.

The Slow Pace of Change

The methods used for hauling and winding improved during the middle of the 19th century as the demand for coal increased. Grand, shining winding engines were installed, such as the one which can be seen at Lady Victoria pit in Scotland. But, except for the intro-duction of dynamite, little changed at the face. The stall and pillar method, and its variants, gradually gave way to the longwall method of extracting coal and led to an increased division of labour, thus altering social relationships and enabling the butty system of piece-work to develop. But coal extraction continued to be done by hand. Right until after the First World War mining was a pick and shovel activity. The task of hewing coal, of loading it and getting it to the pit bottom was mainly done by hand. Only 8.5 per cent of coal was

A winding-engine room.

mechanically cut in 1913. This figure increased, but slowly, until 1939. The use of mechanized transport to convey coal was introduced even more slowly. By 1928 only 12 per cent of the coal output was mechanically transported. About half of the output of coal at the beginning of the Second World War was mechanically cut and conveyed.

This slow encroachment of machines into pit life, slowly altering the skills of mining, diluting some and creating others, continued until the middle of the 1950s. The Nationalization of the mines in 1947 barely altered the pace, even though the Reid Report in 1945 had stated that the industry's future lay with mechanization. "Much of the industry was out of date," the Report stated. "Methods of coal getting and haulage had to be modernised. There was an acute shortage of technical ability . . . We are satisfied . . . that throughout the industry drastic technical re-organization is not only practicable, but vitally necessary . . . Nothing less than the rebuilding of the industry on the most modern lines would do." This, of course, was an indictment of private ownership in coal mining formulated by the committee comprised of people who in the main had played a contributory part in creating the situation it damned so thoroughly.*
The coal industry which had been a satisfactory source of capital for the coal owners was virtually starved of capital itself.

The National Coal Board had other priorities than mechanization at the outset of nationalization. It preferred rationalization and consolidation.

Once these seem to have been achieved the management began to think seriously about mechanization but then, at roughly the same time, the demand for coal started to decline. Thus the possibility of achieving a sharp increase in the supply of coal coincided with a drop in the demand for it. The contradiction was, however, that the need for mechanization as a means of reducing costs was greater in the falling coal market than it had been before.

There were three main separate aspects in coal production: coal cutting, loading and transporting it to the pit head. There were, of course, a large number of related underground tasks providing the context for successful production and others at the surface preparing the coal for distribution. Although these tasks were essential they had no utility apart from actual production so that managerial attention was continually directed at the face where the cutting, loading and transporting aspects occurred, in order to increase efficiency.

* op. sit. The Reid Committee was a Technical Advisory Committee appointed in September 1944 to advise the Government about the technical state of the industry. Its chairman, Sir Charles Reid, had been General Manager of the Fife coal company Ltd. Other members were James Nimmo (General Manager, Mining of the Workington Branch of the United Steel Companies Ltd.), Douglas Hann (Director of Production at Powell Duffry Ltd.), John Hunter (Managing Director of Doncaster Amalgamated Collieries Ltd.)

A Denby miner setting up a wooden prop to make his workplace safe. Many miners resisted the use of iron and steel props because they did not give a warning cracking sound when under pressure.

An early form of mechanization.

The displacement of hand production methods by machines came in a piecemeal fashion. There was such an enormous diversity of coalface conditions; in the thickness and accessibility of seams, the friability of the coal, the presence of water and geological conditions in general, that a uniform approach to mechanization was difficult. These conditions created technological problems which colliery management had little incentive to overcome so long as labour power was plentiful and cheap and coal was in great demand.

The manner in which machines were introduced created bottlenecks which retarded overall improvements. It had been the same in other industries such as woollen textiles, where weaving was mechanized before spinning. Technological inventions have rarely been introduced in a co-ordinated, systematic manner so that improvements in different aspects of production have coincided with each other. It has been the case, rather, that inventions in one department have stimulated inventions elsewhere along the line. Mechanized coal cutters increased the amount of coal a shift could cut and conveyors speeded it to the pit bottom but so long as the coal was hand loaded the benefits of machines were limited. Even when power-loading was possible and the three aspects of production were mechanized the full benefits of mechanization could not be obtained until each aspect was integrated into a process. The machines increased the speed at which faces receded but at the end of each shift during which the coal had been power-loaded, the mechanized process was interrupted while the faces were packed by hand in preparation for the next shift. The introduction of powered roof supports enabled the parts to be linked into a single process.

Integrated Processes

The integrated power-loading system operated like a combine harvester. It moved up and down a face cutting coal directly without the use of explosives to loosen it and mechanically loaded it on to a conveyor. Hydrostatic steel props supported the roof instead of wooden ones and pushed the conveyor belt forward as the cutting advanced. Men followed the cutter to adjust the props and the conveyor belt so that conditions were satisfactory for the cutter to return. The whole operation was continuous. The stage was set for automated, manless coal cutting.

Machines invaded the face but not the whole face environment. A face was a particular length of seam. In order for the cutter to move along it recesses at each end, called stable-holes, had to be made in advance of the cutting. The coal was then sliced off as with a bacon machine. The stable-holes had to be cut by hand. Similarly most development work involved cutting new roadways and preparing new faces had to be done in the traditional manner. It was a problem to get ripping machines which could cut through hard rock and, in

A coal face in the Rams Seam at Bickershaw colliery, Leigh, Lancashire in the 1970s.

any case, in the stable-hole the loading had to be done by hand. There were machines available by the end of the 1960s which could cut and excavate roadways in a single operation, tunnelling like moles, but they were expensive and slow and generally less productive than hand methods.

The conventional faceworker retained a few jobs which remained unchanged but these were ancillary to the main task of coal production which was done by machines with the aid of faceworkers. The work situation was transformed. Less men were needed on face work. They required different skills. They operated in a different supervisory situation. They experienced less physical effort but they lost control of the work pace. For miners the mechanization of coal production had implications far beyond the fact of increasing productivity.

These implications descended on miners like an avalanche. Once powered hydraulic roof supports were introduced the slow encroachment of machines on hand-done tasks reached a pace which was unprecedented in the history of the industry. In 1955 only 9.8 per cent of total output was power-loaded. This proportion reached nearly 38 per cent by 1960 but within the space of the next five years it had risen to 87 per cent and by the end of the decade 92.2 per cent of all coal was power-loaded. There were differences between the areas. Where geological conditions were most favourable as in Nottinghamshire and the East Midlands virtually all coal was obtained through mechanized methods. Pick and shovel coal-getting became a subject for curiosity in a few, isolated pits, and for historical analysis in so far as coal-getting in general was concerned.

CHAPTER 6

EXPLANATIONS

The Pressures for Consensus

British miners in the post Second World War period were continually subjected to explanations as to why they should submit, acquiesce, even be enthusiastic about disruptive changes in their work situation. In this respect there was a marked difference compared with the inter-war years when coal owners had no need to explain away their dramatic decisions because miners were weak and they were strong. From the onset of nationalization the miners collectively were potentially powerful. A recognition of this potential and an intense desire to frustrate its realization invoked many words from the National Coal Board and the Government about the importance or otherwise of coal in the national economy.

The explanations which were given were not presented to closed minds. Miners were well aware of the economic and political needs of the time. In one sense explanations to justify changes in the coal industry were necessary because they were implicit in the economic and political environment of the post-war years. This can be seen from a cursory examination of the issues which influenced the industry.

Nationalization created an atmosphere of euphoria amongst miners and Union officials. There had been many years of political propaganda about nationalization which had, in effect, projected public ownership of the mines as a panacea for the ailments of the industry. Miners believed that the mines belonged to the nation and indirectly to themselves. They had great expectations and, in general, they were prepared to work in order to fulfil them.

Throughout the period there was either the aftermath of war crises with calls for national reconstruction or severe economic crises. There was always some question of national economic urgency which could be evoked in order to persuade the miners to accept one type of change or other. There were always cogent, persuasive economic arguments which could be used to justify action to be taken or to legitimize action already taken. There was the need to provide cheap power to industry, to expand exports, to compete with oil, to overcome the fuel crisis. The N.C.B. and the Government were never lost for crises.

Then, for 10 of the post-war years up till 1968, Labour Governments were in office. From 1945 to 1950 the Labour Government had a large majority committed to a wide-ranging policy of social and economic change which fitted the mood of miners. It was this Government which nationalized the mining industry so miners owed it a special debt. The Government had started on a Socialist programme and miners possessed an unquestioned commitment to Socialism. They recognised that the Government, and, therefore, Socialism, could only succeed if industry became efficient and they knew the vital part which coal had to play in that process. There was no doubt that miners in general understood the implications of having their own Government and a nationalized coal industry.

Some of the elements in the immediate post-war situation had altered by 1964 when a Labour Government followed 13 years of Conservative rule. The aura surrounding nationalization had largely disappeared and the feeling that the Labour Government could solve the social and economic problems of the country had also been substantially modified. It still remained possible, however, for a Labour Government to tap the loyalty of miners to the Labour Movement and to gain acceptance of policies which under other political circumstances they would reject.

Miners were never free to stand aside from all of these pressures to assess what they were being told about themselves and their work. The explanations, moreover, were rooted in the pressures and generally re-inforced them. The complete ideological apparatus in society, especially the mass media, was utilized to appeal for responsibility, a commitment to the nation as a whole, an acceptance of consensus between all classes. This occurred irrespective of the political complexion of the government. Indeed the pressures on miners to believe in consensus were greatest when Labour Governments were in office. There was no lack of volunteers to tell miners why they should believe the main explanations given to them. There were Government Ministers, politicians from all the political parties, members of the National Coal Board and the national officials of their own Union. All of them were eager to convince miners why they should not use their apparently enormous collective strength, why they should not push their achievements to the limits the market could bear, why they should not make up for all the ruthless damage which had been done to them in the inter-war years.

Miners' Media

Views were usually expressed about miners in the press, on the radio and television when there were crises in the coal industry of one sort or another but the most potent of them were those made within the mining industry, presented continually and without ambiguity. There was no national miners' union journal before 1968. Three areas of the N.U.M., Scotland, South Wales and Derbyshire published their own journals at different times but often they reinforced the arguments of the Government and the N.C.B. The Government issued its own reports and publications but the basic medium for the expression of Government and N.C.B. ideas about mining was the Coal Board's own monthly journal, originally called *Coal Magazine* in the pre-contraction days and changed in format, style and title by Lord Robens when he became Chairman of the N.C.B. in 1961. *Coal News,* the new name for the magazine, became a means of conveying to miners established managerial ideas about productivity, mechanization and pit closures. More than two-thirds of the total mining labour force received a copy, the price of which was deducted from their wages. Even after the N.U.M. published its own journal as many as about 15 per cent of the miners still depended entirely on *Coal News* for their information about the industry. Miners were confronted with a continuous flow of information and argument, justifying, rationalizing and legitimizing the decisions of the N.C.B. When there was resistance, senior officials of the N.C.B. and of the N.U.M. made forages into the coalfields. Past chairmen of the N.C.B., Lord Hyndley, Sir James Bowman, and Lord Robens could always be relied upon to don miners' helmets and proffer explanations, supported by the successive presidents of the N.U.M., Sir William Lawther, Ernest Jones and Sir Sidney Ford. In the face of this bombardment miners not only gave in to official explanations but refused to listen to alternative ones.

Relating Levels of Experience

The explanations given to miners about changes in their industry related to two levels of experience. There was the social, economic and political milieux within which the changes were taking place on one level and the day-to-day reality both within the pits and outside them. At the first level there were perfectly plausible explanations about the centralization of coal production, for the closure of inefficient pits and for the mechanization of coal-getting processes. These explanations, however, had to relate to the hard concrete reality of the impact of such changes on everyday life. No matter how plausible the first level explanations were the harsh reality of everyday mining life invoked spontaneous, gut-like subsistence reactions which were invariably initially resistant to change. For this reason, explanations had always to be made to the miners directly concerned.

The explanations of change in the mining industry were implied in the different phases of contraction. During the early years of nationalization and up till 1957, miners were told that coal was basic for the economic recovery of Britain and that due to the neglect of the industry in the inter-war years priority would be given to rationalizing the existing structure. The argument was put to miners that unless they cooperated to make the industry more efficient in terms stipulated by management, including improving their own work performances, they would jeopardize the success of the Labour Government and, in consequence, of Socialism itself.

This argument had credibility by itself only in particular economic circumstances; that is, with an expanding coal industry in the general context of full employment so that closure and displacement did not result in unemployment or even temporary hardship. When, after 1957, pits other than the small and geologically inefficient ones were closed different arguments had to be used. The case for modernization was not relaxed, however, when contraction began in earnest; indeed it was intensified on the grounds that without it the industry would not survive at all. At first, however, after 1957 the main explanation for contraction was that it was really a relatively short-term phenomenon due to a temporary depression in trade caused in large part by Government policies. This was certainly the argument advanced by Union leaders. When the Union organized demonstrations against closures the banners called for an expansionist government policy or a new government to apply such a policy. When Union leaders met the Minister of Power, Mr. Richard Wood, in November, 1959, they requested help in the transitional period for the industry because they did not believe that contraction was inevitable. They wanted help to reduce coal stocks, cuts in open-cast mining and a re-examination of the use of coal for generating gas and electricity as well as assistance to blunt the social impact on miners themselves. Many miners had experienced the trade fluctuations of the inter-war years and they were neither surprised nor alarmed by their consequences. Moreover as if to confirm that the cause of the contraction was a trade recession, matters improved in 1963, a pre-election year influenced by pre-election political tactics. Trade improved, the number of collieries which were closed fell compared with 1962; there was a sharp drop in those miners involved in closures and in those made redundant. The number of miners leaving the industry voluntarily fell sharply; even the number of strikes fell from 1,205 in 1962 to 987. No matter which indice was taken 1963 seemed to mark the end of what the union leaders in 1959 had called the 'transitional,' period. Then in 1964 a Labour Goverment was returned to office, pledged to initiate a co-ordinated national fuel policy in which the coal industry would produce 200 million tons annually.

The explanation of the contraction between 1957 and 1964 turned out to be a misinterpretation of the events by the N.C.B. and wishful thinking by union leaders. Measures which had been taken to economize on coal when coal was relatively scarce came to fruition. Coal began to be displaced by oil on an increasing scale as the coal/oil price ratio altered in favour of oil. In addition oil was projected as being cleaner, less polluting, more efficient and generally more preferable all round than coal. Then, as if to emphasize the rightness of the trend of events, natural gas was found in the North Sea in the autumn of 1965 in sufficient quantities to replace town gas extracted from coal.

The Labour Government revealed its intentions to the N.U.M. slowly after its election, by innuendo, by refusing to commit itself when reminded of its election manifesto and by substituting oil for coal in public services, as for example when oil was used to heat an army camp at Aldershot in 1965. Its first public indication of its intentions for the coal industry came when the National Plan was published in September, 1965. The Plan envisaged a drop of 30 per cent in mining manpower by 1970. Then in November of the same year the N.C.B. announced an accelerated pit closure programme. The contraction of the industry was seen for the first time as an inevitable, irreversible, rolling phenomenon. The announcements were confirmed by experience. The industry contracted more sharply than ever before in its history. But, in case there were people who misread the signs, the Government published a Command Paper on Fuel Policy in November, 1967, spelling out very precisely the dismal future of the coal industry.

The explanation this time was incontrovertible, or so the miners were told. Indeed few people spent any time on explaining to miners why their jobs were disappearing and their villages were becoming derelict. Miners were told simply and crudely that uneconomic pits would have to be closed. They knew, however, that the term "uneconomic" covered a muliplicity of sins. Indeed many miners took it to mean that the N.C.B. could close any pit at any time. In so far as the term "uneconomic" was understood, it was as a manipulable device. I remember being with members of the executive committee of the South Wales Area when they received news of a batch of closures. They exclaimed, almost in unison, 'all the bloody militant pits.'

Fatalism

The manner in which pits were closed encouraged an attitude of fatalism. Almost anything could happen and nothing could be done about it. The general explanation encouraged this attitude. Everything was all so self-evident. It was all happening through the cold, rational, impersonal, uncontrollable operation of the price mechanism. Oil was cheaper than coal; the demand for coal, therefore, must fall. The demand had to fall, otherwise the system would be put out of gear, in disequilibrium, in an imbalance. The minds of politicians, trade union leaders, members of the Coal Board and most miners were so much conditioned by capitalist ideology that it did not occur to them to question the autonomy of this mechanism which supposedly put every factor of production where it was supposed to be - including miners increasingly on the dole.

The Government Paper on Fuel Policy revealed the tram-lines along which such thought processes travelled when it stated: "Further decline in the markets for coal could not be prevented even by holding back the expansion of nuclear power and the development of natural gas unless the present level of coal protection were raised to an extent which would lead to a big increase in the general level of energy prices, or unless coal prices were heavily subsidized. But excessive protection for coal would lead to a misallocation of manpower and capital to the detriment of the economy as a whole . . ." (Cmnd.3438, p.41). The reasoning in this statement did not have to be spelled out. It was enough for the statement to be made for it was backed by libraries of books and decades of propaganda about the virtues of free competition. The coal industry was as clearly doomed as barges were as the primary means of transport. The explanation evoked no questions, except how quickly and easily could miners get out of the industry.

CHAPTER 7

RESPONSES

British miners responded in two main ways to their changed industrial situation. They did so collectively through the National Union of Mineworkers and individually, in that order. The Union reaction largely determined the character of the individual ones.

The Importance of the Union

It is not possible to understand the industrial behaviour of miners without first recognising their commitment to their Union. The National Union of Mineworkers is still the public face of the coalfields based, semi-autonomous county unions which comprise its Areas. The Areas of the Union embody the solidarity between miners. Their influence moreover is not confined to the pits for the consequence of pit work dominates and pervades all facets of the lives of miners and their families. The Union has a presence in the churches, the local government, the Cooperative Movement, the Workingmen's Clubs. It has views on most issues which confront miners. Some miners, of course criticize their Union but, since the end of Spencerism, they have rarely repudiated it and have never broken away from it.

A key factor, then, in the whole of the period up to the late 1960s was the policy of the Union. There was, of course, an interaction between the collective view and the individual attitudes of the miners for they reacted on each other. Individual miners determined the Union policy but they did so in collective situations which were markedly different from their individual ones, in their homes with their families. Their collective situations contained special factors such as the acceptance of a responsibility for the coal industry after the Second World War, a determination to make a success of nationalization, an obligation to give encouragement to the first post-war Labour Government. Miners as individuals, however, like individual workers everywhere, were motivated primarily by questions of subsistence, the level of earnings, the hours worked, the conditions of work. They did not ignore these questions when they met collectively but put them into a different context, and in some way subordinated them to the wider issues.

The Union took its class and national responsibilities seriously and embarked on a policy of almost complete collaboration with the Government and the N.C.B. after 1947. Some officials in the Union found collaboration easy because they came from Areas, like Nottingham, which had traditionally worked closely with the coal owners. Others collaborated from the political conviction that nationalization should be made to succeed through a Labour

Government. The most articulate in this second category were members of the British Communist Party. It was these people, personified by Arthur Horner, the General Secretary of the Union, who gave the Union policy its drive and meaning.

The Meaning of Collaboration

What did collaboration involve? It was not simply a case of cooperating with the N.C.B. in evolving policies for the coal industry but of accepting N.C.B. policies as its own and being in part responsible for their application and execution. It meant moderating Union demands, sometimes almost to the point of extinction, at a time when the Union was in a powerful market position. The Union, for example, obtained a Five-day Week Agreement in 1947 and almost immediately suspended it in an attempt to raise productivity. It accepted voluntary Saturday morning working against a history of pressure for shorter working hours. It took action against miners who engaged in unofficial strikes and absenteeism. It accepted pit closures and defused local protests about them.

The attitude of the N.U.M. in the early years of nationalization was reflected in a speech by Arthur Horner to the N.U.M. Annual Conference in 1948. "On July 13th or 14th," he stated, "you will see in your newspapers reports of the first year's work of the National Coal Board. There will be people going through that Report with a microscope to detect faults in order to condemn the Board because they want to condemn nationalization. We have to say to these critics that together, the Government and the Union, we have saved the economy of this country, for without us it could not have been saved. We will continue to work for the recovery of the economy of this country, and if in the first year there is a relatively trifling loss, which is largely a book-keeping loss, then who is to worry about that when it is related to the great achievements that enables you, Mr. Minister, to promise your colleagues in the Government actually to maintain your policy of full employment . . . We can say to the Board. You have done well, but we will continue to help you do very much better."

Collaboration did not stop with the demise of the Labour Government in 1951, nor when the experiences of nationalization turned sour after 1956. When the decline of the industry first started the officials of the Union tended to blame it upon Conservative policy decisions but fairly quickly they came to accept the logic of the case for contracting the industry. The political divisions amongst miners reflected differences in emphases not basic attitudes. Communist Party members, such as Will Paynter the General Secretary from 1959, Bill Whitehead, who succeeded Paynter as the President of the South Wales miners, Abe Moffat the President of the Scottish miners and his brother Alex who succeeded him as well as others in official positions around the coalfields continued to advocate continuity in the Union's policy of cooperation with the N.C.B. They were in agreement on this issue with those who were their political antagonists, such as Sidney Ford, the Union President, Sam Bullough, the President of the Yorkshire Area and Jack Lally, President of the Midlands Area. The Union revealed no significant sectional differences over the important issues which faced it. On the question of contraction it insisted that the decisions to close which pits, when and where, were the prerogative of the management. The Union intervened only to facilitate the closures by assisting to alleviate the hardships which might result from them.

There was no consultation about the extent and intensity of the closure programmes. The N.C.B. announced its first major closure programme to Union officials in December 1958 without leaving any room for amendment. The same procedure of pulling the programme out of a hat was repeated in November, 1965 when accelerated closures were announced. These unilateral acts still did not upset the harmony between the Union and management or endanger the concessions the Union was willing to make. For instance, right in the midst of the contraction process, late in 1964, the N.C.B. informed the Union that there might be large coal shortages and a need, therefore, to revise working on Saturdays. The executive of the N.U.M. agreed, in the event of that happening, to summon a special N.E.C. meeting to authorize Saturday working. In the light of the Union policy to demand shorter working hours this was a major concession. Forty-three pits were closed in 1964. It so happened that there was a mild winter so that a shortage of domestic fuel did not materialize. The N.C.B., therefore, told the Union that it had no need to consider Saturday working any longer. The Union did as it was advised by the management.

From the beginning of the contraction until 1964, when the Conservative Government was still in office, the Union officials constantly repeated that the only guarantee of stopping the decline was to return a Labour Government. Abe Moffat, the President of the Scottish Area, stated in 1961 that "if we are going to solve our problems in the mining industry, the best guarantee is to get this Tory Government out of office." A Labour Government was returned in 1964. A year later it published its National Plan which indicated that it accepted the reasoning of the previous Conservative Government about energy resources and intended, therefore, to continue the contraction programme. The rate of closures was, in fact, intensified. The pledge given to miners by the Labour Party before the election was repudiated. Despite this the N.U.M. was not deflected from its policy of collaboration with the Government. The president of the Union emphasized this in his 1967 presidential address when he endeavoured to illustrate that the Government was not guilty of a breach of faith. He said that "all the many undertakings and statements have to be read in the context of the first objective of nationalization . . . viz. 'To reorganize and modernize the coalmining industry so as to produce more efficiently the coal required' and the belief that progress would be made in this connection . . . and . . . let me remind you, it was made clear by the Minister of Fuel and Power in 1946, that it was not the intention of the Government that the activities of the Board should be bolstered up by 'concealed subsidies;' there was, he said, 'no charity about the proposals for the industry' . . . Study Labour Party and/or T.U.C. decisions and official documents and publications and you will find such phrases as 'efficiently-mined indigenous coal'; everything depends upon efficiency, costs and the resulting prices,' says the 1966 General Election Manifesto of the Party." Ford added that, "if the industry is to survive it must be reasonably price competitive . . . What we have to ensure is that the industry's capital equipment and its manpower are utilized to the best possible advantage. This can be achieved in two ways. First by concentrating production on the more efficient collieries, and secondly, by the more intensive utilization of the available mechanical aids and equipment within each week." In effect, Ford believed that the Labour Government was justified in not carrying out its pre-election declaration about the level of coal output if its reasons were based on the need to improve efficiency. Moreover, his advocacy of the need to concentrate production implied an acceptance of pit closures as a necessary consequence. The Labour Government did not have a more firmly committed supporter.

The Depoliticization of Miners

This attitude of the Union was a positive one in relation to the Government but it had negative consequences for ordinary members for in effect it endorsed the view that the coal industry did not have a future, that it was an industry to vacate. It gave licence to miners to try to get alternative work. More importantly it turned the minds of miners away from protest by encouraging them to accept the inevitability of decline and, in doing so, it depoliticized them. Miners were diverted from seeing their situation in a political context, with political causes and political solutions. They were encouraged to think there was no solution. The issue was converted into one of self-preservation, of looking after oneself and ones family. This, of course, was a central consideration in any case because it lay at the core of the dominant capitalist ethic, namely individualism. But this was an instance of a collectivist organization encouraging by its actions the antithesis of its own ethic.

When people become depoliticized it is a resignation from effective decision-making, an abrogation of the responsibilities of citizenship, a retreat into disillusionment about the present and pessimism about the future. It is a condition most Governments try to encourage in action, though not necessarily in words, for it destroys opposition. It is sometimes brought about, at other times facilitated, by negative collaboration between unions and employers, and unions and Governments. In capitalist societies virtually all such collaboration, even that in nationalized industries, is of the negative variety.

The Union was not alone in encouraging miners to leave the pits. The N.C.B. played an important part in this operation through its prime spokesman, its chairman Lord Robens, and through the dissemination of information and comment in the N.C.B. tabloid newspaper, *Coal News*. Robens was of enormous value to Governments for he diligently executed their policies whilst maintaining a profile of an aggressive, independent critic who was in some ways closer to the interest of miners than their own officials. He addressed each Annual Conference of the N.U.M. during these years, frequently getting standing ovations, regularly attacking the Government for some aspect or other of its energy policy. I heard him on many occasions making out the case for consensus which meant accepting management's policy, isolating militant miners as unreasonable, unthinking people, consistently using economic arguments which were impeccable so long as their assumptions were unquestioned, yet projecting himself as the champion of the miners' cause.

When Robens addressed the Scottish Trades Union Congress at Perth in 1964 he started by saying that the miners never had a better friend than Alf Robens and that they would have been in a mess if he had not gone to the N.C.B. He projected himself as 'one of them.' Though he was at Perth as a guest, he said that he could have been introduced as a fraternal delegate, a fellow trade unionist or a Socialist. This approach served the N.C.B. well. The attitude of Robens towards the N.U.M. and his approach to the coal industry are well depicted in the autobiographical account of his chairmanship of the N.C.B., called *Ten Year Stint*. He made, for example, the following statement: "There was a continuing tendency for some of the miners' leaders constantly to look to the Government to save the industry from contraction, and at the same time to ensure substantial improvements in wages and conditions. This attitude did not further the interests of the miners, because it took their eyes off the economic ball. Efficiency alone determined the size of the industry and consequently the number of people it could employ. They really believed that under the Labour Government life would be different, and it was some time before the disillusionment came. I took the opportunity of the annual conference speech time and time again to try to show the realities of life under any Government. . . I told them that they had all thought that with a Labour Govern-

66

ment life would be easy for the mining industry. Now they knew differently. 'You will live by pulling yourselves up by your own bootstraps. You cannot look to Governments to save you anymore . . .' I repeatedly tried to show that in the end it was the customer who decided the size of the industry. Once it was cheaper or more convenient to use another fuel, sentiment would count for nothing." (pp. 49-50). These were half-truths, even under capitalism. They bore no relation to the ethical intentions of nationalization. But they were plausible and he was persuasive.

The Bias of Coal News

The ideas which Lord Robens propagated in his speeches were much more systematically spread through *Coal News* which carried managerial accounts of events direct to the majority of miners with little contradiction from Union sources except in Scotland, South Wales and Derbyshire. The management insisted that the *Coal News* reporting was factual. In some instances it was objective, such as when it reported the details of wages agreements, but the selection of facts and the manner of their presentation supported the notions about the industry which management possessed. The reporting legitimized whatever decisions management took. It would have been a rather disruptive house magazine if it had done otherwise.

The meaning of a fact depends upon a person's relation to it. A figure by itself is not a fact. Thus neither 40 by itself nor £40 is a fact until either one is given a context involving a relationship. The figure £40 can be repeated *ad nauseum* without causing anyone the slightest concern. If we write "a £40 wage" this has more meaning but remains uncontroversial until we asked whose wage. When we write "a £40 wage for surface workers in the mining industry" we are stating something which in one sense in an incontrovertible fact for "a £40 wage for surface workers in the mining industry" is "a £40 wage for surface workers in the mining industry" and nothing else. But its meaning depends upon whether one is a surface worker or in a mining job which has a relationship to surface work. It has a different meaning for management and, if the surface workers are campaigning for an increase because, for them, £40 is inadequate, it may have a different meaning for Government. Thus the very sight of this fact on the page of *Coal News* can arouse different emotions and reactions. If we look further and examine the context of this simple sentence we will find that the emphases will increase or decrease the emotions. The fact of the Government's 5 per cent norm for pay increases in 1978 and 1979 had a different meaning for government, for employers and for employees; and amongst employees its meaning depended on whether a person was highly paid or lowly paid. Clearly, once a number is put into a social

67

context it takes on different meanings and is subject to different interpretations.

Lord Robens believed that *Coal News* was performing an unbiassed service to miners when it gave details of a wages negotiation, often before they could be provided from union sources. "When the delicate matter of wages is being discussed," he stated, "it is imperative that every employee should be fully aware of all the facts. The mineworker is entitled to have, not only the details of an offer on which he may be required to vote, but also the reasons why the Board are unable to offer bigger increases, what the effect on prices is likely to be, how much business we may lose to the competitors, and how many miners' jobs may be lost if increases are not covered by rises in productivity. This information is needed before the man can make a sensible decision about where to put the cross on his ballot paper. . ." (*Ten Year Stint*, p. 133). In addition to *Coal News* the N.C.B. used direct mail, local press advertising and the joint consultative machinery in order to communicate with miners. Its communications, however, were unbiassed only to management, though even this was not strictly true because management had its own divisions and contradictory perceptions. The communications system of which Lord Robens was so proud strictly served only his level of management in an unbiased, incontrovertible manner.

Strikes Against Closures

Individual miners formulated their opinions about the causes of contraction and what they should do about it from the consensus of advice from their Union, their employer and the Government which together amounted to 'get out while you can, as quickly as you can.' And this is what they did, though not so quickly at first.

There were many cases of locally organized, unofficial protests against pit closures during the period of expansion, when pits were closed to facilitate concentration, and in the early years of contraction. The protests usually had a community basis often involving church organizations and local Labour and Communist Parties, as well as Miners' Union branches. But they were spontaneous, loosely organized and generally without really effective institutional support. Occasionally strikes developed and spread. For instance, 66 underground workers staged a stay-down strike in June, 1959, against the closure of the Devon pit at Fishcross in Alloa, Scotland. The strike quickly spread to other pits until 45 of them, involving 25,000 miners were on strike. The strike, however, was in opposition to the official Union policy and the Scottish Area officials intervened to end it. Miners diplaced from the Devon pit were transferred to the Glenochil pit nearby and when, in 1962, this was also closed there was a further strike of 3,000 workers but this too was short-lived. In 1960 about 12,000 miners throughout the country were involvd in redundancy disputes. It was much the same in 1961 and 1962. But the experience of protest was not a happy one. It was taken in defiance of the Union, the N.C.B. and the Government. From 1962 there were virtually no local collective protests against closures. The miners had lost heart.

The Exodus

From the advent of nationalization until 1968 there was a relatively high level of employment in the country as a whole. Workers had a security of employment which was unique for peacetime. They could, within limits imposed by their skills and location, pick and choose between employers.

In this situation there was inevitably much movement between industries as workers sought satisfaction by moving from one job to another. It was a luxury for miners, more than for most workers, to be able to pick and choose between jobs and they indulged in it. Labour turnover in mining, however, was always relatively high because of the incidence of involuntary movement through sickness and injury, as well as the usual age factor. Altogether, between 7 and 10 per cent of all miners left the industry each year from 1947 to 1959 and of these just over one-half left voluntarily. The percentage of voluntary leavers varied from one year to another. The lowest point was in 1946 when only 11,000 out of a labour force of 697,000 left under their own volition. After that the proportion of voluntary leavers rose slowly until 1950 when it more than doubled and averaged just less than 6 per cent. The problem which the industry faced in those years of expansion was of recruiting miners from ouside the families of miners and then of retaining them. The voluntary leavers tended to be men who failed to adjust to mining as a career.

The character of the yearly wastage began to change from 1960 as the processes of contraction and mechanization began to make their mark on the attitudes of miners. It is not possible to make a straightforward statistical comparison between the years of expansion and contraction in this respect because the N.C.B. figures for voluntary wastage for the years up to 1956 included miners made redundant whereas from 1956 redundant miners were categorized separately. Relatively few men were made redundant before 1956 but even so the voluntary wastage figures for those years were exaggerated compared with those that followed.

From 1960 to 1968 the rate of voluntary wastage was as high as the rate of total wastage had been before. Miners began to leave the industry in a hurry. In 1960, for instance, 58,000 men left out of a labour force of 583,000. It was much the same the following year. More miners had left the industry in the eight years up to 1968 than remained in it. Altogether, 346,300 men looked for jobs elsewhere.

69

In 1968 the total labour force was only 318,700. This mass exodus was accompanied by an increasing rate of redundancy as the contraction process intensified. The peak and unprecedented year was 1968 when in addition to those who left voluntary and involuntarily due to age, injury and sickness, as many as 21,178 men were declared redundant.

The sight of increased redundancy added to the morale breaking factors which were already present. The evidence of those years indicates that many more would have left mining if they had been free to do so. Many miners were too old or too physically incapacitated to be able to get alternative jobs without great difficulty. Some had family ties such as children in education or at work which made it difficult to move from mining where this involved going to another area. So many miners who stayed were involuntary stayers.

The other aspect of this phenomenon was that those who left were the mobile ones and these, almost invariably, were men in their prime as coal getters, between the ages of 25 and 40 years, physically fit and energetic. With the loss of the relatively young miners, and with virtually no recruitment of boys from school, the average age of all miners rose from just over 42 years in 1955 to almost 44 years in 1969. These figures, however, hide the real significance of the ageing process which was that the percentage of miners in the prime age group, 25 to 40 years, fell from 35 in 1950 to 24 in 1968. Of course, with the introduction of fully coordinated mechanization the need for face workers declined but underground mining in all of its aspects is a tiring, onerous activity which can best be borne by the young and physically fit. The response of miners to their changing, deteriorating work situation, encouraged by all the institutions connected with mining, amounted then to an exodus from mining which was unplanned, unanticipated and a burden which the industry could ill afford to bear.

CHAPTER 8

CONSEQUENCES

There were miners who lost their jobs and miners who did not but both experienced the consequences of the combined pressures of the pincer made up from contraction and mechanization. They faced, in different ways, difficult, unsettling social and economic problems. Most of those who lost their jobs were, until 1967, given the opportunity of work in other pits in their own or other coalfields. There occurred a migration between coalfields which was greater than anything similar since the growth period of the coal industry. The movement was largely of Scots, Welsh, Lancashire, Northumberland and Durham miners into Yorkshire, Nottinghamshire and the Midlands. The insularity of the receiving coalfields was penetrated by colonies of strangers who settled in them. Sometimes, as at Knottingley in the North Yorkshire coalfield where many Scots migrated to work at the new Kellingley colliery nearby, villages were transformed by the scale of the movement.

For all of the miners, their wives and children there were problems due to having to uproot themselves from established social and family relationships, changing homes, finding new friends, fitting into different institutions, sometimes acquiring new skills and becoming acquainted with different work environments. For those who left mining altogether the transition involved more radical and unsettling changes and included an almost complete write-off of their human investment in mining, a rejection of their skills acquired through years of commitment, learning, effort and exposure to injury and disease. The skills which miners acquire are of little use anywhere except in mining of one sort or another. The miners who stayed experienced consequences which were dramatic, unanticipated and disturbing.

Human Capital

None of these factors was taken into account when decisions to contract and mechanize were made. Indeed the mining industry, in common with other capitalist industries, was never concerned about human capital. It is doubtful whether employers have ever regarded labour power as a form of investment either in relation to their own interests or to those of the men and women who have been compelled to sell it, except perhaps in a few instances concerning people with expensive, highly specific skills. It is certainly the case that the coal owners did not identify labour power as human capital, let alone equate it with finance capital. All along, throughout the development of capitalist industry, finance capital has had an unapproachable status and value. All considerations have been subordinate to those

71

Pit brow women workers in the early years of this century. (1)

Pit brow women workers in the early years of this century. (2)

concerned with increasing the value of finance capital. In fact the term capital refers only in common usage to the accumulation and use of property expressed in money terms.

The matter can be stated in more mundane terms. The coal-owners were never concerned about the treatment and the condition of its labour force unless they were forced to be so. In general they acquired labour where they could, men if possible but if not then women and children. They accepted no responsibility voluntarily for the depreciation of their employees through sickness, injury or excessive work.

Managerial attitudes towards the conditions under which labour power was exploited changed after nationalization though not in essential ways. Nationalization did not result in enhancing the value attached to human capital. The N.C.B. continued to regard labour costs as first targets when cost pressures were mounted. Contraction was conducted with some consideration but mainly because the N.C.B. was able to reshuffle its labour force through the local labour shortages it experienced in the midst of a general surplus. In general the N.C.B. responded to its own needs and not those of its employees. Redundant miners were not given the kind of protection which the Limited Liability Act gives to employers to limit their financial losses and protect their personal wealth. Miners who lost their jobs were subjected to the ruthless exposure of the labour market until the N.C.B. from 1962 cushioned its impact with some compensation but this failed to cover the financial costs and did not even pretend to relate to the social costs of dislocation. The depreciation of labour and the burden of dislocation and re-organization in coal mining have always amounted to a social cost which was degrading for any society considered to be civilized. In the main it has been borne by miners themselves and their families.

Mining Families

Mining families, centred around women, have functioned as vital elements in the organization of mining. In what might appear to be an incredibly uncanny fashion every detail of the immediate environment of the miners - their leisure, their homes, family relationships, wives and children - has served the structure of their existence, namely the provision of labour power with given skills in required quantities at the requisite times. Nothing and no one has been spared; no humanity has been allowed to intrude. It has not been a machievellian operation; there have been no villians. It has been simply a case of the basic structural needs of the situation dominating everything else, moulding everything to suit its own peculiar requirements. In this process women and wives have been adapted to meet the needs of mining as effectively as miners themselves.

This process of adaptation has taken place since the seventeenth

74

century with the emergence and development of the mining industry. It has communicated the changing needs of the industry as mines became deeper, more numerous, mechanized, involving more danger, different skills, increased labour power and a reliable source of labour power. The emergent set of social relations, however, was the product of the interaction of mining industry requirements with the appraisal by the men and women in mining of these requirements in relation to their own struggle for subsistence. The result has been a sort of weak compromise with the market influences dominating.

The family has always been at the core of social relationships because it is the institution through which all the immediate questions of subsistence are mediated. Because of its close proximity to production it reflects the dominant relations of production in its own character, organization and administration. The position of the man, the activities of the woman, the socialization of their children, their inter-relationships and the demands which these all make upon other kinsfolk in a capitalist society reflect the essence of capitalism itself. It should be remembered that although the family unit in the working class is crucially concerned with the subsistence of its members this is not its primary purpose. Primarily its purpose is social reproduction - producing a labour force of the kind, in the quantities that capitalism requires.

This is seen most clearly in the case of mining. Women invest their skills in mining, contribute to its organization, its viability and its success in capitalist terms, by ensuring the continuity of a suitable supply of labour power.

Under capitalism, unlike in earlier and other forms of society, production activities extended beyond the family household and came to be concentrated almost exclusively in the hands of men. Indeed only that production which occurred outside of the family and which was the result of the interaction of market forces was accorded a value. Thus men derived power and status from their involvement in market-determined production while those activities which remained within the family household were devalued, being accorded neither prices nor status. Men worked and played outside the family and returned to it only for certain physical comforts and to replenish themselves for the next shift.

The task of social reproduction became the responsibility of women, of wives, mothers, sisters and daughters who serviced the men by washing, cleaning and cooking, who cared for the children and socialized them in the ways of mining. Thus women ensured through a variety of activities that the coal-owners would have an adequate supply of male workers tramping to the pits each day, for each shift whether it be at night or during the day. This function was performed at no cost to the employers for the domestic labour of women had no price on it and was not paid for. It was not even

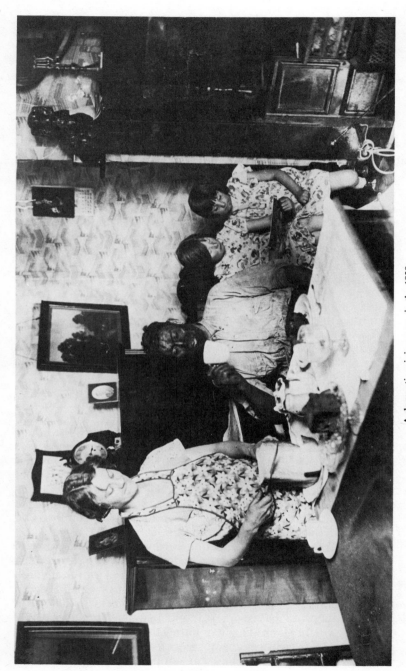

A domestic mining scene in the 1930s.

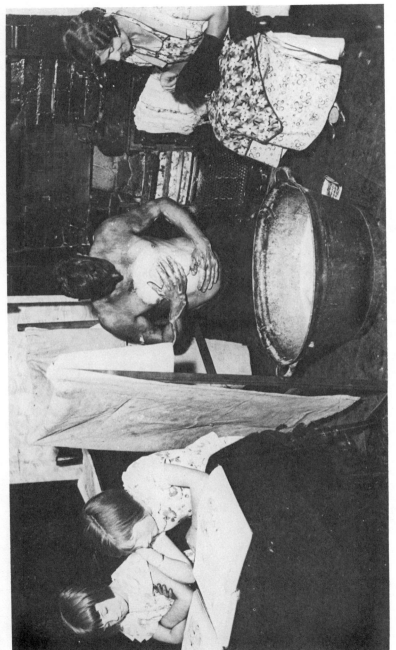

Before pit-head baths.

Domestic, unpaid labour for the coal industry.

designated as work. Women received only their subsistence, paid in kind, in return for their labour.

In some coalfields women combined this all-consuming task with full or part-time wage labour in cotton textile or woollen mills, in pottery manufacture or with home-working activities for the benefit of employers. All of this was done relatively cheaply because women were able to be regarded as a reserve army of labour. They were released from the confines but not the responsibilities of family households as and when the capitalist system required it. So long as domestic labour was not treated as a marketable commodity and home-working was dismissed as a peripheral phenomenon then family services could be regarded as free goods for employers and female labour could be degraded in whatever form it was used.

The manner in which a division of labour was wrought between miners and womenfolk was as effective as any that had been created in the production process and was as necessary for that process. It was supported and justified by ideas about women and their relationships with men which had a basis in women's experience. Women concerned about households wanted regular wages so they preferred miners to be consistent and responsible workers, abstemious workers, hard workers. The 'good worker' in women's terms was a conscientious worker in employers' terms. The bad worker from the employers' point of view was stigmatised in his own home just as Walter Morel was stigmatised in the D. H. Lawrence novel *Sons and Lovers* for his drunkenness, his neglect of his wife and children, for his depravity.

The state of affairs which put men into pits and left women as unpaid domestic labour to provide back-up services for the industry was encouraged, sustained and legitimized in the eyes of women and men by the circulation of ideas about 'man's work,' the responsibility of the women in the home, the virtue of obedience to a man's wishes, of subordination to his needs. The ideas, communicated through education, religion, literature and the mass media consolidated the division between men and women by becoming part of their consciousness, expressed in the conviction that the division was right, indeed natural. Miners and womenfolk lived out a condition in the interests of the capitalist exploitation of coal which became discriminatory and oppressive towards women. This condition was modified slightly as the industry experienced its post-war contortions and women were compelled to get jobs themselves as a buffer against insecurity and declining living standards but the legacy of sexist attitudes and practices remained.

The importance for mining of the free, do-it-yourself method of sustaining the supply of human capital and of nurturing the rejects is self-evident. The significance of the free do-it-yourself method of reproducing human capital to suit the needs of mining is not so

A miner's wife in New Sharlston, Yorkshire, 1979.

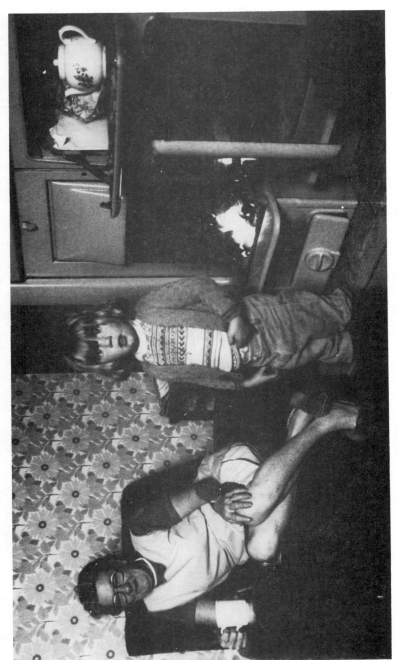

Waiting for the end of a shift, New Sharlston, Yorkshire, 1979.

Wives and workers in New Sharlston, Yorkshire in 1979.

Miners of the future in New Sharlston, Yorkshire, 1979.

self-evident because who, knowing the incidence of disease and injury in mining, would encourage any person to work down a pit. Yet the majority of miners come from mining families. Relatively few men who are strangers to mining want to endure its risks voluntarily. Only those who grow up in the environment of mining, for whom the costs are an everyday feature, become immune to them. The mining family, therefore, serves to perpetuate the mining industry. Anything then which destroys mining families is creating problems for the future of the industry.

The Loss of Managerial Control Over the Labour Supply

Contraction destroyed mining families. Through the disillusionment it created, resulting in about 40 per cent of the miners who left the industry in the decade after 1957 leaving voluntarily, mining families were transformed. The focus of many families ceased to be on the pit. The production of social personalities required for mining was curtailed slowly but surely as the industry was contracted. Disillusionment about the future of the industry was not confined to those who left so that in many families emphases about mining as a career were altered. To the customary hesitations about a job underground because of its dangers was added one about its terminal future. It is impossible to assess the full extent of damage to the future supply of human capital for mining caused by the high toll of mining families. It was not, in any case, considered to be important so long as the industry seemed not to have a future.

The National Coal Board dutifully executed the decisions of Governments in the 1960s in the belief that they would achieve their intended results. Lord Robens, presiding over the N.C.B. during that fateful decade, at the pinnacle of the pyramid of control which professional management had constructed to supervise the extraction of coal, believed that his decisions would vibrate through the organization in precisely the way he intended. "Close those pits in Ayr but not those in Fife, concentrate only on the efficient pits in Lancashire; shed labour here but not in Yorkshire and Nottingham" - all according to the blueprints which described the logistics of successive Government policies. On paper it was so neat and sensible, expressed diagramatically showing how output could be increased from a declining number of pits because the productivity of the few which remained would be raised. It all showed the British coal industry of the 1980s consisting of a relatively small number of large highly mechanized pits concentrated mainly in Yorkshire, Nottingham and the Midlands.

Lord Robens, however, like managers in general, was in a sense living in a world of his own making, to some extent a fantasy world, where problems were simply communications difficulties and resources, animate and inanimate, responded as decisions about them

84

were made. But people have perceptions and attitudes and behave in a manner which can negate managerial intentions. In addition, decisions taken to resolve contradictions create consequences which are unintended. In the process of resolving contradictions others are created which may intensify rather than ease the problems. The image of managerial life is real, however, to the extent that decisions have some consequences. The managers of the coal industry did close pits and they did reduce the labour force drastically. What they did not do, because without absolute control over the whole workforce they could not do, was to transform into experience the details of their blueprints.

Once the contraction began, the Government and the N.C.B. endeavoured to justify it to those who were directly affected by it. The effect of the explanations, however, could not be confined to the particular miners who were compelled to leave or readjust. The Government appeared to be legitimizing leaving the industry and this, in effect, encouraged anyone and everyone to leave it. Miners disappeared from the industry irrespective of management decrees and no matter whether their pits were scheduled for closure or expansion. Many miners who left voluntarily went from pits which were still producing. In consequence the N.C.B. was in the ludicrous position of having localized labour shortages within the labour market it desperately wanted to cut back.

It seemed obvious, moreover, that an industry without a projected future would lose its young, fit, mobile workers. This is precisely what happened. The N.C.B. lost its most skilled face workers. Inadvertently the management created for itself, as was shown in the previous chapter, an ageing labour force which was not well-equipped for such an industry as mining. Older miners found it difficult to cope with the work situation changes, especially the handling of machines. They had less stamina than many of those who had left and were more prone to absenteeism, accidents and sickness. It so happened that many of the men who left were those with fairly young families, involved in the social reproduction of miners. Their departure had immediate and longer term conse-quences for the industry. In total, the planned contraction got out of hand. If the events after 1968 had not reduced the flow from industry it would virtually have wasted away by the mid 1970s, destroyed by an inept, short-sighted miscalcaulation about energy supplies. Once the process had been started both the N.C.B. and the Government were helpless to stop it. Only a decision to halt all pit closures, to stand the Government's energy calculations on their head and to put its propaganda mechanism in reverse would have helped in this matter.

The End of Piecework

The reason for intensifying the process of mechanization was to increase productivity with a smaller labour force but there were other possibilities too. With an integrated process of mechanized tasks from cutting to conveying with hydraulic roof supports there was the possibility of management being able to control the machines, and, therefore, the pace of work, in a way in which they could not control men. Before the introduction of power-loading machines the process of coal-getting had been broken into three distinct shift operations: there had been coal-cutting, loading and then preparations for cutting such as moving roof supports. Actual cutting had been confined to one shift a day. The integrated process of mechanization enabled management to cut around the clock if they wanted to do so.

Under the piecework system of wage payment the actual levels of earnings of face-workers were determined by the rates set for each face. They were issues of great contention for the ability to extract coal varied according to geological conditions so that a rate fixed at the beginning of a face could become inappropriate as the ease of coal getting worsened because of changing conditions. The matter was especially important for the face workers for if they hit a geological fault their earnings dropped sharply. There were, as a result, constant struggles between groups of face workers and colliery managements over rates, resulting frequently in strikes. The outcome of the struggles varied, sometimes within pits. Well organized face workers confronting relatively weak managements were able to push their rates up in comparison with others. Where it was difficult to change the rates because of district collective agreements it was always possible for changing working circumstances to be met by additional payments or allowances negotiated on the spot, at the point of production, not with colliery managers but with deputies who had to work with the miners and who inclined, therefore, to be more conciliatory than more remotely situated managers.

The earnings of miners, from the second world war period, were fixed within the context of district agreements supported by nationally negotiated wages agreements. At the end of the war, although about one third of the earnings of pieceworkers was not related to effort, there remained much scope for local variations. The differing geological conditions and collective pressures created a maze of variations between faceworkers and between faceworkers and others underground and on the surface which management could not control. Such differentials had been consistently opposed by the miners where they represented different rates for similar work but they did not constitute an issue for the coal-owners. After nationalization, however, with a centralized management, the inability to introduce order into wage negotiations and to remove anomalies to regulate differentials to suit and serve a manpower policy was regarded as a major managerial deficiency, a threat to effective management. The N.C.B. therefore, set its sights on achieving a national comprehensive and rational wages structure but it was not until the early 1960s that this became a possibility. With power-loaded faces the management believed that it no longer needed piecework. Moreover, without it there appeared positive advantages such as a reduction in the incidence of strikes and, perhaps, better labour and management relations in general. On the whole, the crude, self-operative, anarchistic piece-work system appeared to be an anachronism in the emerging age of computerized operations and manless faces.

The management had cause to believe in the 1960s that it was in full charge of events. A day-wage method of wage payment was introduced in 1966, productivity improved substantially and the incidence of strikes declined dramatically. But the belief was short-sighted and led to a costly complacency.

The Day-Wage System

The longest surviving issue of policy of the Miners' Federation of Great Britain was to secure a wages system which removed anomalies between similar work and which stabilized earnings. Until the middle of the 1950s, however, it was an issue which was never scrutinized to discover how it would be applied, who it would effect and how it would operate. In 1955 a national daywage structure was agreed. Almost all surface and underground workers other than at the face were paid on a daywage basis. In all there were about 400,000 of them employed in more than 6,500 local job categories. The intention under the new agreement was to evaluate each one according to skill and responsibility and to recategorize them so that anomalous differentials could be removed. About 360 job descriptions were eventually used. It was discovered, however, that the differentials between districts and within them were so wide that the N.C.B. was not able to equalize rates either up to the top because the manage-ment considered it was too costly or below the top because the N.U.M. would not agree to a levelling down process. So a partial and gradual wage equalization method was agreed. It was envisaged that men on the highest rates would not benefit fully from future wage increases and that as day-wage workers changed jobs they would forfeit, if necessary, personal allowances which pushed their earnings up. The Daywage Agreement also categorized piece-workers under work studied job descriptions and grades but the day-wages applied to them were so low that they barely acted as fall-back rates.

The N.C.B. later attempted to construct a national piece-work wages structure in which equal effort was rewarded by equal wages irrespective of the conditions or the method of working but it was never satisfactorily finalized and was not put to the Union. The range of variations between earnings and between tasks was so great that a schedule could not be devised even to act as a basis for negotiations. This was a trickier business than with time-rated workers because pieceworkers were much more group conscious, resistant to adverse changes and prone to use the strike weapon.

Irrespective of the attempts to get a national wages agreement there was a slow accretion of district power-loading agreements, starting with a Scottish one in 1948 so that by the early 1960s the task of achieving national uniformity had become, in part, one of reconciling different local agreements. The General Secretary of the N.U.M. explained the difficulties they met when he addressed a Special Conference on wages in March, 1965. He stated: "We had to face the facts of life as far as power-loading is concerned. It is true that generally throughout the British coalfields power-loading is accommodated within divisional agreements, and we took a return from our Areas to discover just exactly what kind of agreements were existing in the various coalfields. Some are based on straight time rates where task work and piecework are not contained in the agreements. Others are based on task work with incentive bonuses. Others are based on straight piecework, so much for each yard of advance of the face, with a pro rata payment for any excess over the norms that are agreed . . . but not all the coalfields are covered by divisional agreements. We have certain important coalfields, like the North West . . . where all the agreements are on a pit basis and some of them on a seam basis . . ."

The Union was also faced with the problem of wage rates for the daywagemen. These rates were low in absolute terms but were also low in relation to pieceworkers so that the question of narrowing the differential between surface and faceworkers had to be confronted. It was one with which the N.C.B. was also concerned, though for different reasons. By 1965 the interests of the N.U.M. and the N.C.B. were converging on the question of a wages structure but the outcome was by no means clear. The view of the Union executive in March 1965 was that the rates for daywagemen and a power-loading agreement were separate issues and that a national power-loading agreement based on time-rates would be unacceptable to the majority of face workers. Time rates for pieceworkers were, according to Paynter, "too revolutionary a change . . ."

Between March 1965 and April 1966, when a Special Conference on wages was held the view of the N.E.C. about the desirability of introducing time rates for power loading had changed. Will Paynter, in a speech lasting almost 2 hours moved the acceptance of a draft agreement which set up a completely new daywage agreement for 100,000 workers on power loaded faces. Miners working on conventional faces were left to operate their piece rate system but they were a rapidly declining section of the industry. The agreement was accepted by the Conference without any serious opposition but was ratified in the Areas by a relatively small majority, namely 269 votes in favour and 226 against. It was signed by the N.C.B. and the N.U.M. in June 1966.

The agreement established standard shift rates for power-loading teams on all new mechanized faces, except in Scotland and Durham where all mechanized faces were covered. At the beginning the standard shift rates varied between Wages Districts and were related to average face workers' earnings in those Districts but the intention was to reach a uniform national rate by the end of 1971 by holding back the rates of the highest paid and allowing the rest to catch up with them. The agreement entailed a reduction in real earnings for many miners over the five year transition period and it was in anticipation of this that so many of them voted against it. The N.U.M. would have liked to have had uniformity from the outset with every one brought up to the highest rate but the N.C.B. would not agree: indeed Paynter said that the N.C.B. did not want uniformity written into the agreement at all.

The most significant factor during the negotiations was the swing of opinion of the N.U.M. national executive in favour of a national daywage for face workers with no element of bonus or incentive in it. During the course of the year the case for daywages became so compelling that it transcended the belief that the miners would not accept it. Paynter's own conviction that uniform daywages would be equitable and unifying was important as was the N.C.B.'s realization of the possible benefits for management. The attitude of the N.C.B. was stated in its annual report for 1966-67: "Piecework was becoming increasingly inappropriate as a means of payment for men on mechanized faces where productivity depends less on physical effort than on the utilization of machines. Agreements based on piecework, moreover, needed constant revision and re-negotiation and they were the source of many stoppages and disputes in the industry. Deployment of men can be more flexible than when earnings varied from face to face and, with a standard shift rate, wages can be more effectively controlled; in particular, the disproportionate gap between the earnings of faceworkers and men employed outbye and on the surface . . . can be more easily remedied . . ." The N.C.B. did not anticipate, nor indeed did the officials of the N.U.M., how important wage determination under the agreement could become as a means of unifying the miners. At the time, in 1966, everything was sweetness and light.

The Decline in Strike Action

The management seemed to gain all round from the effects of

mechanizing a contracting industry. Productivity rose substantially. The national average output per manshift at the face increased from 65.8 cwts in 1955 to 132.4 cwts in 1970 while the output per manshift for the industry as a whole went up from 24.7 cwts to 42.5 in the same period. This impressive improvement in efficiency was accompanied by a dramatic fall in the incidence of strike action. The coal industry had always been noted for its strike proneness. Miners would strike, it was often said, at the drop of a hat and until the 1960s this seemed to be the case. Miners had a special place in the mythology of struggle which set them apart from others. In 1956 as many as 78.4 per cent of all strikes in Great Britain occurred in mining. The statistics are illuminating. There were 2648 strikes in all industries and services in Great Britain in 1956 and 2,074 of these were in coal mining. Every year afterwards the proportion of mining strikes in the total for the country as a whole fell until 1970 when it was a mere 4.1 per cent. That is, out of 3,906 strikes in Great Britain only 160 were in mining.

It was the case, of course, that there were many fewer pits at the end of the decade than at the beginning and as most strikes were colliery based their number was bound to fall. But there was a real fall in the incidence of strikes. A common explanation for the decline was the establishment of the daywage system. The N.C.B. Report in 1967-68 stated, for instance, that the "policy . . . to eliminate piecework had a beneficial effect upon industrial relations, as is shown by the sharp reduction in output lost through disputes. Only 439,000 tons were lost in this way in 1967-68 compared with 1,707,000 tons in the previous year . . ." There is no question that the new daywage system had an effect but the decline preceded the introduction of the National Power Loading Agreement. Miners were disillusioned and defeated. In so far as they sought solutions they did so through individualist means, by escaping to other jobs in other industries. They had little heart for collective resistance.

Alterations in Underground Relationships

The work situation for miners changed in essential disturbing ways. Managers started to manage by directing, supervising in a manner so different from before. The activities and powers of colliery managements took place within a context of mining legislation which prescribed managerial qualifications and obligations. The self-operating piecework system had a built-in supervisory function which relieved under-officials from the task of constantly watching, correcting and ordering. They spent time on wages questions but, under conditions laid down by the Mines' Acts, their main responsibility lay with health and safety.

The functions of under-officials altered first with the intensification of mechanization which gave them the facility to control

From a painting by Gilbert Dakin. Dakin was killed with five other miners in a major roof fall one hour before the end of his shift in 1939. Daking was then 53 years of age.

the pace of work. They changed even more once the direct monetary incentive was taken out of work and the efforts of miners were regulated by direct supervision. As the under-officials assumed important supervisory functions they increased both in number and as a proportion of the number of face workers. Face workers began to feel that they were breathing down their necks and with some justification. In 1968 there was one under-official for every 4.5 face workers compared with 6.5 face workers ten years earlier. This amounted to an increase of nearly 39 per cent.

This alteration in the supervisory situation was accompanied by upsets in other conventional relationships underground. Power loading systems diluted the skills of face workers and thereby undermined their elite position among colliers in general. On the other hand the position of the craftsmen who installed and maintained machines was altered. They became more numerous and more important for the coal getting process. Their status improved. In a small but inevitable way they began to challenge the authority of face workers which had remained intact since the division of labour had created specialisms at the face. The short-term consequence was to create a position of instability between groups underground, to undermine established relationships and to introduce an element of unpredictability between them which was bad for morale. Stable, predictable social relationships underground are an essential pre-requisite for coping with the dangers and arduousness of mining.

Death, Injury and Disease

Machines, in addition, affected the working lives of miners by making work intitially more dangerous. Life underground was already exceptionally hazardous. In 1955, before the pace of mechanization had intensified about one in every three workers had an accident of some kind involving at least three days off work while the number of fatal accidents averaged more than one a day. 408 miners were killed at work in 1955. Figures do not always speak for themselves. When the deaths and the injuries are spread out over the weeks and months and are scattered among the collieries in the various coal-fields they tend to be ignored. It is only when there is a disaster that people suddenly become aware of the hazardous nature of mining and even then it becomes a ten day wonder until the next time.

The Wilberforce Report in 1972 stated that "other occupations have their dangers and inconveniences, but we know of none in which there is such a combination of dangers, health hazard, dis-comfort in working conditions." Men descend as far as 3000 feet below the surface, as in the Monktonhall colliery in Scotland. They travel as far as 5 miles from the pit bottom to the face by man-riding facilities and on foot, as at Woolley colliery in Yorkshire. They work coal seams as narrow as 18 to 24 inches as at Caphouse colliery

Pit disaster at Lundhill colliery, Barnsley in Yorkshire in 1857. One hundered and eighty-nine miners lost their lives on this occasion. Miners used candles for lighting in this pit.

in Yorkshire. They have to be protected continually, vigilantly, against floods of water, gas explosions, falls of rock.

The possibility of disaster is forever present. One simple act of forgetfulness or one taken in ignorance of the real dangers can have devastating consequences. No other industry has such a catalogue of mass killings which have continued despite statutory controls and management and union regulations to prevent them. An explosion at Hartley colliery in Durham in 1862 cost 204 lives and resulted in the statutory provision that each mine should have two shafts. More than 200 men died in the Blantyre explosion in 1877. Yorkshire had its worst disaster at Oaks colliery, near Barnsley in Yorkshire, in 1866 when 361 miners were killed. In this explosion, as in all the others, fathers and sons and brothers were among the dead. At Combs pit in Yorkshire 139 miners were killed in 1893. The biggest death toll of any mining disaster in Britain occured in Senghenydd, South Wales in 1913 when 439 died. South Wales suffered more than most coalfields for 176 died in Monmouth and 87 in Glamorgan in 1890; 112 died in Glamorgan in 1892 and 290 died there in 1894. In 1910 as many as 344 miners died at Hulton in Lancashire through a coal dust explosion while at Whitehaven in Cumberland 136 miners died in the same year through an explosion caused by fire damp. These are samples, admittedly the worst, from the long catalogue. Recent disasters have not matched those for human devastation but they are still too large and too frequent. In 1973 alone there were disasters in Lofthouse in Yorkshire, Markham in Derbyshire and Seafield in Scotland. On these three occasions 29 men died.

Face workers suffer the greatest exposure to danger. Dust circulates in all areas of underground work but it is most intense at face workings. Pneumoconiosis, emphysema, bronchitis and other respiratory diseases are common. The fatality rate is high. Between 1951 and 1971 more than 17,000 miners and ex-miners died from pneumoconiosis alone. The real incidence of debilitation and death from respiratory diseases which have their origin in pit work is incalculable but phenomenal. The cost of coal can never truly be calculated.

Machines with their own attendant dangers were introduced and squeezed into this already hazardous and spacially limited environment. They made matters worse for underground workers in important respects. Men had to learn to operate them. In the early 1960s, lack of expertise with machines caused the N.U.M. much concern. The most important factor was most probably that of coping with the presence of machines, remembering that they were fixtures occupying precious space with pipes and cables serving hydrostatic and pneumatic equipment trailing everywhere and around, over and under which miners had to step, stoop, crawl and

Commemorating the centenary in 1977 of the Blantyre explosion in which more than 200 miners died.

Working by Candlelight.

A putter tramming coal from the face at Tinsley Park, South Yorkshire. He is using a candle instead of a flame safety lamp either because there is little firedamp present or because it gives off a better light. In any event the practice was dangerous.

A haulage worker in Tinsley Park colliery, Derbyshire before the First World War. The cables are already beginning to accumulate.

Coal-getting in Derbyshire in 1980

wriggle, careful not to trip or do damage to themselves or the machines. In conditions where the managerial priority was to cheapen production it was not easy for miners to take satisfactory precautions for they were under continual pressure to produce coal.

The difficulties miners faced were reflected in costs to themselves. There were less fatalities but many more reportable accidents. The fatal accident rate per 100,000 manshifts covering all workers was almost halved between 1955 and 1968. There was a slow, uneven downward trend in the pit death rate resulting from more stringent precautions by the Union and management as well as changed methods of production. The rate of serious reportable accidents remained roughly stable but the rate for other accidents involving at least 3 days' absence increased. 1968 was not a bad year for accidents yet the accident rate was 27 per cent higher than in 1960. There were 161,000 reportable accidents in 1968 when the labour force was about 320,000. The worst year was 1965, the last year until 1978 when machines were used under a piecework system. In 1965, of course, many miners were still relatively unaccustomed to power loading. The number of accidents for every 100,000 manshifts had increased by 45 per cent over the 6 year period leading to the end of 1965. The main increase in these years was in the category described as 'machinery, use of tools and appliances and stumbling and falling.' The rate of accidents directly due to machinery about trebled.

The work environment was affected by machinery in other adverse ways. For the first time noise became a problem as noise levels at the face tended to rise above tolerable limits. The dust problem became potentially greater because machines created finer dust, particularly from stone, which was more difficult to control. Moreover as machines increased the rate of extraction face workings moved more rapidly than hitherto from the pit bottom and, in order to ventilate these remoter workings, the velocity of the circulation of the air had to be increased so that the finer dust was carried in the air for longer periods.

In general the miners' work environment in the period of contraction was unpredictable and uncertain. It was one with which miners could not easily cope. The miners, moreover, were given no financial inducement to try and cope. On the contrary their relative real wages fell. Everything seemed to be consistently calculated to persuade them to leave mining.

The Fall in Wages

The market mechanism works in many devious ways and not at all like the text books say. When the demand for coal was falling and miners were being penalized for it the reason given was that it was all due to the operation of the market. Yet when coal was in great demand and there was a scarcity of labour miners were not correspondingly rewarded. In 1948, when coal was scarce, the earnings of miners were relatively high at about 29 per cent above the average paid to workers in manufacturing industries. This figure declined slowly until 1954 and then quite rapidly until in 1958 it was about 16 per cent above the average. But none of these figure reflect the rates of pay miners could have obtained in a free market for two reasons. Firstly, the N.C.B. operated a low price policy for coal in order to stimulate British industry. Secondly, the N.U.M. refused to exploit its bargaining power in the interest of the British economy as a whole. In consequence coal was subsidized for the private and public sectors at the expense of miners' earnings.

With a characteristic lack of justice and fairness, the miners were not shielded from the full effects of the market pressures when the demand for coal fell. Nor were they recompensed in any way for the sacrifices they had volunteered after the war. The market mechanism worked in its most unfeeling way. As the demand for coal fell costs were squeezed to try and make coal more competitive. Labour power is always the first cost to be scutinized and attacked. So it was in mining. Indeed while the attack on labour costs was mounting the suppliers of machines were having a profits bonanza. The position of the miners was exposed by the falling demand for mining labour. The N.C.B. had no need to bother about the level of wages as an inducement to attract or keep labour because they wanted to shed it. So down went miners' wages. The average weekly earnings of miners were only 7.4 per cent above the average for manufacturing industry by 1960 and by 1970 miners were earning 3.1 per cent less. From being top of the wages league table after the war they had fallen to twelfth place in 1970. The relative earning power of miners fell by more than 30 per cent in that period. There is no doubt that the earnings of miners conveyed, as they were intended to do, a message of rejection.

It would be misleading to think of miners' earnings in relative terms only. The relative changes came about through a depreciation in the absolute position of the miners and through marked and substantial improvements in manufacturing industry. Miners were consistently less able to maintain their living standards after the 1950s. Surely and inexorably they became the 'hand loom weavers' of the twentieth century, being forced by absolute deprivation to seek other jobs, or to adapt to the disturbing, unfamiliar changes underground with falling real wages. They were encouraged to be fatalistic, to accept their rapidly deteriorating positions as inevitable. This they did, but in doing so they became despondent and disillusioned as individuals and demoralized collectively. Their responses fitted this degenerate pattern.

CHAPTER 9

EMPLOYER

From Private to Public Management

Who were the miners confronting during the years of decline? Private owners had disappeared with the nationalization of the mines and the National Coal Board had taken over the function of employing miners. But was the N.C.B. an employer in the classic sense? Or did it have an ideology which differed from the coal-owners and which related in some way to the Labour Movement's concept of nationalization as socialization under public ownership.

The National Coal Board, the central governing authority for the coal industry, had its powers and duties specified by the Coal Industry Nationalization Act of 1946. This Act stipulated that there should be a financially unified mining industry but made no comment about the managerial and administrative organization of the industry which was rather hurriedly contrived in the first instance and then adapted and modified in subsequent years as views and experience of centralized as against decentralized decision-making altered. The management structure in 1947 was highly centralized with the N.C.B. at the top of a rigid pyramid of committees. There were eight divisional boards mediating between the N.C.B. and 48 colliery groups. Within this formal set-up there was confusion because the details of management organization had not been worked out. Private company management organizations, in consequence, were perpetuated and used by colliery managers.

The management personnel consisted mainly of those who had worked for the private coal-owners and former officers from the armed services. Neither group was particularly committed to the idea of nationalization, though a few favoured a radically re-organized industry and saw nationalization as a means of achieving this. The nationalized industry, of course, had no alternative but to employ managers from the privately owned collieries. There was no other source. Colliery management qualifications were specified by statute and could not be acquired easily or quickly. There were similar, though not so exacting, constraints on the recruitment of managers in other functions. First priority was given to qualifications and experience in administration, accounting, labour relations and the like. The only place for discretion in appointments was at the level of the composition of the national and area boards but this discretion was not taken up by the Government to ensure that the non-executive directors at least believed in the intention of nationalization. Indeed the reverse seemed to be the case.

It was offensive for Socialists to witness anti-Socialists running a prize nationalized industry but fortunately the social and political

102

characteristics of the members of the national and area boards had relatively little impact on the course taken by the industry. Not even the chairmen of the N.C.B. were able to alter the context within which the industry operated. The various chairmen from the first one, Lord Hyndley, to Sir Derek Ezra differed in their flamboyancy, in their sensitivity to the problems of miners, in their facility to communicate but when one takes a deep close look at the industry the chairmen were as window-dressing, like successive monarchs in a parliamentary democracy. As with monarchs, some filled the role better than others. There is no doubt that the facility of Lord Robens to appear as a champion advocate for mining, even to miners, smoothed the way for the draconian cuts in mining activity. But nothing would have been substantially different with anyone else in charge. A point to remember also, is that the mixture of private enterprise managers, ex-army officers and former N.U.M. officials which manned the newly nationalized industry had evolved by the 1960s into a professional management, much like the Civil Service, competent to administer whatever decisions were made for it but at its own momentum and within its own framework of rules and procedures. The changes wrought by chairmen, with only a few exceptions, made only dents on this organization.

From the outset the nationalized coal industry was organized to achieve better physical performances than had been the case under private ownership. It became, therefore, as alert and sensitive to production costs and selling techniques as any private employer had been. It concentrated its attention on variable costs which were labour ones so, like private mine-owners, the N.C.B. was continually pre-occupied with wages and effort and contributory factors such as labour turnover and absenteeism. The N.C.B.'s emphasis on labour costs was not simply due to their variable character. Labour costs in 1947 amounted to 62.1 per cent of total costs. Changes in wage rates or effort reacted immediately on prices because they so dramatically affected total costs. Even after the extensive mechanization of coal production in the 1960s labour costs still amounted to around 50 per cent of total costs.

Profit-Making by the N.C.B.

The Nationalization Act imposed constraints and obligations on the N.C.B. which ensured that it acted like a private employer. The Board had to search for financial profitability though at first not very rigorously. Section I, part 4 of the Act stated: "The policy of the Board shall be directed to securing . . . that the revenues of the Board shall not be less than sufficient for meeting all their outgoings properly chargeable to revenue account on an average of good and bad years." This directive remained unchanged until 1961. In the intervening years, however, the pricing policy was dictated by the

Government to the disadvantage of the N.C.B. which complained in its 1965-66 Annual Report that its "operational results were affected by government policies during the years of coal shortages between 1947 and 1956. In that period, the Board had to bear a heavy loss on coal imports; and coal prices generally were kept below the level which the market could have yielded. As a result, the Board were unable to build up adequate financial reserves." The N.C.B., nonetheless, still had to meet its statutory financial obligations to the former coal owners. When it wanted to engage in substantial schemes of capital expenditure the absence of reserves compelled it to borrow, thus increasing the burden of interest charges.

The N.C.B. acquired a variety of assets from the coal owners and compensation was assessed for each type. Compensation for collieries amounted to £164,660,000 while that given to former royalty owners was fixed at £78,457,000. These, plus the compensation for other assets made it a daunting liability which was a continual source of controversy. After 1946, interest charges turned a profit into a loss during five years out of ten. These were not just the cost of compensation for the N.C.B. had to meet the interest on capital borrowed since vesting day as well but it was compensation which, in the years of expansion, formed the most formidable and politically sensitive element. After 1956 the operating margin between profit and loss narrowed and the liability of compensation became even more important as a perceived and real drag on the industry. Then, more than ever, the ethic underlying the payment of rewards to coal owners who had long since recovered more than their due return on the capital they had invested was questioned by miners who had never been adequately, let alone fully, compensated for their human capital investment.

The financial obligations of the Board were altered in April, 1961 when the Government stated that "Surpluses on Revenue Account should be at least sufficient to cover deficits in Revenue Account over a five year period: in arriving at the surpluses and deficits for each year there should be charged against revenue and items normally so chargeable (including interest, and depreciation.)" Following this announcement the Minister of Power agreed that the N.C.B. should be able to break even by the end of the first five year period. Its ability to do this, however, depended upon maintaining the market for coal at its 1962 level and that was impossible. Inevitably, therefore, the Board's financial position deteriorated and its obligations had to be altered again. In 1967 a limit was fixed on the size of the deficit it was allowed to incur.

For an assessment of the profitability or otherwise of the coal industry we have to turn to the published accounts of the N.C.B. This is an unreliable source because of the scope for manipulation which accounting provides. The outcome of a set of accounts depends upon the nature and number of the items included. It is possible to transform substantial real operating surplus profits into accounting losses or minimal gains and this is what frequently happened to the N.C.B. accounts. The first thing that is noticable from the published, summarized accounts is that in most years when there was a profit after interest had been paid, the amount of interest was just slightly less than the profit before it had been paid. The similarity is too common for it to be coincidental and gives rise to the suspicion that the accounts have been so arranged to show a minimal surplus or none at all.

The N.C.B. made a profit before the payment of interest every year after 1947. Even on the basis of formal accounts the industry was not doing too badly. The operating surplus, however, was much greater than the accounting surplus. The reason for this was explained in some detail in *A Plan for the Miners* in 1964. This stated that the N.C.B. had a discretionary category for depreciation into which sums were allocated after the calculation of the operating surplus. The Board could decide for itself what figures it put down for depreciation and they did not have to tally with real replacement costs as far as these could be calculated. The pamphlet stated that the "Presentation of the accounts is made arbitrary by playing fast and loose with the amount reckoned as depreciation: this means that over a range of several million pounds the N.C.B. can choose to record a larger or smaller surplus or deficit - and to do so just as it suits them . . ." It stated further that the N.C.B. and the Government had been deeply concerned to conceal the great and growing surpluses which were arising.

This allegation of manipulation was rejected by both the president of the N.U.M., Sidney Ford, and the chairman of the N.C.B., Lord Robens, at the 1964 Annual Conference of the N.U.M. Ford called it "assiduous propaganda" and said that "the charge that part of the industry's resources are being 'salted away' by 'arranging depreciation' and is thus being deliberately diverted from the pockets of the mineworkers, must inevitably, as indeed it is designed to do, create doubt, suspicion and deep resentment in the minds of the great mass of the membership." He then went into some detail in order to explain the need for depreciation provisions in terms of the N.C.B.'s aim to become self-financing. This, of course, was not disputed. The issue was taken up by Lord Robens who explained and justified the morality of charging interest on borrowed capital and gave a condescending example, as if to school-children, of the purpose of a depreciation fund. But neither he nor Ford dispelled the suspicion that the depreciation provisions were varied to create an image of an industry which was always either in the red or barely profitable. There is no doubt that the real situation was that the industry was more profitable than miners were led to believe and that deficits or small surpluses were recorded for political reasons, namely to convince miners that it was futile for them to hope for real wage advances.

The freedom which the N.C.B. possessed was largely an accounting one for it operated within severe constraints. It had a legal commitment to cover costs, it carried excessive financial obligations to the former coal owners and it was not in control of its own pricing policy. Its operations, moreover, were strongly influenced by the decisions of successive Governments. The consequence was that the N.C.B. developed into an unhealthy hybrid with the appearance of a private profit-making monopoly but without the capacity to survive as one. For management the consequence was a continual commitment to the grind of profit-making within most unfavourable circumstances.

A Compliant N.U.M.

When an industry has problems the first conventional reaction is to blame the unions. The management of the coal industry could hardly do that. It could point to miners as individuals or in small groups and deplore the rates of absenteeism and strikes but it could not point disparagingly at the N.U.M.

The N.C.B. had a statutory obligation to recognise the unions in the industry, to establish collective bargaining relationships with them and to set up joint consultative machinery. There was no mention in the Act of power sharing; the intention was simply to establish tried procedures in the belief that they would lead to 'good' industrial relations. But even if there had been no statutory provisions the power situation in mining would have compelled the N.C.B. to collaborate with the N.U.M. From 1947 coal was scarce and so were miners. The N.U.M. was a powerful Union in a favourable market position. The N.C.B. could not have acted as a critical, hostile employer for fear of arousing the N.U.M. to use its collective strength. Fortunately for the N.C.B. the N.U.M. wanted to cooperate more than anything else. The Union was polite, cooperative and sensitive to the need to make the industry technologically efficient and nationalization a political success. Everything was sweet and light for the management. An employer could not have had an easier passage through economic difficulties.

The eagerness of the N.U.M. to collaborate resulted from good intentions but in one respect it matched the reality of its power position. Miners were powerful but divided. So long as wages were determined on a piece-work basis there was no issue of sufficient importance to transcend coalfield differences and unite miners on a national level. This situation changed in principle in 1966 when the

106

National Power Loading Agreement introduced a daywage system and created a unifying influence.

From 1966 the N.C.B. as an employer was in a contradiction which it did not recognize. It did not have to bow to the superior power of the Union in any sense for the Union had been seriously weakened by the sharp fall in its membership. The N.C.B. did not have to make concessions to attract and retain miners. It could behave as it wished and it did so but in company with the N.U.M. itself for the leaders of the Union believed that retaliation could make matters worse for the miners. However, by behaving in this manner, the N.C.B. unwittingly began a courtship with a national strike.

The situation for miners was also contradictory. Whenever the N.U.M. stirred itself to make a wage demand it was confronted by the apparent lack of profitability glaringly publicized by the red figures or small black ones in the annual accounts. Yet the miners knew that the industry was an efficient one. There had been a considerable increase in productivity. The output per manshift at the face had increased from 58.4 cwt in 1947 to 137.7 cwts. in 1969. Overall productivity had risen from 21.5 cwts. per manshift to 43.4 cwts. in the same period.

Though the real state of the industry was hidden and distorted by the annual accounts it was never without difficulties. Many miners asked themselves why the N.C.B., a large monopoly providing an essential commodity, even though for a contracting market, under improving technological conditions, could not be an economically viable, self-financing institution with a rising profit rate. They were certainly not to blame, self-suffering and compliant beyond reason as they were.

Nationalization for Capitalism

The primary cause of the problem lay in the original terms of nationalization and the way in which they were interpreted by the N.C.B. and successive Governments. Except where it was sold directly for domestic consumption coal was not a profit-making commodity. The demand for it was derived from that for commodities which consumed coal in their production and the profit which accrued to it was a share of the profitability of those commodities. In this sense it was like labour power. When coal supplied virtually all the power of the country its profitability moved directly with the state of the economy: up, when trade was good and down, when trade was bad. As the sources of power became diversified then the demand for coal was linked more directly with those industries which mainly consumed it. Coal had always been most profitably **produced in conjunction with the main processes which largely** depended on it, such as the iron and steel and gas industries. Its profitability had always been greatest as part of vertically integrated processes.

The coal owners had recognised this economic factor as far as market forces and their own capital resources permitted. They were often steel masters or steel master were coal owners. Employers who produced commodities which depended heavily on coal tried to assume the control of coal production, while coal owners attempted to control the processes which used coal. This was not done tidily or systematically under private enterprise because economic sense had always to be knocked into the heads of capitalists by the imperatives of cost, falling profit, threatened bankruptcy. One of the advantages of public ownership was that the relationships between parts of production processes could be planned, linked, integrated.

To make economic sense, public ownership had to be initially so widespread that it could transcend the false distinctions between commodities which private enterprise imposed through its basic tenet that everything which commanded a price must thereby have its own market and be a separate commodity. Nationalization, however, was always advocated for separate, conventionally defined industries, like coal, iron and steel, and railways, largely through pressure from unions in them so that when the Labour Government in 1945 launched its nationalization programme the items in it were there for political reasons. There was no question of looking at public ownership in its economic context as a tool for planning related productive processes.

The coal industry was nationalized on terms satisfactory to capitalist enterprise in general. It was isolated from other processes, a single product concern, fully exposed as a basic cost factor with no value in itself except as a source of domestic heating. In the conditions of post second world war Britain no reasonably intelligent capitalist would have wanted to own and control the coal industry on the terms entrusted to the N.C.B., namely to be confined to "the working and getting of coal." But a reasonably intelligent capitalist faced with the inevitability of nationlization, would have wanted coal to be so isolated, to be exploited as a subsidizing factor, as it was until the late 1950s and to be castigated for its cost raising qualities, as it was afterwards.

It would have been interesting to have listened in on the discussions between the coal owners and government representatives about the assets to be nationalized - collieries but not the steel plants, coke reduction plants but not those in the steel industry, brick-making dependent upon the use of shale, and a variety of activities unrelated directly to mining or the use of coal which the owners wanted to jettison. Land, houses, farms, hotels all came into the possession of the N.C.B. but not the control of wholesale and retail distribution.

Coal Distribution

The N.U.M. was consistently concerned about the effects of the exclusion of distribution from the Nationalization Act. On some occasions it pressed for the nationalization of distribution. In the later disillusioning years of the 1960s it simply asked for the rationalization of distribution. Both requests were denied. All that happened was the *ad hoc* process of re-adjustment between private firms which takes place within capitalist markets. When the Price Commission reported on the "Distribution of Domestic Coal and Solid Smokeless Fuels" in 1976 there were 280 wholesalers and 7,800 retailers dealing with coal distribution. The National Coal Board controlled over half of the wholesale trade but only 5 per cent of the retail sales. About 15 per cent of the retail market was in the hands of co-operative societies. The remainder was a private enterprise activity comprising firms of varying sizes. In some areas, particularly in the South East of England, large retailers dominated the market. Compare this situation with that of the multi-national oil companies which not only tightly control the retail outlets for oil products but have infiltrated coal distribution by persuading coal distributors to handle competitive heating oil.

Although most coal goes for industrial uses, including electricity generation, the domestic market for it has always been a significant, though declining proportion of total sales. Domestic consumption fell from 19 per cent of the total in 1950 to round about 10 per cent in 1978. This represented a fall in consumption from 38 million tons to 11 millions. Nonetheless the market has remained important in the struggle to maintain the size of the industry and politically important because it is there that the general public confronts the nationalized coal industry. What happens to the price of coal from the pit head to the consumer is of importance to those who want to illustrate the positive features of the industry.

The N.E.C. of the National Union of Mineworkers claimed in 1967 that the irrational distribution of coal frequently resulted in domestic consumers being charged more than double pit head prices. The Price Commission looked into this question in its report in 1976. It found wide disparities in coal prices between different types and qualities of solid fuel, between different regions, within regions, sometimes within small towns, and between different sizes of retailer. The Price Commission found it difficult to identify a representative price for coal or to compile a typical list of items which made up the retail price. Coal consumers had no means of knowing whether or not they were paying fair prices for their products. There was evidence, though ordinary consumers had no means of knowing it, that they were being exploited by distributors for the Commission stated that the process of conveying coal from the pit to the consumer normally added 70 per cent to the pithead price and could add considerably more than this. In so far as domestic consumers were concerned the contortions going on in the industry in order to improve efficiency were of academic interest only for the pithead and retail prices of coal had no logical connection.

Bad Management

The Coal Industry Nationalization Act of 1946, constrictive though it was, allowed the N.C.B. some entrepreneurial scope. Chapter 59, Section 1, Part 2 of the Act stated that:

> "The function of the N.C.B. shall include the carrying on of all such activities as it may appear to the Board to be requisite, advantageous or convenient for them to carry out in connection with the discharge of their duties . . . and in particular:
> (d) producing or manufacturing any goods or utilities which are of a kind required by the Board for or in connection with the working and getting of coal or any other of their activities or which can be advantageously produced or manufactured by the Board by reason of their having interests or facilities for the production or manufacture thereof in connection with the working and getting of coal or any of their activities, and supplying and selling goods or utilities so produced or manufactured.
> (e) any activities which can be advantageously be carried on by the Board with a view to making the best use of the assets vested in them by this Act."

The N.C.B. then had statutory powers to pursue a policy of self-sufficiency; to enter into manufacturing and repairing mining equipment and to do so on such a scale as would enable it to provide its equipment and services to other mining industries. There were possibilities of substantial savings in costs here through eliminating the profit margins and distribution costs which private manufacturing and repairing entailed. Increasing mechanization after 1947 provided enormous scope for technological inventiveness and manufacturing capacity just as did experimentations in coal utilization. In 1947 the most modern face was equipped with only a coalcutter and a conveyor, costing about £20,000 whereas in 1975 the fully mechanized face involved an investment of about £½ million. In many cases the advance was from pick and shovel to mechanized cutting and loading with self-advancing powered supports. The N.C.B. in 1947 knew, as the Reid Committee before it knew, that the path to higher productivity involved increased mechanization.

The N.C.B. set up a small manufacturing capacity but decided not to manufacture mining equipment. This was not so important in the early years of nationalization when the main emphasis was on maximizing output from existing methods of production but it became of crucial importance later in the 1960s during the pit prop revolution. In retrospect, however, it is clear that the decision to manufacture mining equipment should have been made at the outset of nationalization. The decision not to do so, to permit the private exploitation of mining interests, allowed a rich harvest of profit to be reaped by a small number of companies, eventually only three, from an industry which could ill-afford to pay it. The decision was a major act of organizational incompetence and a betrayal of the true purpose of nationalization at the same time.

It should have been clear all along that the social objectives of nationalization could not be achieved while the coal industry could be exploited by private manufacturers. Moreover as the profit making potential of these private manufacturers was dependent upon policy decisions made by the National Coal Board there was scope for financial corruption by senior management and, in consequence, for the purpose of nationalization itself to be distorted. Once decisions in the coal industry were being made which in one way or another were related to the pecuniary interests of some members of the N.C.B. management, then the integrity of nationalization was being damaged.

The possibility of corruption existed when senior executives of the National Coal Board and their close relatives acquired shares in mining machinery manufacturing firms in the 1960s during the boom in hydraulic roof supports. In 1960, Gullick Ltd., a mining machinery firm, invented a new form of self-advancing roof support with an articulated base. The invention was patented. Then, in 1965, the patent was surrendered to the National Coal Board on the understanding that it would be put out to tender. This was not done. Gullick Ltd. lost from the transaction for the N.C.B. transferred much of its custom to another firm, Bonser Engineering, which had begun producing a roof support similar to the patented one, and in which Mr. Alfred Robens, * the son of Lord Robens, then Chairman of the N.C.B., and the wife of Mr. W.V.Sheppard, Director General of Production in the N.C.B., held shares. When Gullick Ltd. threatened to take its complaint against the N.C.B. to court it was persuaded to agree to an arbitration process. The arbitrator was Mr. W.V. Sheppard who settled in favour of the N.C.B. and, in consequence, of the firm in which his wife held shares. Questions about Lord Robens and Mr. Sheppard were raised at a meeting of the Parliamentary Select Committee on Nationalized Industries in July, 1969, and were followed by a Government request to Mr. Michael Kerr, Q.C. (later Justice Kerr) to carry out an independent inquiry into allegations of impropriety by these two people. Mr. Kerr concluded that there was "no *prima facie* case whatever for any further or formal investigation of any of these allegations, either against Lord Robens or Mr. Sheppard." The Government accepted this report in November, 1970. **

* In October, 1967, Mr. Alfred Robens married Patricia Bonser, the daughter of the chairman of Bonser Engineering.
** Select Committee on Nationalized Industries, Session 1974-75. The Purchasing of Powered Roof Supports and Spares by the National Coal Board, Appendix 25, pp. 496-497.

The matter came to light again through a series of articles by *Private Eye* in 1971 and 1972.* The main allegations by *Private Eye* were summarized by the Parliamentary Select Committee on Nationalized Industries in 1974 and were as follows.**

"(i)   That Gullick surrendered an important patent for the Board to implement its normal patent policy, which is to put the designs out to Tender, and this was not done.

(ii)   That the patent was passed to Bonser Engineering only, a firm without experience in the field of Roof Support equipment.

(iii)   That Lord Robens' son was a Director of Bonser Engineering.

(iv)   That Gullick protested, threatening to take the matter to law.

(v)   That Gullick eventually accepted independent arbitration, which did not appear to be independent, as the sole adjudicator was said to be a senior N.C.B. official, now Deputy Chairman, whose wife at this time held shares in Bonser.

(vi)   That at a later date, the treatment of Gullick was remedied by greatly increased prices.

(vii)   That at the time Bonser's powered support interests were sold to Dowty, 50 per cent of the supports supplied by Bonser were under complaint by senior N.C.B. engineers.

(viii)   That Dowty paid £1,400,000 for Bonser, including an amount of £900,000 for Goodwill. (The Thomson McLintock report states that at the time of purchase Bonser had no orders for powered supports from the N.C.B.). The allegation is that this could only be recovered from the N.C.B., the sole customer. Who promised this recovery, by what means and under what terms; indeed under what authority?"

The *Private Eye* allegations were the subject of an internal N.C.B. inquiry conducted by the Board's own auditors, Thomson McLintock who, in January, 1973 reported on the issue of share-holding in machinery supply firms by stating that "in 1964 the powered support revolution was getting under way and the prospects were good. It was therefore quite natural for productive people who had some money to spare for an investment and particularly local production people who knew the Company's products and possibilities to seek an investment where they could keep and eye on how things were going. An investment in such a quoted company did not contravene any staff rules ." *** The N.C.B. accepted this Report. A month before, however, the Chairman of the N.C.B. had sent a letter to all staff members stating that none of them should become financially involved in companies. The British Association of Colliery Management which represented the N.C.B. managers regarded the McLintock Report as a vindication of current practices and, in March, 1973, called for the withdrawal of the Chairman's letter.

---

*   The articles were in issue No. 239, 12th February, 1971, pp. 20-21; issue No. 260, 3rd December, 1971, pp. 21-22; issue No. 269, 7th April, 1972, p. 24; issue No. 272, 19th May, 1972, p.22; and issue No. 274, 16th June, 1972, pp. 22-23.

**   op. int., Appendix 13, p. 420. Sections (vii) and (viii) relate to the merger in 1969 when the two large mining machinery firm, The Dowty Group, bought the mining machinery side of Bonser Engineering. The assets of Bonser Engineering were reputedly worth about £500,000.

***   ibid, Appendix 3, pp. 272-278.

The real basis for concern about the behaviour of the management of the N.C.B., however, lay in documents prepared in detail and with great thoroughness by two N.C.B. employees, Dr. David Leigh and Mr. Alan Grimshaw, who separately examined aspects of the N.C.B.'s purchasing policies but jointly alleged that the firms supplying roof support equipment made excess profits of £74 million in the three years, 1969-72.

Dr. Leigh was an operational research scientist in the N.C.B.'s Operational Research Executive, while Mr. Grimshaw was an N.C.B. manager based in Doncaster who specialised in buying underground equipment. Neither person made allegations of corruption but simply detailed practices which could only be described as corrupt. Their evidence showed that the purchasing policy for roof supports had been allowed to pass out of the control of the N.C.B. and into the hands of three large private firms and that in consequence these firms were able to charge excessively high prices for their products. The firms pursued a policy of proliferating the types of replacement parts for powered roof supports causing the N.C.B. to invest large sums in spares and have high write-off costs which would not have been necessary if the N.C.B. had insisted on the elementary principles of standardization and the scrutiny of prices. Whenever parts changed they were given new and higher prices. This proliferation facilitated hidden price increases.

In some instances the proliferation was not real in the sense that the parts were mechanically different for they were simply given different numbers. A spare part became different if it had a different number. This is how Mr. Grimshaw described the practice in his evidence to the Select Committee on Nationalized Industries:

"For many years up to 1973 Suppliers used an advice note printed "Part Number Ordered," "Part Number Supplied." Part numbers, in total thousands, were changed without advice to the users of the equipment, or to the staff provisioning the equipment. This facility given to the Supplier resulted in number proliferation, increased prices and stocks of items not required, as well as creating a situation where Stock Control and Budget control of spending was impossible.""[*]

In other instances parts were altered by trivial and expensive additions to them. Once they were altered they had new numbers and new and higher prices. Mr. Grimshaw estimated that in the 3 years, 1969 to 1971 inclusive, in excess of 10,000 new part numbers, at new prices, covering assemblies, components, and spare parts, were introduced by powered support manufacturers. It should be noted that the significance of the numbering of parts was not only that it facilitated price rises but caused the N.C.B. to replace components unnecessarily. If a colliery manager wanted to secure a new spare and he found that its number had changed then he had to

[*]   ibid, Appendix II. "A reply by Mr. W. A. Grimshaw to investigations by Thomson McLintock into criticisms made by the both Dr. Leigh and Mr.Grimshaw," p.392

replace not just the part but the complete unit to which it belonged. It was this practice which resulted, as Dr. Leigh claimed, in excessive write-off costs.

The activities surrounding the purchasing practices of the N.C.B. showed how the efficiency of the coal industry was adversely affected by a relationship with private industry which need not have existed. The practices which Dr. Leigh and Mr. Grimshaw described were not imposed on the N.C.B. by an overpowering private enterprise but resulted from initiatives by the N.C.B. itself. For example, following the mergers of powered support suppliers in 1969, sponsored by the Industrial Re-Organization Corporation and the National Coal Board and which reduced the suppliers from eight to three, a conference of Purchasing and Stores Department senior personnel in the N.C.B. was told by the Director-General "that for various reasons, it was not possible to go into detail about recent developments, but that three new groups would now supply the Board on 'agreed' lines."* We can surmise from the subsequent purchasing practices of the N.C.B. what the 'agreed' lines were.

As a result of the exposures by Dr. Leigh and Mr. Grimshaw the N.C.B. initiated an internal inquiry by Thomson McLintock, the Board's auditors. The auditors, which at the same time considered shareholding in supply firms, reported that there was no evidence to support the allegation that prices were too high.

The N.C.B. accepted the McLintock report which had taken six months to prepare and during which time no consultations were held with Leigh and Grimshaw. No one in the senior management of the Board seemed concerned that the inquiry was conducted by auditors already in the pay of the Board.

The Leigh and Grimshaw allegations were taken further to the Select Committee on Nationalized Industries which for the second time faced the problems of N.C.B. management. Its Report contains much damning evidence which does not seem to be related to its conclusions. The Select Committee did not meet to examine possible corrupt practices and did not, therefore, query systematically and purposefully the involvement of N.C.B. officials in the supply firms. Its purpose mainly was to examine the purchasing policies of the N.C.B. which lay at the core of the allegations. On this matter, as indeed on all other matters, the N.C.B. was vindicated. There was a slight stricture in the Conclusion which stated that "the investigation, both of the matters criticized by Mr. Grimshaw and Dr. Leigh and of aspects of the subject which they did not mention, has revealed a number of areas in which the Board's management and procedures in the past have been less effective than they should have been, and **where room for improvement still exists . . ."** But this meant**

---

*   ibid, Appendix 13, para 74 "Mergers in 1969," pp. 431-432.
**   ibid, Part VI Conclusion, p. lx

nothing for the main charges were dismissed.

Inquiries into the allegations stopped with the Select Committee Report despite the fact that one of the suppliers refunded the N.C.B. the sum of £1,339,000 just before the Select Committee Report was published and even though the N.C.B. revised its purchasing policies in what amounted to be an admission that the Leigh and Grimshaw allegations were valid. At every stage after this time obstacles were raised against holding an independent or judicial inquiry. The Government resisted pressure for further investigations from such M.P.'s as Mr. Dick Kelley and Mr. Dennis Skinner and seemed to engage in a self-protecting embrace with the N.C.B. The National Union of Mineworkers was motivated by the allegations of profiteering to demand, in 1974, that the Government authorize the N.C.B. "to be the exclusive manufacturer of all mining equipment." But it was rather late for such a resolution for the industry was nearing the end of a technological phase. The real profits from powered supports had already passed into private hands. In any event, as the secretary of State for Energy commented, the N.C.B. already had "extensive powers to manufacture the equipment they needed. . ."

The only sufferers from this sordid episode were the two people whose motives and actions were beyond question, namely Dr. Leigh and Mr. Grimshaw.* They were put under discipline after the McLintock report was completed. Both were called before the N.C.B. in March, 1973 to explain why they had acted as they did. Mr. Grimshaw lost his staff and his function and was ostracized in his job. Dr. Leigh whose only occupation had been as a mining engineer with the N.C.B. left it for a job unconnected with mining. After he had given evidence to the Select Committee Mr. Grimshaw was declared redundant by the N.C.B. As a result his case was referred to the House of Commons Committee of Privileges on the grounds that he had been dismissed because of his evidence to the Select Committee but it decided against him. He became unemployed and suffered a considerable financial loss for showing concern about the misuse of public money and the bad management of a nationalized industry. It was an ironic end to the matter, though not necessarily to the practices which were central to it.

The N.C.B. had, it seems, an innate preference for encouraging the private exploitation of its activities. It set up Central and Area workshops to do cyclical repair and maintenance of mining equipment but always used outside contractors as well. In 1963, for example, outside contractors were given business worth £4.6 million. Craftsmen within the N.U.M. who persistently protested to the N.C.B. about its failure to utilize the repair and maintenance capacity of the

* See *The Role of Parliament in the Grimshaw Affair*, a privately circulated document by Mr. Alan Grimshaw, for details of the treatment of both people.

industry, were repeatedly assured that work would not be put outside which could be carried out competitively in the Board's own workshops, but they never saw a solution to the problem.

The Board behaved in much the same way over the use of private contractors for development work, such as opening new faces. This aroused more hostility than the craftsmen's issue for it involved the militant face workers, yet it too remained unresolved. The N.C.B. employed its own development workers, paid at agreed face work rates, who often worked in the same pits as private contract workers doing similar work at very much higher rates of pay. The reason for using these private contractors was never functionally clear for their skilled labour was invariably recruited from the Board's employees and they brought no competence to bear on the work of development which the N.C.B. itself did not possess.

The final phase of isolating and exposing coal as the only source of profit in the industry was the asset-stripping one. The N.C.B. disposed of assets such as earth moving equipment and lorries and then hired them back; it sold its offices to property companies and rented them back and then, after 1971, it ridded itself of ancillary activities such as brickmaking. Under the Coal Industry Act of 1971 the N.C.B. was required to report to the Government on its ancillary activities and on the activities of companies in which the N.C.B. shared an interest. This was a prelude to the last possible asset-shedding the Board could engage in, unless the absurd were contemplated and profit-making collieries themselves were sold off.

The primary purpose of the National Coal Board was to work and get coal. In order to do this it had to employ a large number of men and some fewer women. Its responsibility as an employer was to these men and women; to provide congenial working conditions and adequate rewards. Its position, however, was indivisible. What the N.C.B. did as an employer was dialectically related to its activities as an entrepreneur and this meant not simply getting coal but operating as a viable, financial, profit-making entity. How it did this depended on the way in which it used the skills it bought but also on its own skills in management and investment, in risk-taking.

The N.C.B. was in a peculiar position. It was required to manage a publicly-owned enclave in a private enterprise economy along lines consistent with the morality of capitalism.

It was this situation which produced a hybrid with fairly low survival qualities. It made the N.C.B. into a body of aspiring capitalists who continually hit their heads against obstructions created by advice and controls by hostile or incompetent governments and their own ambivalence. It is little wonder that they diverted Coal Board activities so frequently to private enterprise operators, or dabbled in private firms making mining machinery.

Through ambivalence towards its purpose, through the advice

given by Governments and the controls they imposed, through its own incompetence, the National Coal Board was a bad entrepreneur. While successive successful capitalists were diversifying, integrating, ensuring control over supplies and outlets, the N.C.B. was moving in an entirely opposite direction. This did not occur because the coal industry was not and is not a capitalist undertaking but is a nationalized industry for if the coal industry had not been simply publicly-owned but organized to serve society then the Government would have allowed none of the options which the N.C.B. took.

Because the N.C.B. was such an inefficient entrepreneur it was also an ineffective employer with neither the resources to act positively in response to miners' demands nor the authority to oppose them. It was rescued right until the end of the 1960s by the extraordinary compliance of the National Union of Mineworkers. When that compliance was replaced by confrontation then the incapacity of the National Coal Board to handle labour relations was quickly and clearly exposed.

CHAPTER 10

LEADERS

A Successor for Will Paynter

A small gathering of miners' representatives from Kent, Derbyshire, South Wales, Scotland and Yorkshire met at the County Hotel in Sheffield on Saturday, 5th August, 1967 to discuss the possibility of obtaining a left-wing successor to Will Paynter who was retiring from the general secretaryship of the N.U.M. in December, 1968. There were rank and file members there and also full-time officials, some of whom were influential in Area affairs. Jock Kane from Yorkshire was elected as chairman. They had come together after discussions at the Annual Conference of thé N.U.M. at Eastbourne in July of that year about the quality of future leadership in the Union.

All Union conferences have different facets such as formal policy-making, forging informal alliances and jamborees. The N.U.M. conference held at a seaside resort in the summer often has a festive, rather carefree, aspect. There is much opportunity to meet friends, to chat and celebrate. The friends usually have similar political commitments. This was certainly the case with the delegates who got together at Eastbourne - Michael McGahey and Lawrence Daly from Scotland, Emlyn Williams and Dai Francis from South Wales, Jack Dunn from Kent, Sammy Taylor and Jock Kane from Yorkshire, all of whom were full-time union officials, and some rank and file delegates such as Ron Rigby and Arthur Scargill from Yorkshire. The state of the Union was a common topic of conversation. The question of finding a successor to Will Paynter was raised. It was agreed that the matter should be pursued further and discussed by a small but representative meeting as soon as possible. One person in each Area was given the task of deciding the representation within his Area. Will Paynter was invited but he declined to attend because he did not want to be seen campaigning for his own successor. He did point correctly, however, to the person he thought should succeed him. Overlooking the N.E.C. and travelling around the coalfields he had good opportunities of assessing likely candidates.

There were two important reasons for calling the meeting. First, was the need for a single candidate to represent left-wing interests. At earlier elections for national positions the progressive forces had weakened, in one case squandered, their chances of success by presenting a multiplicity of candidates. It was the practice of the N.U.M. to use the transferable vote system whereby miners listed candidates in order of preference. A successful candidate had to get a majority of all the votes cast. If no candidate was in that position after the distribution of first preference votes then the bottom one was eliminated and the preferences on that candidate's ballot papers were distributed to the other candidates. This process continued until one of them obtained a majority. It is possible to influence and predict the first preference votes but the rest are distributed in a random manner and are, therefore, entirely unpredictable. There is no guarantee that a voter who gives his or her first preference to a left-wing candidate will order the remainder in a consistent political way; anything may happen after that depending upon information and propaganda about the candidates and which coalfields they come from. Under the preferential vote system it is possible for a candidate to be elected who does not represent the majority interests of members of the union. This is most likely to occur when those interests are competed for by a number of similar candidates.

The election for the presidency of the Union in 1960 was ever in the minds of the delegates for it was a stark reminder of what could happen when there were competing left-wing candidates. Four prominent left-wing candidates stood in that election polling 57 per cent of the total votes between them. Only one of these candidates, Alex Moffat from Scotland, had any serious acknowledged support outside of his own area. He was a Communist nominated by Cumberland, Kent, Scotland, South Wales and Yorkshire. W.L. Ellis was nominated by Nottingham; Jim Hammond received the Lancashire nomination and Bert Wynn had the Derbyshire nomination. Each of these was supported by his own Area. If all of the votes cast for the left-wing candidates in the first round had gone to Moffat he would have had a pronounced majority over the remaining candidates.* Some voting, of course, was parochial but even so it is likely that Moffat would have won on the first count if the other left-wing candidates had withdrawn. Moffat topped the poll in the first round. He maintained his lead until the last of the preference votes were distributed when he was overtaken by Ford and lost by 10,000 votes out of a total of 412,556. As a consequence the N.U.M. had a president who not only had never worked down a pit but had been employed for most of his working life as a clerk in the N.U.M. offices. With this experience in mind the Sheffield meeting had no difficulty in deciding there should be only one left-wing candidate.

The second reason for the meeting was to obtain a candidate who could fit the mould of the two previous general secretaries. Both Arthur Horner, who had been the first general secretary since the

---

* The actual first round voting was:

W. L. Ellis (Nottingham & left-winger)	61,389
S. W. G. Ford (C.O.S.A. & right-winger)	43,084
J. Hammond (Lancashire & left-winger)	28,853
T. Holliday (Northumberland & right-winger)	47,264
Alex Moffat (Scotland & left-winger)	116,174
J. H. Southall (Midlands & right-winger)	33,752
H. W. Wynn (Derbyshire & left-winger)	32,040

Arthur Horner, General Secretary of the N.U.M., 1946-58. Previously President of the South Wales Miners' Federation, 1936-46.

formation of the Union in 1944, and his successor, Will Paynter, were intellectual giants in the trade union movement, of the highest political integrity and outstanding orators. Both were Communists from the harsh, unremitting pre-war environment of depression and repression in the South Wales coalfield. They were difficult men to follow but it was important that someone of the same calibre, cast in the same broad political image, though not necessarily Communist, should take over from Paynter. Both Paynter and Horner were seen as models. Will Paynter was brilliant on each occasion he spoke, cogent, persuasive and intellectual. I heard him many times in varied situations but he did not vary. It did not matter whether he spoke at conferences, in public meetings or in open air gatherings in the rain, he captured attention and worked on opinions. He was a Communist but he gave high priority to his Union. His job was to present Union policy, to act as the servant of the N.E.C., and this he did meticulously even though, in many instances, the views he presented were contrary to his own. Inadvertently, but unavoidably, the brilliance of Will Paynter served to consolidate the power positions of those who comprised the majority on the N.E.C. who were contemptuous of his politics and who opposed and contained him by their majority position. He did for them what they were incompetent at doing for themselves. Intellectual ability on the post-war N.E.C. of the Miners' Union always resided in its left-wing members and this was epitomized by the Union's outstanding general secretaries. Paynter knew, moreover how he would be treated by the N.E.C. if he refused to act as its servant and express its policies. He had before him the example of Arthur Horner who once defied the N.E.C.

Horner and Paynter as N.E.C. Servants

Arthur Horner went as a delegate to the 27th Congress of the General Confederation of Labour in Paris in October, 1948, at the same time as the French miners were striking for a wage increase. Shortly after arriving he was told that Will Lawther, the N.U.M. president, had made a public statement opposing the French miners' strike and he was asked for his reaction. In his autobiography, *Incorrigible Rebel*, Horner stated that he refused to comment because it was not his job "to engage in controvery with another official of the union in a foreign country." But, he added, he would give his views on the French miners' strike in his fraternal speech to the C.G.T. Conference. At the Conference, Horner gave his support to the strike. He said "No British miner has authority to speak against the French miners' strike, and if he does so it is entirely unofficial . . . . You must resist any interference from Great Britain in your affairs as we would if you intervened in ours and I am sure, however, that in spite of propaganda that when the British miners know the full facts of the French struggle they will rally to your support." When Horner was interviewed by reporters on his return to Britain he said much more, especially about his position as a Communist and a union leader and put it into the context of the developing climate of the Cold War. The incident occurred in the wake of the introduction of Marshall Aid which broke up the wartime alliances between Communists and Non-Communists. Horner was openly critical for the first time of the intentions of the Labour Government both on a national and international level.

There was a prompt reaction from the N.E.C. of the Union. At its meeting on 28th October, 1948, both Lawther and Horner made statements about the miners' strike in France after which it decided that Horner's "statements were contrary to union policy, were unauthorized and are therefore disclaimed by us:

(ii) that the action of the President in repudiating the statement by the Secretary and the President's adherence to Union policy be confirmed;

(iii) that in dissociating ourselves from the unauthorised action of the Secretary we warn him that a recurrence of such conduct will not be tolerated . . ." A sub-committee was set up to reply to the allegations made by Horner and to define Union policy. The sub-committee produced a lengthy report which focussed primarily on Horner's membership of the British Communist Party in order to attack international Communism. It questioned Horner's credibility in a number of respects, accused him of megalomania. It amounted in all to a denigration of Horner's character and it was circulated to the membership.

Nothing was recorded about what the N.E.C. would do if Horner offended it a second time. Horner had made the charge that a decision had been made to remove him from office, a logical consequence, it seemed, of the wave of anti-Communism which was spreading throughout the trade union movement from the General Council of the Trades Union Congress downwards. The sub-committee replied that the charge was untrue, adding: "Mr. Horner can only be removed from office in accordance with the Rules of the National Union of Mineworkers, and the charge he makes is a serious reflection on the integrity of those persons who would be called upon to attend any Conference of the Union and whose duty, as delegates, it would be to deal with such a situation." The N.E.C. could have set in motion the process of dimissal which, according to the 1947 Rules of the N.U.M., would have had to have been based on a resolution of a national delegate conference, but, with Scotland and South Wales firmly behind him and supported by his incredible oratory, it is unlikely that enough delegates would have agreed to it. In any case such a Conference would have been the setting for exposing the activities of the president, Will Lawther, as much as

Lawrence Daly, General Secretary, N.U.M., 1968-, addressing a Scottish Miners' Gala in Edinburgh, flanked by Dennis Skinner, M.P., on his left and Michael McGahey on his right.

those of Horner. Wisely, nothing was done to remove Horner. He survived until his retirement in 1959 but within constraints which he did not challenge again.

Will Paynter was a prisoner of his own integrity, just as Horner before him had been. Shortly after he became general secretary the president designate, Alwyn Machen, died, leaving a vacancy which the right wing believed it could not win and which would be lost to another Communist. It was suggested to Paynter that he might contest for the presidency and if he did and left the general secretaryship vacant he would not be seriously opposed. He refused even to contemplate the transition. He hated intrigue. I remember the contempt with which he regarded the proposal. The presidency, in the event, was won by a right wing candidate who had never been a miner. By that act Paynter sealed his containment but he could not have acted otherwise.

He made substantial intellectual contributions to all the Conferences as he did at Eastbourne but he failed by and large to influence policy. At Eastbourne there were no divisions. The opinion of the N.E.C. on every motion was accepted by the Conference. If the N.E.C. said 'remit' then the motion was remitted; if it said 'support' it was passed and if it said 'oppose' then it was lost. All the motions which appeared to the N.E.C. to be correct in principle but awkward in practice were remitted for consideration by the N.E.C. even though, as one delegate put it, that was equivalent to handing over to a burial board. The consensus was complete. The N.U.M. on this showing did not provide encouragement to the few people who were anxious to break the collaborative attitude of the union.

Lawrence Daly

The candidate chosen by the Sheffield meeting was Lawrence Daly who was the general secretary of the Scottish Area. Daly seemed an ideal choice. He was one of those miners who somehow had enough time and energy after work to combine political and trade union activity with a voracious appetite for reading prose and poetry. When he left the Communist Party in 1956 he moved into the mileaux of intellectuals who comprised the New Left and published first the *New Reasoner*, then the *Universities and Left Review*. He was then a face worker at Glencraig pit in Fife but he was completely at home with university teachers and writers. He was an intellectual in conventional terms. He read, analyzed and reasoned. And although he had left the Communist Party and had campaigned against its influence in Scotland he had the respect of Communists. His transition from face worker had been rapid. He remained a face worker until 1963 when he became a full-time Union agent in Fife. Two years later he became the General Secretary of the Scottish Area. Now, two years after that he was on the point of being nominated for the General Secretaryship of the National Union. He had been a member of the National Executive Committee since 1966.

Lawrence Daly was in the same intellectual category as Horner and Paynter. He was also an outstanding orator who frequently used the language of poets. His main disadvantages were that he had moved so rapidly through the Union hierarchy that he had not had time to acquire the skills which go with union leadership, in particular the ability to resist intellectual arguments in the interest of solidarity, and that he was relatively unknown to miners outside of Scotland. Will Paynter had noted his ability on the N.E.C. in 1966 and had earmarked him as a possible successor, adding that it was important that he should become more widely known in the different coalfields. Once it had been decided that Daly should contest the election for Paynter's successor then it was necessary to project him throughout the major coalfields in much the same way as a new packet of soap flakes was introduced to consumers. He had to be taken around to places frequented by miners in as many Areas as possible so that his obvious talents, his contagious warmth of personality, became known and appreciated by them.

Policies not Personalities

The Sheffield meeting made other decisions which turned out to be more important in the long run than the selection of Daly. It decided that the election should be waged around policies and not the personalities of the candidates. For this to happen policies had to be formulated, published and debated which challenged the logic of the consensus explanations. 1967 was not an auspicious year for miners. Its events did not encourage miners to rebel, as the proceedings of the Annual Conference had indicated. All the mechanisms of constraint on protest which had operated in the 1960s; the collaboration attitude of the N.U.M., the plaintive reasonableness of the N.C.B., the projected impotence of the Government to alter what was happening and the possibility for individual miners to escape to other industries, were still present. There seemed to be little possibility of reaching the minds of the miners with anything which challenged the dominant explanations. Attempts had been made before and had failed so what chance was there in 1967 of doing better?

Those who wanted to alter the consciousness of miners seemed to be caught in a vicious circle. The deteriorating mining situation created an attitude of disillusionment amongst miners which facilitated and encouraged the deterioration. How could the disillusionment be tackled? In the absence of external forces in the energy market there was no way of altering the situation without getting at miners themselves and they did not want to listen or read. Getting

125

out, subsisting, coping, each man for himself, were dominating preoccupations. There was only one course open and that was to engage the miners in argument through leaflets, pamphlets and public meetings.

This, in part, had been attempted before in 1964 when the Derbyshire Area had published a pamphlet called *A Plan for the Miners*. The exercise had not been successful. The pamphlet dealt with the same issues as those which were pertinent in 1967: pit closures, investment policy, wages and working conditions. Its publication received much publicity. The president of the N.U.M. devoted almost the whole of his presidential address at the 1964 N.U.M. Annual Conference to an attack on it. The chairman of the N.C.B. used part of his speech at the same Conference to refute allegations made in the pamphlet about the financial practices of the N.C.B. Both Bert Wynn and Bill Whitehead referred to it in their speeches. This created the impression that the pamphlet was having a propaganda effect. It was treated as a subversive document, peddling ideas of proscribed organizations which were not named. Its reception that week in July, 1964, confirmed my general belief that there is nothing quite so subversive as an attack on prevailing ideas. But the influence of *A Plan for the Miners* largely ended with the Conference. It was bought and read by miners who were mainly the converted. Its ideas produced no changes in policy, in attitudes, in practice nor, of course, could they do so in a vacuum. Other conditions had to be present. The small group which gave rise to the pamphlet widened its membership and met for the last time in January, 1966. The convenor of the meetings Bert Wynn, the Derbyshire Area Secretary, died shortly afterwards. Bill Whitehead, the South Wales Area president, who had been an active and consistent participant, resigned from his Area post in 1966. Will Paynter, at the centre of the group, began to adjust to the idea of retirement. The group disintegrated without having made any visible contribution.

The Broad Left Alliance

There were reasons, other than the deadening effects of the fatalist perception of the condition of mining, which made the task of altering the consciousness of miners so difficult. The most important was the absence of an organization which could sustain a campaign around the ideas being discussed. Pit closures were not an issue which could excite, unite and generate action. Like unemployment they divided miners from each other and demoralized them. Wages were not an issue either. Until 1966 there was no common interest in wage negotiations and for a couple of years afterwards the significance of day-wage negotiations was not realized. There was, moreover, no unity between the left wing Areas.

126

The attempts to get a debate going before 1967 were dominated by South Wales and Derbyshire. The president of the South Wales Area at that time, Bill Whitehead, was a militant, highly articulate Communist and he provided much of the initiative. Whitehead had cooperated with Bert Wynn, the ex-Communist secretary of the Derbyshire Area. Will Paynter had also been involved. The president of the Scottish Area, Alex Moffat, however, had consistently refused to commit his Area and had never attended a meeting. Both Alex Moffat and his predecessor, his brother Abe, saw no grey area between Communism and anti-Communism. Their experiences in Scotland, particularly during the Cold War period, gave them little evidence to believe alliances with members of the Labour Party could work without Communists being subverted. Hence their aloofness in Edinburgh. But without Scottish commitment and involvement there could not be an effective minority opposition in the Union. The combined votes of Scotland, South Wales, Kent and Derbyshire were far short of a majority in conferences and on the N.E.C. they amounted to an uncertain block of five, sometimes with a couple of votes from other Areas, out of a total of 26. The Union leadership believing in collaboration with the N.C.B. and the Government irrespective of its outcome, was firmly in control of the National Executive Committee and its sub-committees. There was no left wing member, excluding the General Secretary, on the powerful Finance and General Purposes Committee and on other committees they sat usually as solitary watchdogs. There was no left wing member on the Business Committee of the Annual Conference which arranged its agenda, decided on priorities for resolutions and framed composite motions.

The position of the National Executive Committee was strengthened by the fact that there was no inconsistency between its intentions and the Annual Conference. Whatever the N.E.C. decided it could carry at the Conference. In this situation the N.E.C. could diligently follow the Union constitution in the spirit as well as the letter. Rule 8 of the Union constitution stated that "The Government of the Union shall be by Conference as provided for in Rule 23. In the periods between Conference the National Executive Committee shall administer the business and affairs of the Union and perform all duties laid down for it by resolution of Conference, and it shall not at any time act contrary to, or in defiance of, any resolution of Conference." This rule presupposed a consensus in the Union and in the 1960s this existed because the people who controlled the N.E.C. also controlled the Conference. The N.E.C. was quite happy to take instructions from the Annual Conference for they were of its own making.

When the meeting at Sheffield decided on its course of action there was no apparent reason to think that it would be any more

Michael McGahey, President of the Scottish Area of the National Union of Mineworkers, 1967- and National Vice-President, 1973 -.

Jack Dunn, Secretary of the Kent Miners, 1960-1980, at the point of retirement.

successful than its predecessor. Yet it was different from the earlier one in important ways. The composition was different. The Scottish Area was represented for the first time, and by its general secretary, Lawrence Daly, and vice-President, Michael McGahey. In 1967 the president of the Scottish Area, Alex Moffat, was ill and McGahey acted for him. McGahey's presence was important, not only because it committed the Scottish Area to whatever campaign was launched, but because McGahey's energy and emerging leadership qualities were devoted to it. McGahey was as unknown in the English and Welsh coalfields in 1967 as was Daly but he quickly, informally, assumed the leadership of the widely based forum for democratic discussion and decision-making which began to emerge. His qualities were a combination of unreserved self-less commitment to the miners' cause, a belief in trade unionism and the possibility of positive action through the N.U.M., and an exceptional degree of political acumen. He used them with daunting vigour. He always argued and spoke with authority so that it was difficult not to be impressed, if not persuaded by him. He was an intellectual who did not intellectualize his arguments but expounded them as clearly as the issues themselves were clear. He was one of a small, select band of orators who could attract the attention of a meeting after his first sentence. These added up to rather special leadership qualities. McGahey and Daly, friends since their days together in the Young Communist League, comprised an impressive Scottish contingent.

The other members of the meeting brought with them similar qualities of commitment and application but with differences in manner and approach. In their respective spheres they were leaders, not afraid of making decisions and able to issue commands. But at Sheffield and subsequently, Michael McGahey quickly and easily, without a vote, without even a formal position, imposed himself as one who supplied initiatives. It would be a mistake, however, to see this group as one which was led by any one person. Its members were much too skilled in analysis, argument and rhetoric to be dominated by one person.

Jack Dunn, a Communist and secretary of the small Kent Area was present. His special contribution was a terrier-like intellectual quality. He rarely raised a point, let alone pursued one, which was not researched and backed by documentary evidence of the most conventionally impeccable kind. The South Wales Area was represented by Dai Francis, its general secretary and Emlyn Williams the Area vice-president. Dai Francis combined a curious mixture of Communist and Welsh religious non-conformist principles and in those days he was not easy to work with. He applied his strict principles of social as well as political behaviour as a standard for everyone around him as well as for himself. Working with him was like being perpetually scrutinized under a giant microscope. No one

Dai Francis, General Secretary of the South Wales Area, N.U.M., 1963-1976.

Left to right: Sammy Taylor, Tommy Degnam who had been a prominent militant Yorkshire miner, and Jock Kane. Taken in 1962 on the occasion of "Deg's" 65th birthday.

was spared. His Communism had a flair of individualism so that his interpretations of events, his stand on particular issues were sometimes slightly maverick. This trait was not uncommon amongst South Welsh Communists. Dai Dan Evans, who was the previous general secretary, had combined membership of the Communist Party with a fervent belief in Syndicalism. Emlyn Williams belonged to the Labour Party but that was the only factor which distinguished him from McGahey, Francis and Dunn for he joined with them in his analyses, his commitment and his loyalty. In fact he displayed loyalty more than most by frequently putting his own personal interests aside to preserve unity. The then president of the South Wales Area, Glyn Williams, played no part in this conscious-raising process and this gave Emlyn Williams much scope to exercise his leadership talents.

When the Scottish, South Wales and Kent officials made decisions they were able to commit their respective Areas to them. This was the case to some extent with Derbyshire. The difference in this Area was that Bert Wynn's successor, Herbert Parkin, was much more ambivalent about attacking the N.U.M. establishment than the others who attended the Sheffield meeting. His ambivalence however, was on this occasion compensated for by Tom Swain who accompanied him. Swain was the Member of Parliament for North East Derbyshire and was to become the Chairman of the Miners Parliamentary Group and ex-officio member of the National Executive Committee of the National Union of Mineworkers a few months later. He was a constant reminder of the basic ethics of the Labour Movement. He understood the mechanism of capitalism with great simplicity and could locate the miners in it precisely. He had been a miner and forever remained one, whether in Parliament or out of it. The seductive glamour of Parliament made no impression on him. Unfortunately Tom Swain did not carry influence in the decision-making process in the Derbyshire Area. Although Dennis Skinner, later to make a reputation as a vociferous left-wing M.P., was the president of the Derbyshire Area and Peter Heathfield, later to be an outstandingly progressive secretary of that Area, was the full-time Compensation Agent, they were not able to counter the influence of Parkin and commit Derbyshire unequivocally to a left-wing campaign. The main seat of power in Derbyshire was unquestionably occupied by the Secretary.

The other Area represented at Sheffield was Yorkshire. Two full-time officials were there, namely Jock Kane, the Yorkshire Financial Secretary, and Sammy Taylor, the Area Compensation Agent. They were both committed Communists and tough and unyielding over principles, but they were entirely self-effacing, unconcerned about their own positions, disinterested in projecting themselves. Both of them had had rough lives involving unemployment and political victimization. It was always something to be wondered at that people such as Taylor and Kane could survive the destructive pressures of a hostile environment without blemishes on their principles and integrity. It was the case, of course, that they were never alone. Both of these men had substantial followings in the Yorkshire coalfield. Some of their exploits in strikes had become legendary already. Each of them attracted support because they were open, abrupt and honest in their relationships. Sammy Taylor was the more reflective of the two though he appeared as a stereotypical Yorkshireman. Jock Kane, a Scotsman who had been forced to migrate to Yorkshire, had his trade union base in Doncaster. He was forthright in his opinions and in the language he used to express them. He made an ideal chairman because he recognized no distinctions between members of the group. Each one was treated to the same disarming cutting language.

The other two from Yorkshire were Tommy Mullany and Owen Briscoe. Both were working miners from Doncaster and were prominent in the Doncaster panel. They were able to speak on behalf of the Doncaster miners though, because of the parochialism in Yorkshire, not for the Yorkshire miners as a whole. In any event the Yorkshire Area, despite the official positions held by Taylor and Kane, was firmly controlled by conservative, strenuously anti-Communist officials. The Yorkshire Area Council which comprised pit delegates and the Yorkshire Executive Committee which was an elected body, both reflected the conservatism of the Area President and General Secretary. Yet the Area had important contradictions which the positions of Taylor and Kane reflected. Yorkshire had a higher average incidence of strikes than even the left wing Areas and it was through this sphere of activity that miners such as Mullany and Briscoe asserted their leadership. Each of these miners was to make important contributions to changes in the Yorkshire Area. Tommy Mullany was the more assertive and articulate of the two and might have achieved high office in the Union if he had vacillated less in his policies and allegiences. He did not readily subordinate his own aspirations when they conflicted with majority decisions so that he increasingly found himself isolated. Owen Briscoe, on the other hand was solid in his commitment to left-wing policies. He eventually became the General Secretary of the Yorkshire Area.

There was one respect in which Tommy Mullany and Owen Briscoe differed from the increasing number of militant Yorkshire miners who joined up with them subsequently to campaign for changes. Mullany was the chairman of the Doncaster Panel and, with Briscoe, could influence its decisions. No other militant miners in Yorkshire were in that position.

The Panel system in Yorkshire was an informal arrangement whereby the Area was divided into four sections, North Yorkshire,

Doncaster, Barnsley and South Yorkshire reflecting early N.C.B. divisions but persisting after those divisions had been abolished. Each section had its own representative committee, with a chairman and secretary, which met to discuss local and national issues and to give mandates to pit delegates who comprised the Area Council. The panels became instruments for rank and file influence over policy which eventually achieved semi-official status in the Area. They reflected local loyalties and were competitive in their relationships. The Doncaster panel prided itself for its militant policies, for initiating strike movements in the Area and its decisions played a prominent part in activating Yorkshire miners to adopt more progessive policies. Therein lay the importance of the presence of Mullany and Briscoe at the Sheffield meeting.

The meeting at Sheffield differed from earlier ones not simply in its composition but also in its intentions. It decided to organize a campaign about policy issues around the forthcoming election for the General Secretaryship and to draw on left-wing resources in every coalfield. The election provided a finite and specific purpose but the aim was to alter the consciousness of miners with implications well beyond that election. It intended, moreover, to convert right-wing Areas to left-wing policies and to start right there in Yorkshire.

CHAPTER 11

STRATEGY

It would be pretentious even to imply that the small number of miners who were preparing to campaign for the projection of Lawrence Daly in 1967 as a candidate for the General Secretaryship of the N.U.M. in November, 1968, and who wanted to use the occasion as a means of transforming the policy of the Union, knew what to do. They were not in a position to choose tactics and conditions to suit their own purposes. Their methods, their tools, in total their strategy, were derived from their own limited experiences and knowledge and from the constraints which a hostile environment placed on them.

Their experiences had been shared by many others and their knowledge was common. None of them was a celebrity or a national figure with access to the mass media, except for the columns of the *Morning Star*. Some did not even have Area status. They were not sought after by reporters of newspapers, sound radio or television for their opinions about the coal industry. In order to communicate with other miners and to influence opinion outside the coal industry they had to use the methods of early nineteenth century reformers, namely pamphleteering and oratory. The revolution in electronic communications has little significance to people with no property, except to carry information and ideas to them.

The tasks, however, were made easier because the economic and industrial context of mineworkers was altering to favour protest. Firstly, increasing unemployment began to block the usual escape route for disaffected miners. The N.U.M. in 1967 was in the midst of the biggest ever closure programme with more men involved than ever before. In that year 34,300 miners were directly affected by closures and of these 12,900 were made redundant. No more than 2000 miners had ever been declared redundant in any previous year. The number of redundant miners as a proportion of all miners who left the industry rose dramatically from 2.8 per cent in 1966 to 21.7 per cent in 1967. The N.C.B. was no longer able to relocate all those men who were involved in closures and who wanted to stay in the industry.

The rise in redundancy coincided with increasing difficulties in obtaining alternative work. Redundant miners received small lump sum payments as well as weekly payments of compensation but, except for those nearing retiring age, these did not recompense for the loss of paid employment. The Labour Government which had been elected in 1966 gave its priority to the balance of payments, embarked on a policy of public expenditure cuts and caused a rise in the numbers unemployed from 1.7 per cent for males in Great

Britain in 1965 to 3.2 per cent in 1967. Some of the coalfields were in the traditional depressed areas which had relatively substantial employment problems.

Miners in 1967 were confronted with a new post-war situation which was the beginning of a worsening trend. They could no longer easily seek individualistic solutions to their problems. The conventional wisdom about the uncontrollable, all-powerful laws of the market disseminated by the Government, the N.C.B. and Union officials appeared rather sour to miners faced with the prospect of unemployment. Those who lost their jobs had no alternative but to cope as best they could as individuals. Those who were dissatisfied with their conditions of work lost the option of leaving the industry easily and had to stay and tolerate them or to struggle collectively to improve them. After placidly accepting closures for so long it was difficult to go into reverse quickly and protest. They did not protest in 1967. In that year there was not one recorded dispute about redundancy.

But the basis for protest was laid once miners recognized they could only improve their individual positions by action inside the industry. Quite suddenly there was a mining audience which was prepared to listen to alternative explanations to those which had been given to them for so long. And coincidentally there was a group of miners willing and capable of providing the explanations. This is a simplification of the real situation but essentially the scene was set for changing the attitudes of miners. Arguments about mining conditions, spoken and written, reasoned and shouted, began to penetrate the pits and influence the minds of miners as they had not done for decades before.

The Yorkshire Campaign

The left wing activists recognised that one or more of the large right wing Areas, Nottingham, Durham or Yorkshire, had to be won over in order to ensure a continuing influence over policy-making. Winning in this respect meant filling leading Area positions with progressive miners as well as dominating the Area executive and council. It was a difficult assignment under any circumstances but in the case of Nottingham and Durham it was complicated by the methods they used to select their leaders. In each of these Areas it was impossible for an ordinary member to challenge for a leading position for the leaders were selected from existing full-time officials. Even if a left wing miner became a full-time official he could be isolated and effectively neutralized for the Area bureaucracies exercised a fairly tight control over the electoral machinery.

It was only in Yorkshire that the method of election allowed for a real possibility of challenging the Area leadership. The tenure of the President and General Secretary had only a few years to run.

Arthur Scargill, President of the Yorkshire Area of the National Union of Mineworkers, 1973-

And there were miners there prepared to mount the challenge. Yorkshire had the added quality of being the largest Area, with almost 80,000 members. For these reasons Yorkshire selected itself as the target for left wing attention.

A vital asset was a local nucleus of support for progressive policies without which a campaign could not have been started at all. Each Area of the National Union of Mineworkers controlled its own territory very much like an autonomous county union of pre-amalgamation days. It surveilled its own members and protected them from external influences as far as it possibly could. The officials from other Areas were not able to enter another on Union business without the permission or invitation of the local officials. There was even likely to be resentment and suspicion if an official from another Area was seen around socially or perhaps at the invitation of a non-mining union organization such as a local trades council, the Labour Party or the Communist Party. In this respect Yorkshire was in some ways more chauvinistic than the other coalfields.

The Yorkshire coalfield possessed its own transforming contradictions with, in consequence, its own contending forces. It had for some years contained an active Communist Party which had provided an organizational basis for militant action. In 1967 opposition to the Area leadership was centred around the two Communists, Sammy Taylor and Jock Kane who were full-time Union officials. The opposition comprised a mixture of Communists, ex-Communists and left wing members of the Labour Party. The demands of the campaign tapped the leadership qualities of this group and fairly quickly a number of miners emerged as potential union officials.

The most important organizational innovation in Yorkshire was the formation of the Barnsley Miners' Forum by Arthur Scargill, a faceworker and delegate from Woolley Colliery, near Barnsley. Scargill had been active as a militant rank and file miner since the late 1950s. The Forum was held on Friday evenings at Barnsley Cooperative Hall and was attended by hundreds of miners who listened to speeches by Lawrence Daly, Michael McGahey, Emlyn Williams, Jack Dunn and others. For the first time many young miners heard arguments against pit closures, in favour of high wages and a shorter working week. Through this medium Scargill acted as a catalyst in the Barnsley district and beyond. He worked closely with a small group of Barnsley miners including Peter Tait, George Wilkinson, Ron Rigby and Don Baines. They met in a room of a Barnsley hotel where Roy Mason, who became Minister of Power in July, 1968, often drank in an adjoining bar.

Fairly quickly these miners developed a cohesion which had not been present before. They were competent branch officials who until now had struggled in the isolation of their branches. They had never controlled the Barnsley Panel but collectively they began to discover that they could influence its proceedings. Within a relatively short period they controlled it in much the same way as the Doncaster one was controlled by Ian Ferguson, Jim Oldham, Owen Briscoe, Mick Welsh and Tommy Mullany. These representatives of the Barnsley miners began to meet with the Doncaster ones to discuss policy and strategy. There was never anyone present from South Yorkshire; while from North Yorkshire the only representative was the irrepressible Communist, Jimmy Miller, the Scottish secretary of the large, modern Kellingley colliery.

A succession of propaganda meetings was organized consisting of evening lectures, day-schools and weekend schools. Lawrence Daly was so well-publicized in the branches and the Miners' Clubs that the miners throughout the coalfield voted to invite him to be an official main speaker at the Yorkshire Miners' Gala in May, 1968. This was the first sign of a break in the right-wing control of the Area. Then he was selected as the Yorkshire Area's nominee for the Union General Secretaryship. After this the official Area leadership was in a precarious position. The combination of the aggressive determination of miners such as Arthur Scargill and circumstances propitious for campaigning ensured that left-wing influence would continue to grow. That is what happened.

This period proved to be a learning experience for Scargill. He always acted competently with confidence but he was rarely at this stage given more than grudging respect by the others. He was, and still is, essentially a shy person who projects himself as compensation for his shyness. Those miners who worked alongside Scargill in the newly formed left-wing grouping in Yorkshire, however, did not engage in personality analysis and treated him as they found him. There was a tendency, therefore, for them to react to his brashness by trying to argue him down before looking at the merits of his case. He perpetually had to defend his stance from criticism by miners such as Ian Ferguson, Jimmy Miller and Ron Rigby who could always detect the wider political consequences of action in the Yorkshire coalfield. Arthur Scargill selects himself for attention because of his later achievements but in the early days of the campaign it would have been difficult to identify the future leadership pattern in Yorkshire because the field was so rich with talent.

Policy-Making in the Areas

The campaigning tasks were less onerous in the left-wing Areas though Daly still had to be introduced to them and alternative policies had to be discussed there, breaking the sense of impotence and futility which had gripped them during the years of decline. Periodically various Area representatives met for weekend discussions, clarifying different emphases, reconciling contrasting experiences, to reach a common understanding. Much of this understanding went into a pamphlet called *The Miners and the Nation* by Lawrence Daly, published by the Scottish Area and distributed throughout most of the coalfields early in 1968. The pamphlet posed problems and gave answers. It examined the whole field of energy policy, projected a Socialist case, formulated a programme for miners and outlined the strategy miners should pursue. Daly advocated industrial action. He stated: "By adopting more militant attitudes to secure a change in fuel policy we could save Britain from over-dependence on foreign fuel supplies. But we could also protect our mining communities from the worst effects of redundancy and win conditions and rewards that would attract and hold young, skilful and intelligent men in our modern coal industry. . ."

The arguments Daly projected were ignored by the Government and the N.C.B. to their eventual cost. The threat of militant action was not taken seriously. But miners in the coalfields read and listened for what was said made sense to them. This was reflected in the election for the national secretaryship in December, 1968, when Lawrence Daly obtained 52.3 per cent of the total votes thus beating his one opponent, Joe Gormley, the secretary of the Lancashire Area.

The initiatives that were taken during the election campaign, as was intended, had wider implications than the election of Lawrence Daly for they began the arduous process of raising the consciousness of miners in general. For this process to be successful, however, it had to end with changes in Union policy and behaviour. As the Union policy was decided at Annual Conferences it was important that their procedures and power were examined. They were the core of the democratic procedures that made up the constitution. Each year rank and file delegates met under the chairmanship of the national president of the Union to debate resolutions on policy, changes of rule and to decide important Union elections. Conferences elected the national vice-president and the Union's nominees for the T.U.C. General Council and the Labour Party executive as well as lesser positions at the T.U.C. and Labour Party conferences. The conferences gave instructions to the N.E.C. Their decisions, it was believed, could not be countermanded. They were formal constitutional repositories of power in the Union.

The Union constitution was practised, however, in a way which was unintended by its architects. On many issues the delegates were mandated by their respective Area policy-making conferences. They always voted, not as individual representatives, but as members of Area delegations. On issues where there were no mandated instructions Area delegations decided how to vote. The really important decisions, therefore, were made in the Areas or in Area delegation meetings outside of the conferences. The national conferences were places where the votes were added. There was always the possibility that an Area delegation could be persuaded to adopt a particular position or change its attitude but this was not the normal practice.

The National Exectutive Committee exercised considerable influence over the conduct of the conferences. The conference procedures were interpreted by a Business Committee, consisting of Executive members, which also determined the order of business and, in some instances, its substance. It made decisions about wording of composite motions and decided the order for discussion. A motion could have a vital word eliminated or altered in meaning through pressure from the Business Committee or it could be relegated to the tail-end of the conference when the press was absent and the delegates had their minds on getting home. A struggle for control over the conference had to take account of the activities of the Business Committee.

The National Executive Committee intervened directly in the affairs of the conferences by expressing opinions about the motions and giving delegates advice about how to vote. On virtually every motion the Executive would tell delegates to accept, reject or remit it. Voting, therefore, was not simply about policy but was transformed by the attitude of the N.E.C. into expressions of confidence in itself. A defeat of a motion supported by the Executive was interpreted as a rebuff for it. Within this context it was difficult to swing a conference to vote against the advice of the National Executive Committee. Some way had to be found of constraining the Executive's powers in the manner stipulated by the Union constitution.

Tactics at the Annual Conference.

The left-wing miners' leaders were clear about what they wanted to achieve. They wanted to be able to control the National Executive Committee through asserting the superior policy-making powers of the conferences. According to the constitution the Executive was committed to particular and specific demands by the wording of resolutions. There was obviously a difference for the Executive between being instructed, requested or advised to do something. It was clearly possible to word resolutions to give the Executive degrees of discretion ranging from absolute freedom to none at all. What the left wing delegates wanted was to commit the National Executive Committee to their own resolutions leaving it with no discretion to deviate from them.

It seems all so very obvious now what should have been attempted after 1967 but at the time the issue was far from clear. Clarity came almost accidentally through the wording of the wages resolutions. Hitherto the wages resolutions had usually been vague, simply

Emlyn Williams, President of the South Wales Area of the N.U.M., 1973-

asking the National Executive Committee to negotiate "substantial" increases without any reference to specific sums. The first change was to remove the word "substantial" and to demand specific sums. The second change was to stipulate in the resolutions precisely what kind of action should follow if the actual demands were not met. In this way the National Executive Committee lost its freedom to manoeuvre.

The National Coal Board had set its own pace for wages negotiations in the 1960s. It was never in a hurry. The wages resolution passed in the July, 1968 Annual Conference, for instance, was submitted to the N.C.B. in September, 1968 but was not settled until the Autumn, 1969. That resolution asked for a minimum wage of £15 a week for surface workers and £16 for underground workers. These figures had been contained in a Scottish Area resolution which in turn had been published in Daly's pamphlet, *The Miners and the Nation,* as an appropriate demand early in 1968. The claim was conceded in full, for the first time in the history of the N.U.M. This settlement was influenced by a rather special 1969 strike situation and was part of a package deal, as is described in the next chapter.

The naming of figures for wage increases was not repeated again until the 1970 Annual Conference at the Isle of Man when Scotland, Yorkshire, Derbyshire and South Wales made similar wage demands. The Business Committee attempted to persuade each of these Areas to agree on a single composite motion calling for mimimum rates of £30 a week for face workers, £22 for other underground workers and £20 for surface workers. South Wales refused to surrender its own motion so the Conference debated two wages motions. The composite one was moved by Arthur Scargill, still a working miner, and seconded by Michael McGahey. In his speech McGahey declared that he was pleased that figures were incorporated in the motion "because for too many years and for too long were we fobbed off with what they termed 'substantial increases' . . . We were getting shillings instead of pounds." The conference agreed without opposition.

The reason for the South Wales Area's insistence on its own motion was that it could not get the sting in its tail included in the composite. It demanded a mimimum underground rate of £1 a week less than that mentioned in the composite motion but added that "should the Board refuse to concede this demand, then the British miners take strike action until this claim is met." Emlyn Williams who moved the South Wales motion declared its purpose. "It is a clear mandate," he stated, "to the National Executive Council that unless the figures contained within this resolution are attained, then we are committed to recommend to the coalfield industrial action in accordance with rule . . ." Although there was no opposition to the wages demand there were strong feelings about the South Wales directive to the N.E.C. and the right wing Areas tried to defeat it. The N.E.C., however, for the first time for many years, did not have the support of the Yorkshire Area and the motion was passed by the small margin of 169 votes to 160. The National Executive Committee left the conference as never before, committed to demand a specific wage increase with instructions to advise a strike if it could not be obtained through negotiations. The South Wales resolution became the model for all subsequent ones from the left wing Areas. They always named figures and made provision for national strike action.

The power struggle which was taking place in Yorkshire was reflected at the 1970 conference. The Yorkshire Area moved the composite wages resolution and supported the South Wales one. It gave Arthur Scargill his first important national platform. Outwardly there was nothing of special significance in this. However, the chairman of the conference was Sid Schofield, the national vice-president and the general secretary of the Yorkshire Area. He had taken the place of the president who was ill. Schofield was a tireless opponent of left-wing critics and he devoted some part of his chairman's address to attacking Scargill and others, not by name but by reference to their activities. "We must not allow the minority," he stated, "who are already holding unofficial meetings, to formulate policies that undermine the whole concept of Trade Unionism . . . I am quite satisfied that the minorities in our Union, who are arranging unofficial meetings, printing and issuing pamphlets, ignoring the policies agreed upon at Annual Conferences, have a purpose in mind to try to undermine the status of Area and National Officials of our Union, and to incite our members into taking unconstitutional action, on an issue that they will choose." He criticized, again by implication, the sting-in-the-tail of the South Wales resolution despite his own Area council's unanimous support for it, as a Yorkshire delegate, Henry Daley, was quick to point out. The position of the president and general secretary of the Yorkshire Area was rapidly becoming untenable. Long before they were actually due to retire, they slipped into obscurity.

The determination of the South Wales Area to retain its resolution at the 1970 Annual Conference completed the initial strategy of the left-wing campaign in the N.U.M. There existed by 1970 a cohesive alliance between members of the Communist Party and the Labour Party in which political allegiances only rarely obtruded. There were open, sometimes disturbingly frank, discussions between them. They never voted but always argued until a consensus emerged. There were, of course, personal rivalries but members were quick to jump on those who were seen to subordinate policy matters for their own interests. It was not until later when left wing influence had been consolidated that personality differences emerged in the juggling for official positions. This alliance placed the entrenched majority on the N.E.C. in a constrained constitutional position from which it could see no escape, except to ride with the militants.

Women surface workers sorting coal in the early part of the century. Women continued to be employed in the sidings, tramways and washing and sorting coal throughout the inter-war years, particularly in Lancashire. Their places were taken by men who, in the main, had been compelled to leave facework through injury or disease.

CHAPTER 12

EXPERIENCE

Surface Hours

Each year, in a monotonous succession, the National Union of Mineworkers has made demands to the National Coal Board which have been rejected, stalled or, in some way, simply not met. Some issues have been carried over from one year to another, from one decade to another. Indeed it has become difficult for Areas to discover issues which have not been raised before when they select the three motions each of them is entitled to send each year to the Annual Conference.

If an Area feels strongly about an issue it is not enough for it to submit a motion to the Annual Conference or even to get it accepted as Union policy. It is, of course, a necessary condition for action in many cases to get a matter accepted as Union policy. But what happens thereafter depends upon the priorities of the National Executive Committee and the power position in the industry. Some issues, vitally important for some sections of the workers, are left trailing behind, never able to get anywhere near the top of the list of priorities. In power struggles the weak have only triumphed when principle has pre-empted expediency but all too often expediency has been given preference.

One of these trailing issues in the late 1960s was working hours for surface workers. Surface workers were the cinderellas of the industry. Many of them were underground rejects, men who had not qualified for the rigours of face work, or who had suffered from underground work through injury or disease and had been downgraded. Their work was unpleasant, dirty, draughty, poorly paid. They had no status for they were not coal getters but 'on-cost' workers, depending upon face workers for their livelihoods. They played a relatively minor part in the Union for its leadership at all levels had always been controlled by face workers. They were not of the kind to challenge the initiative provided from underground because so many of them understood from their own experiences that real power lay there and not at the pit head. There were some exceptions, of course, such as the winding enginemen but these had never regarded themselves as ordinary surface workers anyway.

The Miners' Charter in 1947 insisted on a 40 hour week for surface workers. Many of them worked 40 hours, not because the N.C.B had acceded to the demand, but because of the special conditions of their work. Miners connected with winding left work when winding stopped while surface workers who worked continuous shifts had a 40 hour week. But men who worked in the pit yard and on the tips worked an 8¼ hour day plus mealtimes. It was Union

Removing dirt from coal at the Parkhouse screens in a Clay Cross pit. This work was dirty, back-breaking, monotonous and poorly paid. Many of the miners in this photograph were partially disabled through underground work.

Surface workers operating a 'Billy Fairplay' machine at Denby's pit in Derbyshire, around 1900. This was an automatic machine introduced in the 1880s to separate hard coal from slack and indicate the weight of each so that miners could be paid at different rates for different qualities. Its name was a misnomer and it resulted in many disputes.

Surface workers on open-ended tipplers at Denby pit in Derbyshire in 1900. These miners were always lowly paid and neglected by the unions as well as the employers.

policy to erase this anomaly but it persisted.

The anomaly was still present when the 1968 Annual Conference met. Both Derbyshire and Yorkshire had resolutions to deal with it. They were merged into a composite resolution which stated: "This Conference of the National Union of Mineworkers is of the view that the hours of surface workers should not exceed 7¾ per shift and instructs the National Executive Committee to give priority to the submission of a claim for a reduction in the shift hours for all colliery surface workers." This politely phrased request was moved by the Derbyshire Area whose delegate made the main points: the men involved were essential for the efficiency of the pits; they were discriminated against because of the nature of their work; they comprised less than 2 per cent of the labour force and the total cost of meeting the claim would be no more than £700,000. In 1968 the operating profit of the N.C.B. was £28.6 million.

The resolution was remitted to the N.E.C. which raised its content with the N.C.B. in October,1968. The Board agreed to consider the matter. It replied on 30th May, 1969.

The Union had obtained a reduction of 15 minutes a shift in 1960 and was offered a further reduction of 15 minutes in 1963 with the option of taking 7 rest days instead. The option was taken up by the Areas on the understanding by the Board that that settled the Union's claim for a 40 hour week for surface workers. The settlement, however, was unrealistic for the hours anomaly remained and, in any case, the rest days were equivalent only to a 40 hour week exclusive of meal-times, which was less than the miners wanted. Nonetheless the N.C.B. reminded the Union of the 1960 settlement when it replied, adding, however, that it was prepared to make a great advance by conceding a 40 hour week exclusive of meal-times for all surface workers, when Government policy permitted, provided the Union delayed its demand for a shift allowance and refrained from lodging a claim to reduce the hours of underground workers.

Industrial relations in Britain in 1969 was influenced by the Government's 1966 Prices and Incomes Act introduced to put a brake on wage increases and backed by legislative sanctions. This Act was altered in 1968 so that increases could be delayed for up to 12 months. Moreover Government approval had to be sought for reductions in working hours. So when the N.C.B. made its offer it was within the terms of the Government's policy. Miners were told to wait until the next general wages settlement in the hope that they would get Government permission to reduce the hours for surface workers.

The Demand for Action

The South Wales miners, in May 1969, demanded action to reduce surface workers' hours, by striking if necessary. Four areas submitted resolutions to the 1969 Annual Conference which reaffirmed the demand for a 7¾ hour shift, inclusive of meal-times. South Wales miners demonstrated outside the Conference while inside most delegates who spoke emphasized the anger which was building up amongst the members. Lawrence Daly, in his new position as General Secretary, took up the issue with a warning that unless progress was made soon " surface workers in the various coalfields will take action themselves." Delegates from Scotland, South Wales, Kent and Derbyshire lobbied the headquarters of the N.C.B. on 24th September, 1969. On 7th October the South Wales Area executive received a delegation from the Mountain Ash district which informed it that miners there intended to take action, possibly in the form of a one-day strike.

A campaign for strike action was building up throughout some of the coalfields but at the time it was not recognised as such. There was no attempt to bring the different strands together, to unify or even coordinate the rank-and-file initiatives. Left-wing miners' leaders supported the move to reduce the hours of surface workers but could not agree on what methods to use. In South Wales, the president and the general secretary opposed strike action as did their Area executive. Lawrence Daly wanted to deal with the issue through the conciliation machinery. Indeed, the prevalent feeling amongst the officials was that a strike would not have support from the members and that, in any case, it would not alter the attitude of the N.C.B. In fact the hours issue involving a minority of surface workers did not seem to be capable of galvanizing face workers who were the traditional leaders of strike movements. After a decade of humiliating repression what indeed was capable of creating a sense of unifying injustice amongst miners? Pit closures had not done so.

The South Wales executive felt justified in opposing a strike over hours because of its miscalculation in the Avon colliery matter. In April 1969 the N.U.M learned that Avon colliery was to close because of the problems in marketing the coal it produced and the difficult geological conditions in the pit. A delegation from the pit called on the Area executive in May to oppose the closure for it felt that the N.C.B. simply wanted to release manpower from Avon to be deployed elsewhere.

In the following months there was much discussion in South Wales about methods for opposing pit closures. A Special Area Conference was held in June to discuss the issue; a delegation went to London to appeal against the closure although it had been decided in 1968 that it was futile appealing to London; pressure was put on the Welsh Office of the Government in Cardiff to keep the pit open. The N.C.B. was unmoved, confirming the cynicism of the Area executive about protests. So, in August, 1969, the Area executive recommended that unless the N.C.B. reversed its decision, the coalfield would stop working on the day the Avon colliery was closed. This recommendation was rejected by 49 votes to 32 at a Special Area Conference on 20th August. The rebuff to the executive by the members was even more marked in September when they voted against strike action by 30,900 votes to 4,950. This Area ballot result was announced on 23rd September, overlapping with the campaign to reduce surface workers' hours.

Yorkshire as a Catalyst

Despite occasional threats, few people expected a strike to break out in favour of the surface workers. It could hardly have resulted from action by the relatively small number of surface workers who were affected by the demand. The Doncaster and Barnsley miners who had campaigned for the election of Lawrence Daly were pressing for strike action. There were rumours that the Doncaster panel in Yorkshire intended to call a strike on 6th October but nothing of the kind happened. Instead, on that same day, the Yorkshire Area Council agreed to postpone a discussion of surface workers' hours until 11th October so that they could receive a report from the National Executive Committee meeting on 9th October. Johnny Weaver, *a new delegate on the Yorkshire Area Council from the Edlington pit in Doncaster put a motion for action which caused the President to postpone the discussion. He read it out from a piece of paper handed to him by Mick Welsh, later to be a Member of Parliament for the Don Valley constituency in Yorkshire, but written by Arthur Scargill, the Woolley delegate. Both Scargill and Welsh thought that as Weaver was new he stood a better chance of getting the motion debated than did Scargill. At that time any initiative by Scargill in the Yorkshire Council Chamber was a recipe for defeat.

When the National Executive Committee met on 9th October, with Jock Kane attending for the first time, it received a report on the surface hours issue and simply referred the matter back. This inconclusive situation was reported to the special meeting of the Yorkshire Area Council by its N.E.C. representative, T. Burke, in its resumed debate on 11th October and evoked a wave of protest. A motion for strike action was moved by Scargill but the chairman refused to accept it on the grounds that it could result in unofficial action. Then in an almost unprecedented act the chairman, Sam Bullough, who was also the national vice-president of the Union, was voted out of the chair. The Area vice-president, Jack Leigh, took his place and allowed Scargill's motion to stand.

The incisive intervention at this meeting came from Jock Kane, in full Scottish flavour, blunt and in uncomplicated prose, when he supported strike action but reworded Scargill's motion to make it more acceptable to those delegates who were wavering about going

* Johnny Weaver became a rank and file Yorkshire representative of the N.E.C. of the Union in 1979.

on strike. Kane told the delegates that if the rule book stood in the way of a strike then it should be thrown out of the window. Whereupon the Council decided:

> "1 - That we note the report of Mr. T. Burke upon recent developments at national level on the subject of Surface Workers' hours and express our deep regret that our claim for eight hours inclusive of meal-times has not yet been conceded.
>
> "This Council Meeting views with alarm the position now facing the coalfield, and expresses in the strongest possible terms our deep disappointment at the delaying tactics of the National Coal Board.
>
> "We must warn the Board and our N.E.C. that because of this, the Yorkshire coalfield will be at a standstill on Monday morning. This unofficial action will have been taken because the patience of our men has come to an end."

An Unofficial Strike in 1969

This motion was passed by 85 votes to 3. An attempt was made to pass the responsibility for calling the strike on to the N.E.C. but it failed. The delegates were true to their word. On the morning of Monday, 13th October every pit but one in Yorkshire was idle. The remaining pit was on strike by Tuesday. The Doncaster panel was the main organizer and it had its flying pickets, a method used successfully in the 1955 strike, around the coalfield and into Derbyshire and Nottingham from the start. On the Monday night 16 surface workers on the coal preparation plant at Monktonhall in Scotland went on strike. On Tuesday morning a pit-head meeting decided to call all Monktonhall miners out. Craftsmen, many of whom were surface workers, at Bilston Glen colliery in Scotland stopped work on the Tuesday afternoon. The strike in Scotland spread in this untidy fashion. The strike spread to South Wales rather belatedly. The Executive of the South Wales Area met on the day the strike started in Yorkshire and decided to demand a Special National Delegate Conference to call for a national strike rather than to follow the example of Yorkshire. The following day an Area Delegate Conference accepted the Executive proposal and this was confirmed by a 48 to 9 vote among the branches. Yet by 20th October there were 24 South Wales pits, involving 16,000 miners, on strike. Branches which had supported the Executive proposal were on strike; in some cases miners struck against the advice of their own branch officials.

In general the strike situation was chaotic. It had the characteristics of a lack of organization combined with a feeling of trepidation about striking amongst miners. They were being advised from all quarters that they would only damage the industry if they struck. Lord Robens on October 17th stated that "if they stay out on strike they will do terrible damage to the industry. They will lose customers and the pits will close." Sir Sidney Ford, the Union's president said that the strike was a "serious blow" at the Yorkshire coalfield and he was "absolutely certain that unofficial action will solve nothing and could well prevent the N.C.B. making any further concessions on surface hours." Robens expressed the same sentiment. "These unofficial strikers feel they can put a pistol to one's head," he stated in a radio broadcast. "All I can say is that they are very much mistaken."

The leaders on the left were either ambivalent or opposed to the strike. They had not been involved in this kind of nation-wide strike before. They had believed that strikes were counter productive in the declining state of the industry. Some were influenced by the unoffical character of the strike. When the South Wales executive had threatened a strike over the Avon colliery closure Lawrence Daly had written to say that the strike was against the rules and should be called off. On this occasion Daly adopted the same attitude on television and called for the strikers to return to work. But the strike leaders were the very miners who had campaigned so vigorously to get him elected the year before. They were angered by Daly's inability to judge the merits of a case apart from what the rules stated just as they had been impressed by Jock Kane's ability to make that distinction. Daly's reputation amongst his friends suffered and was never fully restored. Miners have long memories where strikes are concerned and still point out the scars of the 1926 General Strike. So, although Lawrence Daly was actively associated with the left-wing until after the 1974 miners' strike and played a prominent leadership part in the 1972 miners' strike, the stain caused by his 1969 intervention was indelible. The striking miners did not expect Daly to advocate an extension of the strike but they did expect him either to argue their case or to keep quiet. It was not an auspicious beginning to his career as a national official.

The strike spread from Yorkshire, its main base, to Scotland, South Wales, Derbyshire, Kent, Nottingham and the Midlands until it involved 130,000 miners from 140 pits. It lasted from 13th to 27th October, 1969. It spread despite poor communications between the Areas. A rudimentary communications system existed but it was not used. The officials and strike leaders in the Areas affected by the strike were too busy trying to control their own situations to liaise with each other. In some instances pits took action on the basis of gossip. There were cases of miners being called out on strike, led back and called out again. Everywhere, except in Yorshire, the strike was a shambles.

The main support outside of Yorkshire lay in South Wales and Scotland. At the end of the first week of the strike 16,000 South Wales miners from 24 pits were involved. The strike spread there in part because of vigorous picketing by some militant pits and against the advice of the Area officials, with the exception of Emlyn Williams

Bill McLean, General Secretary of the Scottish Area of the N.U.M., 1969-1977. Sitting alongside him is Graham Steel, a Scottish Area Agent, who was arrested for picketing the Longannet Power Station in 1972.

who was the Area vice-president. The strike in Scotland spread in a similar piecemeal fashion with some pits striking as others were returning to work, with sections of pits striking, with faceworkers returning to work while surface workers stayed out. A meeting of branch officials in the Ayr coalfield refused to support the strike yet two of their pits did so. The Area officials, including the president Michael McGahey, encouraged the strike to spread but both McGahey and the general secretary of the Scottish Area, Bill McLean,* were members of the N.E.C. and, because of its attitude, were inhibited from taking a public position of support. For this reason no public statement about the strike came from the Area until the strike was nine days old. Then, on 22nd October, a Special Area Delegate Conference declared itself in support of the strikers but refrained from attempting to extend it. Altogether about 18,000 miners out of a total of 27,500 in Scotland were on strike at some time during its duration.

Yorkshire, in comparison with the other Areas, was a model of organization. The four Panels in North and South Yorkshire, Doncaster and Barnsley, came together in an exceptional display of solidarity. They formed a strike committee and through it maintained cohesion throughout the coal field. The militant core was provided by the Doncaster Panel, supported by the small Barnsley group comprising Arthur Scargill, George Wilkinson, Don Baines and Ron Rigby. The president, vice-president and general secretary of the Yorkshire Area were opposed to the strike and were excluded from its organization. The strike ended where it began when eight members of the Yorkshire strike committee got an assurance from Vic Feather, the general secretary of the Trades Union Congress, that he would try to get an independent inquiry to investigate the issue of surface workers' hours.

Whilst the strike was going on negotiations were being held over the miners' wage claim which had been submitted in September, 1968. The claim, without precedent, as quoted in Chapter 11, was granted in full but it was linked with the N.C.B.'s offer of a 40 hour week exclusive of mealtimes to surface workers which the strikers had rejected. The Coal Board offered a package deal which the National Executive Committee of the N.U.M. accepted for it had been as strenuously opposed to the strike as the N.C.B. But when the package was proposed to the Special Delegate Conference on

---

* Bill McLean succeeded Lawrence Daly as general secretary of the Scottish Area in 1969. He had been the vice-president of the Area since 1965 and a full-time Union Agent since 1956. He was a Communist who, alongside Michael McGahey, played an increasingly important part in organizing the Left Wing campaign. After Jock Kane retired in 1972 he became chairman of its operations. He was quiet and unassuming. He did not speak in public with the fluency of McGahey or Jack Dunn. But his lack of rhetoric bore no relation to his intellectual qualities. He gave clear, usually correct advice. He worked assiduously on organizational matters and supplemented the qualities of his close colleagues. He possessed a charm and a warm-heartedness which his friends valued, and occasionally exploited. His sudden death in September, 1977 was tragic. Many of us lost a friend. The Labour Movement lost a committed worker.

Wages and Hours on 30th October, 1969, it was rejected by 168 votes to 165. The Conference agreed, however, to hold a national ballot vote on the issue. The national officials who framed the ballot paper lumped the wages and hours questions together. The acceptance of one was dependent upon accepting the other. The ballot paper required only a single answer. This was a devious but well-known way of getting an unsatisfactory offer accepted. It was known that a majority of the miners would not wish to reject the wages offer which affected them all in order to get an improvement in the working hours of a small minority. The ballot result confirmed this view for only 41,322 miners out of a total of 235,307 voted to reject the package deal. Even in the Areas where the strike was concentrated there were substantial majorities in favour of the deal.

There was some recrimination among the strike leaders, particularly in South Wales and Scotland, after the strike because of the lack of communications between them, the confusion during the strike and the apparent failure to get anything out of it. There was some ambivalence about the achievements of the strike, however, for although the N.C.B. had refused to give surface workers a 40 hour week inclusive of mealtimes it was felt by some that the strike had played a part in convincing the Board to grant the wage demand in full. The National Coal Board was not known for its spontaneous generosity.

The ballot result was a failure in appearance rather than in substance. In retrospect it did not represent success to the National Coal Board or the National Executive Committee of the N.U.M. Many of the strikers appeared to contradict themselves by voting for the package but this was not apparent to them at the time. The unofficial strike of 1969 was more about the phenomenon of striking than about hours of work. In a sense the strike was experimental. For so many years miners had been told that strikes would boomerang and cause additional pit closures, or that they would be detrimental to the industry. Nothing like that happened. They had doubts about surviving financially because in the decade of contraction their personal debts had escalated through hire purchase commitments. How could they retain their cars, television sets, refrigerators and washing machines without wages, without even strike pay? They survived. They had become victims of inertia and cynicism, following their own individual solutions, believing nothing better could be done. The traditions of militant mining trade unionism had come to mean nothing to them, except as folklore. Then suddenly, without warning, with virtually no organization, they had an experience which showed how wrong they had been. After this the future was unlikely to be as placid as the immediate past.

CHAPTER 13

PRELUDE

The consequences of the 1969 strike were immediate and lasting. It is fairly easy now to identify its impact but there was a feeling even at the time that miners had had an important experience. It had, of course, revealed weaknesses in their solidarity. It had shown that the miners' leaders from the left-wing Areas lacked experience in organizing coordinated strike activities; that in some ways their consciousness was not as developed as the rank and file members and that Lawrence Daly in particular was vulnerable to conformist pressures. But perhaps most of all it had shown that the traditional left-wing Areas could not be taken for granted.

It was quite clear that the strike had given a radical twist to the momentum which had been started by Daly's election campaign. A struggle to raise the consciousness of miners began in earnest through leaflets and public meetings.* Although the advantages of the unofficial strike were recognized the left-wing leaders had no intention of repeating the experience. Their immediate aim was to alter the decisions of the Annual Conference and for this end they had to work strictly according to the rule book.

Candidate for the Presidency

Following the strike there was a diversion from policies to personalities due to the rumour that the Union president, Sir Sidney Ford, was contemplating retiring through ill health. The left-wing Areas had to select a candidate for the post.

The position of left-wing miners had altered since Lawrence Daly had won the general secretaryship. Firstly, the campaign has revealed various possible left-wing candidates. Secondly, the task was more complex and delicate than it had been in 1967. There had always been a left-wing general secretary so there was some logic in Daly following Will Paynter. There had never been a left-wing president in office so at no time had the Union had two left-wing national officials.** Many miners saw this distribution between left and right as fair, even as a convention. Moreover, the county parochialism of miners caused them to want to allocate the national posts between different Areas. With one of them occupied by a Scotsman it was going to be difficult, whatever the merits of the person, for a Scot to win the second.

---

* A copy of the first of the leaflets to be distributed is contained in the Appendix to this chapter.

** Alwyn Machen, the Yorkshire president who was elected as the national president in 1960, was more progressive than his predecessors and he looked forward to working closely with Will Paynter. He died before taking office. Sidney Ford was elected to take his place.

160

The choice for the Left turned out to be between Emlyn Williams of SouthWales and Michael McGahey, the recently elected president of Scotland.

McGahey was both a Communist and a Scot but opinion favoured him. He was by now well-known in different coalfields, particularly in Yorkshire; he had shown pronounced leadership qualities. Emlyn Williams gave his support to McGahey in what was recognized as a calculated risk.

The Wages Campaign

When the Annual Conference met in July, 1970, the electioneering, in effect, had begun though Ford had not yet resigned. McGahey moved into the limelight through his participation in the wages debate. The policies with which he was identified were put to the conference by Arthur Scargill, Emlyn Williams, Jack Dunn and others. Real differences emerged between those who wanted to reject the policy of collaboration which had dominated Union activities since 1945 and the main advocates of collaboration. There were signs of bitterness in the exchanges as the right wing majority realised that its position of power was threatened.

The bargaining which occurred after the Union had submitted its wages demand in August took place in a changed political environment. The Labour Party had lost the general election and the Conservatives, led by Edward Heath, with a policy of returning to the free market mechanism, took office. The Trades Union Congress attacked the new Government's approach to nationalized industries while Mr. Heath warned the T.U.C. that State industries would not be able to borrow money to cover excessive wage increases. The Government introduced its proposals for an Industrial Relations Bill, arousing the hostility of all sections of the trade union movement. Political tensions rose sharply after the election.

Miners began to witness changes in their favour. Coal stocks fell as demand outpaced the supply of coal. There was a shortage of smokeless fuel in the domestic market. The pit closure programme has been scaled down. These were visible signs that the coal industry had reached a trough, that the prognostications of doom were, perhaps, wrong, and that its fortunes might even improve. These factors made an impression on the morale of miners. When considered within the wider political context they formed a basis for developing militancy.

The wage negotiations were accompanied by aggressive noises from all sides. On 16th September, 1970, Lawrence Daly stated that "If it takes a massive strike to make people realize miners are no longer prepared to work underground for low wages, I am all for it." Predictably, Lord Robens talked about the possible loss of jobs if the price of coal went up to meet a wage demand; while the Prime

161

Minister appeared on television on 24th September to say that he was prepared to stand up to a general strike if necessary. Leader writers in various newspapers expressed their thoughts about a possible miners' strike. *The Times,* for instance, remarked that "If they strike nationally, the country will quickly be in trouble." (18.9.70). There was a psychological setting for a strike. It began to look as if people would be disappointed if the wages struggle petered out.

The Government was in the midst of the wages battle. It had set a limit of 12 per cent for public sector wage demands and the miners wanted a 33 per cent increase. The N.C.B., on 16th September, guided by the Government, offered less than half of what the Union wanted. The N.U.M. Executive, under pressure from about 1000 demonstrators from all over the country turned down the offer and agreed to ballot the membership to support strike action in pursuit of the claim. The South Wales wages resolution was being carried out to the letter.

The composition of the National Executive Committee had not significantly changed since 1969 but its members had not been able to isolate themselves from the changing approach of working miners towards their problems. This was illustrated by the behaviour of the Yorkshire Area president, Sam Bullough, who had refused to allow a discussion of strike action at an Area conference in 1969 but stated a year later that "We want 100 per cent support for strike action so that we can achieve our just demands." So a ballot paper went out containing an N.E.C. recommendation for strike action. The whole world for British miners was turning upside down. There had not been an official national miners' strike since 1926. There had been more than 2 decades of embarrassingly close collaboration between the Union and N.C.B. Now the Union was contemplating taking on the N.C.B. and the Government.

Behaviour can be a bad guide to ultimate intentions. On the face of it the Union leadership was determined to call a strike if necessary but underneath there were differing approaches. Only a third of the National Executive Committee was really set on pursuing the logic of their decision to ballot, namely to campaign in the pits to obtain strike support and, if given it, to call the strike without equivocation. The rest either saw the ballot as a tactic to force some little extra concession from the Coal Board and with no intention of following it through or supported it to be with the majority. The campaign for strike action was very uneven. In Scotland, South Wales, Kent and Derbyshire it was intense. The Scottish Area officials and members of the Area executive addressed pithead meetings for each shift at every colliery. They distributed leaflets to miners and their wives. In Yorkshire the campaign was conducted by an unofficial group with members of the Barnsley and Doncaster panels playing a

162

leadership part, but with no access to Area resources. Where the campaign was conducted intensively there was a dialogue between officials and members and discussions among members. It has always been the case that the left wing Areas have been the most democratic and that attempts by left-wing miners to campaign in other Areas have activated the democratic process. Right-wing Areas of the N.U.M. have been consistently dominated by inertia. There is no doubt that there is a direct correlation between the involvement of miners in union affairs and their criticism of official, whether union or government, explanations and policies.

Almost 260,000 miners participated in the ballot and just over 55 per cent of them voted in favour of strike action. In the left-wing Areas overwhelming majorities favoured it. In South Wales the majority in favour was 82 per cent, in Scotland 77 per cent, in Kent 67 per cent, while in Yorkshire the percentage was as high as 62. The problem was that although a simple majority of the miners favoured strike action it was less than the two-thirds majority required by the rule book. The N.E.C. could not call a national strike. It refused, moreover, to sanction strikes in those Areas where a majority of the miners were in favour, as requested by the Scottish Area. Instead it returned to the negotiations in the hope that the N.C.B. would increase its offer after it had learned the strength of feeling amongst miners for strike action.

Unofficial Action Repeated

Four days after the result of the ballot was announced negotiations were restarted. An offer was made amounting to 50p a week more than had been conceded before but this was still much less than the miners were demanding. The night before the offer was made, in anticipation of an unsatisfactory result, the miners in Monktonhall pit in Scotland refused to work. On the day of the revised offer Brodsworth miners in Yorkshire struck and persuaded the Doncaster Panel to support their strike. As the Doncaster miners were diligent pickets the strike spread in Yorkshire. A number of Areas, including South Wales, were involved in the strike by 2nd November, only six days after the offer was made. The pattern of the unco-ordinated action of 1969 began to emerge. For instance, as the Yorkshire pits came out on strike six Scottish pits went back to work on the recommendation of the Scottish Area Executive Committee. Very little reliable information about the intentions of Areas seemed to pass from one to the other. In any case it took time before an Area could respond to what the others were doing and by then some of them had changed their minds.

The main difference between the 1970 situation and that in 1969 was that the Area executives in Scotland and South Wales endeavoured to respond to the strike initiatives made in the pits rather than

163

to impose their will on them. They called Area conferences which made decisions to strike even though they had no right to do so under the rules of the Union. Unfortunately their decisions rarely coincided so that the full impact of their collective strength was not felt for long. There was a period following 11th November when the whole of South Wales and all but 5 pits in Scotland were not working. Altogether 103,000 miners went on strike. This was less than the previous year because only half of the large Yorkshire Area supported it. There was no disciplined end to the strike. It shrank in size and created a sense of isolation amongst those who remained on strike. This encouraged a drift back to work until only South Wales was left, feeling angry and let down. The strike was finished by 23rd November. During its last four days a ballot was held on the offer which had sparked off the strike and almost two-thirds of the membership accepted it. Scotland, South Wales and Kent rejected the offer but about 60 per cent of the Yorkshire miners favoured it.

The strike in 1970 did not leave a feeling of exhileration amongst miners as the 1969 one had done. It produced nothing tangible. The two main left-wing Areas, South Wales and Scotland were in temporary dispute over its conduct. Emlyn Williams, the vice-president of South Wales and strike leader was critical of the manner in which Michael McGahey had handled his Area. Yorkshire, it was realized, was far from being the militant centre it had appeared to be in 1969. The national officials of the Union and the majority on the National Executive Committee had shown how resistant they could be to pressures from unofficial strikes, lobbies and demonstrations. Indeed officials from Leicester, South Derbyshire, Northumberland, Durham, Power Group No. 1, the Midlands, the Power Group, Lancashire and Nottingham, who comprised the majority on the Executive, issued a statement on 11th November condemning the "unconstitutional methods now being employed by certain Groups in the N.U.M." Full-time officials from some of these Areas had met at Snibston Miners Welfare Club in the Midlands to discuss how they should react to the developing strike situation. They feared the violence which was generated and spoke of seeking police protection when they attended the next Executive meeting in London. Branch secretaries in the Midlands Area were circulated with details of the meeting and the text of the statement.

The Reaction of the Employer

The National Coal Board did not know how to cope with the mood of militancy which reflected a rejection of both the collaborationist policies of the 1960s and the attitude of paternalism which had been fostered under the chairmanship of Lord Robens. Paternalism became a provocation. The N.C.B. sent details of its offer to individual miners at their homes before the strike ballot even though the Union had already informed the miners of it. Some members of the N.C.B. tried to influence miners by telling them falsely that if they went on striking they would lose their entitlement to super-annuation. Lord Robens made public statements which, in their effect, put the Union in a bad light. He made his views known on radio and television. The whole business, he said on sound radio, was a Communist plot; it was a case, he said on television, of "a group of people who are breaking all the rules, all the agreements, in order to demonstrate the fact that they do not like this final offer." He likened the activities of pickets, when he spoke in Edinburgh, to Fascist dictatorships; and when he visited Doncaster he was met, he said, by a "yarling mob." At the end of the strike, which had cost the N.C.B. almost 3 million tons of coal, Lord Robens explained to the British Institute of Management that he accused "the militants of this country, backed by a Communist conspiracy, of trying to do what the Russians have not been able to do in this country and western Europe." The relationship between the N.U.M. and the N.C.B. deteriorated. The N.E.C. of the union felt obliged, at its meeting on 12th November, 1970, to "condemn any interference by the Chairman of the Board or anyone else in the internal affairs of the Union." It also agreed to discontinue the practice of alternatively acting as host with the N.C.B. to a dinner at Christmas.

The miners had learned in 1969 that they could strike and survive; that striking was therapeutic. Their experience in 1970, however, contained different elements. This strike was a bitter one. Miners have always been serious about their strikes and they were part-icularly serious in 1970. They used roving pickets to extend the strike as the Yorkshire miners had done in 1955. The Doncaster miners were again particularly active in this respect. They toured Yorkshire and adjoining Areas in cars and put pressure on non-striking pits. Some pits even waited for the pickets to arrive before making a decision to strike or not to strike.

Rule 43

The 1970 strike was not tentative and experimental. It was a struggle to obtain a wage increase. Coal stocks had run down. Industry was beginning to feel the impact. The striking miners could see that they could win. Their main obstacle was their own disunity and this stemmed from the opposition of the N.E.C. to the strike because, under the Union rules, there had been an insufficient majority in favour of the strike. Rule 43, which stipulated that there had to be a two-thirds majority before a national strike could be called, was seen as the main obstacle to a truly national official strike.

The mood in the Union was propitious for an alteration of the rule. Even before the 1970 unofficial strike was over the Derbyshire Area had proposed to the N.E.C. that the rule should be altered to enable a strike to be called when a simple majority was in favour. This was unacceptable to the N.E.C. which chose to support a compromise of 55 per cent and supported this figure when a motion containing it was proposed to the 1971 Annual Conference. Only a few Areas resisted making striking easier. The left-wing ones supported the compromise as being preferable to no change at all for, after all, if the figure had been 55 per cent in 1970 there would have been a national official strike.

Election for President

Rumours about the health of the president, Sir Sidney Ford, ended on 4th March, 1971, when he informed the N.E.C. that he intended to retire in June. The election campaign began in earnest from the moment of the announcement. Only two candidates were eventually nominated, namely Michael McGahey and Joe Gormley, secretary of the Lancashire Area and unsuccessful candidate in the election for the General Secretaryship.

The election of the president was governed by regulations and directives laid down by the N.E.C. except that the Union rules stipulated it should be conducted on the principle of the "transferable vote" as defined in the Representation of the People Act in 1918. In general, trade union elections have always been conducted with the minimum of electioneering. Unions have endeavoured in different ways to introduce equality in elections by minimizing and regulating the publicity any candidate could create for him or herself. The formal attitude of unions towards elections has not altered since they first drew up their rule books. It is only the context of union elections which has changed. The rules of unions still, in the main, either prohibit canvassing completely and give no publicity to any candidate other than printing names and nominating branches on ballot papers, or limit it to a bare biographical statement with a few lines about motives. There is no union in Britain which, like the International Typographical Union of the U.S.A., encourages electioneering in the style of party politics.

The National Union of Mineworkers is no exception to the British rule. The National Executive Committee had hitherto refused to permit any candidates to issue leaflets or to engage in any other form of publicity. This practice had been criticized after Daly's election in 1968 so when the Union's Organization Sub-Committee met in March, 1971, to determine the procedure for the election it proposed "That each candidate be given an opportunity of submitting personal biographical details not exceeding 250 words which subject to vetting by the Organization Sub-Committee should be distributed to Branches in the form of a poster." This proposal was applied but its effects were negated by the contents of a letter from the General Secretary to the Areas on the conduct of the elections. When the election for the General Secretaryship was held in 1968 the retiring General Secretary, Will Paynter, announced that the practice was to be that of earlier elections, making explicit reference to the prohibition of canvassing. When Lawrence Daly circulated a letter on the conduct of the election for the presidency there was no reference in it to canvassing. This omission was interpreted by Gormley, though not by McGahey, as licence to canvass. Gormley's interpretation was confirmed by the acting president of the Union when the Scottish Area protested about the electioneering activities of Lancashire miners in Scotland. Schofield stated that the procedure for holding this particular ballot did not prohibit "the issue of leaflets or other forms of publicity in support of candidates." This change of policy resulted from an administrative decision. Daly did not make it. He simply signed a letter prepared for him. The Executive did not discuss the matter until the campaign was well advanced. Indeed the change was not explicitly stated until the acting president made his ruling. Those who worked for McGahey considered the letter to be a campaign trick which was designed to benefit Gormley though they did not know whom to blame. As the architects of union constitutions doubtless realized, unrestricted electioneering feeds on prejudice and bias and leads to bitterness and acrimony. This was certainly the case in this election, to the considerable disadvantage of Michael McGahey.

The election was won by Gormley. In a 67 per cent poll he received 117,663 votes compared with 92,883 votes cast for McGahey. This result upset the euphoria which the left-wing of the N.U.M. had been experiencing. Rough pre-election calculations based on reports from the Areas had given McGahey a comfortable majority. These were undoubtedly a figment of left-wing optimism.

The ability of Gormley, his determination to win and the built-in disadvantages of having a Scottish Communist as a candidate had been underestimated. McGahey was characteristically consitutional in his approach to the election. He published a pamphlet called *Miners and the Energy Crisis* before the close of nominations and then sat tight. He decided not to send delegates into the right-wing Areas because he considered that it would be offensive to miners to do so. There was election activity in favour of McGahey, then, only in those Areas where he already had support. The weak Areas remained weak. Virtually nothing was done to get him support in Cumberland, Durham, Leicester, Midlands, Northumberland, North Wales, Nottingham and South Derbyshire. There was no activity to curb anti-Communist and sectarian attitudes which McGahey's commitment invited.

Joe Gormley had none of the inhibitions about union propriety

167

which influenced McGahey. He used to the full the licence to campaign and his Area executive allowed him to spend up to £12,000 of its funds for this purpose. His supporters, without loss of pay, campaigned in South Wales, Yorkshire and even Scotland. They made the biggest impact in Yorkshire where the conservatism and anti-Communism of the North and South Yorkshire panels were tapped. Gormley himself moved about and between the Areas like a will-o-the-wisp, exploiting McGahey's weaknesses and occasionally stealing his clothes. It is a disadvantage of candidates of the left that they cannot emulate their opponents. In a "no-holds barred" election only Gormley stood to gain. In general the mistake was made of believing that the rising militancy of the miners indicated a desire for a permanent shift to the left in the running of the Union. If McGahey had become president in 1971 it would have had important political consequences for the Union, the T.U.C. and the Labour Movement. The miners were not yet prepared for such a change.

MINERS

Our demands in 1970

The Government says that the market demand for coal is falling : this is no longer true. It says that coal is inefficient compared with natural gas, oil and nuclear energy. What are the facts ? Natural gas supplies will last for only 25 years, and should be used as an emergency energy supply. Oil costs do not include the military defence of oil supplies in the Middle East and Nigeria. Nor do they include the cost of oil imports to Britain's balance of payments. In 1965 we paid £300 million in foreign exchange for oil. Today the cost is considerably higher. Nuclear energy prices do not include the tremendous costs of research, of wastage in capital equipment as processes change, of contamination to the sea and atmosphere because of difficulties in disposing of nuclear waste. Nuclear costs are unpredictable and are soaring like the cost of nuclear missiles.

The prices of natural gas, oil and nuclear energy do not include the cost in human suffering of running the coal industry down ; costs borne by us and our families. Since 1967 alone the Government has had to allocate £185 million to finance the run-down of the industry. This cost is like a subsidy to the oil companies. It should be counted as such. Britain needs a healthy coal industry.

There must be **NO PIT CLOSURES UNLESS THROUGH EXHAUSTION.**

Where pits have to be closed there must be **ALTERNATIVE JOB OPPORTUNITIES ON HAND**

A colliery closed is a supply lost for ever. The policy of indiscriminate closures backfired in the U.S.A. Now they are short of coal. Coal is needed for many purposes. The same is happening here. This year there is not only a shortage of smokeless fuel but a general shortage. While the Government is turning from coal housewives are turning to it. Production is now less than demand. This is the Government's responsibility. But **WE** bear the cost.

Our wages are too low. While the Government responds to the dictates of oil magnates, oil profits rise. Nuclear power station contractors and the exploiters of natural gas make high profit. In the **ENERGY** field only we suffer.

The **Energy Industry** is an expanding industry. It should be treated as a whole. No section of it, neither miners nor oil workers nor any other group should be discriminated against. All should share in its prosperity. This means us.

In 1956 miners were amongst the highest paid workers in Britain. Coal was then a valued commodity. Now we are well down the list. Look at this table :

The Facts

Coal is Britain's only important indigenous fuel.
Coal is still vital for the British economy.

It costs no foreign exchange
It is in abundant supply
It needs no enormous capital outlay

Yet the Government's policy is to contract the industry. The production of coal in 1957 was 212.9 million tons ; in 1966 it was 174.7 million tons ; in 1970 it is expected to be less than 155 million tons. Each year the number of collieries has diminished, 70 closed in 1968, ours may be next.

Each year for the last 12 years miners have lost their jobs. We may be next.

Manpower fell by 57,257 in 1968. In 1957, 704,000 men worked in the industry. By 1970 this figure had fallen to 297,000. The fall is continuing. We may be next.

In January 1970, 23,414 miners were unemployed. This represented an unemployment rate of 6.4%. The national average is only 2.3%.

Price 3d

Changes in Average Weekly Earnings
1956 - 1969*

| | Average Weekly Earnings | | Percentage |
	1956	1969	Change
Mining	£14 14 11	£24 9 9	66%
All Industries	£11 15 4	£24 16 5	111%
Manufacturing Industries	£12 2 2	£25 10 10	111%

*Adult male manual workers.

Our weekly earnings on an average are less than the average for all industries. But the real position is worse than this indicates. A high proportion of miners earn much less than the average. Surface workers are in the worst position of all.

The cost of living has risen almost as fast as our wages. Between 1956 and 1969 the index of retail prices rose by about 54%. So the value of miners' wages has risen by about 12% in 13 years. Less than 1% a year. But the value of the wages of workers in all industries, including manufacturing, has gone up by about 57% in the same period : that is almost 4.4% a year.

And what has happened to our productivity ? It has risen by about 70%. Our O.M.S. in 1956 was 24.8 cwts. Now it is 42.5 cwts. Our share in this has been substantial. But where is our reward ?

Unless we act now the position will worsen. Our families will suffer.

Remember—COAL is a vital commodity in a vital Energy industry. Fight for a living wage.

Remember—The coal industry is efficient. The N.C.B. made an operational profit of £28.9 million in 1968-69. Only after compensation to former owners, amounting to £37.9 million, was paid was there a loss in that year.

No one in mining should receive less than £20 a week

DEMAND : a £20 surface workers minimum

DEMAND : a £21 underground day-wage minimum

DEMAND : a £30 National Power Loading Agreement parity by the end of 1971

DEMAND : an improved wage structure for craftsmen and other categories

Anything less in unacceptable. Force the N.C.B. to concede these demands.

Hours

The Miners' Charter in 1946 demanded a 40 hour week inclusive of meal-breaks for surface workers which 24 years later has still not been won. In October 1969 130,000 men from 140 pits went on strike for a 40 hour week for surfacemen. The N.C.B. refused the demand.

WE HAVE STILL TO WIN THE 40 HOUR WEEK FOR SURFACE MEN.

What about underground workers ? In 1918 the Miners' Federation of Great Britain demanded a 6 hour day, exclusive of winding time.

The Sankey Commission 1919 recommended a 7 hour day and this was implemented in the Coal Mines Act of 1919. After the 1926 General Strike the hours were increased to 8 ; reduced to 7½ in 1932, and to 7¼ in 1964. THEY HAVE NOT YET FALLEN TO THE 1919 LEVEL.

50 years of campaigning have still not obtained a 6 hour day. Make this our demand now.

A decent life requires genuine leisure.

1. 37½ hour week inclusive of meal-times for surface workers.
2. 6 hour day for underground workers.
3. Three weeks holiday with pay.

Militant Action

As miners we were becoming disillusioned by the contraction of our industry. We started to seek individual solutions. Many of us left the industry. Absentee rates were high. We lost faith in our national leadership. Conciliation, negotiation, compromise brought no real gains.

The unofficial strike last October changed all this. The strike forced the N.C.B. to grant its biggest wage increase ever. It rejuvenated the miners. It raised morale. **Militant Action Pays.**

Sections of our National Leadership are not only out of touch with the working miners. They are unwilling to lead us in our struggle. They are protecting themselves behind rigid, out-dated union procedures.

The union constitution must be further
D E M O C R A T I S E D.

1. Simplify the procedure for changing the rules.
2. Make officials accountable to the members by periodic elections.

THE N.U.M. IS OUR UNION. RUN IT IN THE INTEREST OF MINERS.

Solidarity

A revitalized N.U.M. is necessary for a strong trade union movement. The union must ally itself with progressive forces. It must return to its historic role in the Labour Movement.

The attacks on trade unions will continue. We can expect :

A. renewed pressures for legislation to curb strike action.

B. renewed pressures for an incomes policy which is a disguised wage freeze.

C. renewed pressures to force unions to collaborate with employers and the Government.

These pressures will be detrimental to the material well-being and the freedom of all workers. This includes us. The struggle of all workers is our struggle.

PLAY YOUR PART NOW. LABOUR NEEDS A PROGRESSIVE N.U.M.

THE PROGRESSIVE N.U.M. NEEDS A SOCIALIST GOVERNMENT

FIGHT FOR A SOCIALIST POLICY

Signed :
Arthur Scargill, Ron Rigby, Yorkshire
Sam Green, Kent
J. Ritchie, John Philips, Scotland
Councillor W. Woods, Emlyn Jenkins, South Wales

CHAPTER 14

HESITATION

Challenging the Government

The growing awareness of British miners about their wages and working conditions took place within an environment which was dominated by an unprecedented confrontation between unions and the Government. Governments had always tackled unions when the need arose and had done so successfully for, except for a brief period after the first world war, trade unions had avoided confrontation for fear of undermining the conventional parliamentary political decision-making process. It was enough for the Government to shout "constitution" during an industrial dispute for union leaders to go scurrying for cover.

This attitude had changed. Unions were challenging the Government's National Incomes policy in which it was aimed to reduce each successive wage demand by 1 per cent. This challenge did not amount to much in 1971 but it was occurring. The Government chose a relatively weak union, The Union of Post Office Workers, in order to express its determination to maintain its policy. Postal workers were forced back to work after a 7 week strike, dispirited and disillusioned. But they had been prepared to take on the Government. There was a mounting campaign against the Government's proposals for a restrictive Industrial Relations Act. Within weeks of obtaining power in July, 1970, the Conservative Government introduced its proposals and, as promptly, unions reacted against them. The unofficial Liaison Committee for the Defence of Trade Unions organized mass strikes against the Bill. On the day of a Special T.U.C. concerning the Bill on 18th March about 3 million workers struck against it with the support of their unions. Attempts to alter Government policy by strike action were becoming common-place. They entered a new phase, however, when the workers employed by the Upper Clyde Shipbuilding consortium refused to accept its liquidation when the Government declined to provide a continuing subsidy in pursuit of its 'lame-duck' economic policy. 8,000 workers in four yards occupied them in August, 1971 and set a precedent which workers threatened with redundancy in a variety of industries subsequently followed.

Miners in different coalfields identified themselves with the struggles in their various forms. The Scottish miners supported the Upper Clyde Shipbuilding workers. Amongst the Yorkshire miners there was common talk about the need for a general strike to prevent the Government from making the Industrial Relations Bill law. There was anger amongst miners at the Government's treatment of the postmen. The groundswell of anger, resentment, and

171

sympathy which arose because of the Government's policies influenced the miners' perception of themselves. They adopted high wage demands and discussed strike action. They were influenced by the deteriorating economic conditions. Unemployment in the winter of 1971/72 was the highest since 1939. It was particularly high in the coalfields of Durham, South Wales and Scotland. Unemployment in Scotland in the summer of 1971 was 7.5 per cent compared with 4.8 per cent for the country as a whole. At the same time prices were rising faster than at almost any other time since the end of the war. The 1971 annual rate was 9.0 per cent. In 1965 the rate of price increases had been about one-third of that and there had been virtually no unemployment. Pits were no longer closing as they had been in the 1960s but conditions were bad and were deteriorating.

The Mood of Miners

The preference of the miners for Joe Gormley as president of the Union had little immediate meaning for the Union as a whole. The stage was set for him. He simply walked on it and obediently said his lines. McGahey had been rejected but the policies he advocated became the property of the Union. The first Union annual conference presided over by Gormley both adopted the wages demand which led to the 1972 strike and changed the rules to make that strike easier to call. There was no disunity in the 1971 conference at Aberdeen. Those Area officials who so consistently had advised caution, compromise, even retreat in the 1960s were now raising their hands with the militants. It was not that they had changed their political spots. It was that, despite other characteristics, they were having to be sensitive about the mood of their members.

Sensing the moods of members, however, is a difficult task for all union leaders at any time. On this occasion there were many variables and some were contradictory. The miners had made militant gestures in 1969 and 1970; would they do so in 1971 or had the chaotic 1970 experience disillusioned them? The earlier strikes had been partial and undisciplined; would the miners have the energy and determination to wage the first all-out national struggle since 1926 with all the possibilities of hardship and privation which followed then? Miners still, moreover, had the image of the coal industry which the events of the 1960s had created and which had considerably reduced their faith in their own collective power. They had been conditioned to believe that coal was an outdated fuel; how could it suddenly become a fuel with a future? They had been told that coal was no longer essential for British industry so what collective power could they have? They had been threatened with accelerated closures if they went on strike; might not this happen if they called a national strike? There was some evidence to suggest that conditions in the industry were changing but they were inconclusive. The massive

172

pit closure programme had trailed off. The overall consumption of coal was exceeding production and there were signs of an oil crisis. Coking coal stocks, however, were accumulating due to a recession in the steel industry. Coking coal plants in Scotland were in jeopardy and it was suggested by the new Chairman of the N.C.B., Derek Ezra, that pit closures might have to be resumed. It was difficult to know what to conclude from the evidence.

The militant leaders as well as others were influenced in their thinking by such factors. They, in addition, were plagued by alternative strategies. How would the N.C.B. react? What if it made a substantial but divisive offer? What if it attempted to return to local agreements, to establish a productivity scheme? What should the left-wing be prepared to accept? A conflicting factor was the parity agreement drawn up under the Third Day Wages Structure whereby all face workers were guaranteed parity of earnings by 31st December, 1971. This meant that on that day, face workers in the low earnings Areas of Scotland and South Wales would receive quite substantial wage increases to put them in line with miners from Kent and Nottingham. Would the N.C.B. attempt to relate the wages claim to this agreement? It was generally stated on the left-wing that the parity agreement was not negotiable. But how would the traditional militant South Wales and Scottish miners react to a call for strike action when they knew that without a strike they would get a wage increase anyway.

The imponderable elements in the situation in the autumn of 1971 brought the left and right wings of the N.U.M. Executive together on a common strategy. The left-wing members were cautious. They did not want a quick ballot for a strike. The right-wing members did not want a ballot anyway. Both sides, for different reasons, could not envisage a national strike being successful. There was still a feeling of apprehension about using industrial action against the Government.

Personalities

In retrospect it seems odd that men who had struggled since 1967 against what seemed to be insuperable obstacles to raise the consciousness of miners should hesitate at the point where miners in general were not only thinking critically but were prepared to act out their criticisms. But it is often the case that people accustomed to minority struggles need time to adjust to victory. Even the prospect of victory can be daunting and unreal.

In this case the inhibitions came from the interplay of ideas amongst left-wing leaders. They were fearless as individuals. They had suffered ridicule, discrimination and harassment in the pursuit of the miners' best interests and they were quite prepared to take on the Government if necessary. But in the autumn of 1971 they were

173

held back by their collective intellect. They analyzed and argued almost interminably in the open, aggressive but never acrimonious manner which characterises working class activities. They never displayed the false gentility of middle class relationships.

The people who discussed the issues and formulated the policies throughout 1971 were from different Areas with different lengths of experience. The elder statesmen were Jock Kane and Sammy Taylor, both ready to retire within two years. Sammy Taylor, however, was seriously ill during the summer and died, before retirement, on 1st December, 1971. This left Lawrence Daly, Michael McGahey and Bill McLean, with Jack Dunn, Jack Collins and Joe Holmes from Kent, Dai Francis and Emlyn Williams from South Wales and Jimmy Miller, Arthur Scargill, Peter Tait, Ron Rigby and Owen Briscoe from Yorkshire. Frank Ellis from Nottingham had been the solitary representative from that Area in the early meetings of the the Forum but he had dropped out in 1969 and was not easily replaced. Nottingham had the reputation of being the hard core of trade union conservatism, firmly controlled by its president, L.A. Clarke and general secretary, Albert Martin. Yet it had its contra-dictions and through these emerged Joe Whelan, a Communist, who succeeded Albert Martin as the Area representative on the National Executive Committee in April, 1971. On all major issues Whelan's vote was added to those of the left wing though because of his Area he could not consistently vote that way. There were others who figured more or less prominently at this time comprising the cores of resistance in their respective Areas. From South Wales, for example, there were Haydn Matthews and George Rees; from Scotland Eric Clarke and Jimmy Young; from Yorkshire Martin Redman, Ian Ferguson, Sammy Thompson and Johnny Weaver; from Kent Joe Burke and Dave Watkins. Eight of these, not inclu-ding Daly, were members of the N.E.C. In total they provided the leadership for the miners in 1971, gave the momentum for struggle and direction. They never constituted a majority in national de-liberations, whether on the N.E.C. or in conference, but the course the Union took was the result of their initiatives. All others either went along with the initiatives or acted as bystanders. It is a testimony to the strength of the part played by these men that only two of them, Daly and McGahey were members of the 16 strong National Negotiating Committee which directly handled negotiations with the N.C.B. and only McGahey had a vote.

The Wage Claim

The National Union of Mineworkers had decided at its 1971 Annual Conference to demand an increase in weekly pay from £30 to £35 for face workers, from £19 to £28 for other underground workers and from £18 to £24 for surface workers. These figures were drawn from

174

motions from Yorkshire, Scotland and South Wales. They were not calculated initially as a percentage of the wages being received but from the question "what is a resonable wage for a face worker taking into account the skill and exigencies of his work?" The differentials were assessed in the light of the Union's policy of narrowing differentials. The percentage increases were high: 17 per cent for face workers, 47 per cent for other underground workers and 44 per cent for surface workers. But they gave a mistaken impression. What the Yorkshire, Scottish and South Wales delegates wanted was proportionately high only because what the miners actually received was absolutely low. They paid no attention to the Government's incomes policy which restricted pay rises to eight per cent over the year. The resolution instructed the Executive "to consult the membership with regard to various forms of industrial action" if the National Coal Board made an unsatisfactory offer. The figures and the resolute conclusion were supported in one composite resolution by the oddest collection of Areas, namely, Durham, Nottingham, North Western and the Midlands as well as the staunch left-wing Areas which provided the substance.

The Run-up

The demand was too much for the N.C.B. It was submitted shortly after the July conference, presented in some detail in September and answered on 12th October. The response was an offer of an increase to all grades of £1.60 per week without disturbing the parity arrangements under the National Power Loading Agreement. The Coal Board negotiators suggested that money could be obtained for a wage increase by increasing productivity and by pit closures. The N.C.B. negotiators were slow learners. Their offer was not negotiable and they did not have the sense to avoid the sensitive issue of pit closures. In Hobart House, the Board headquarters, they seemed to be completely unaware of the changing mood of the miners. The National Executive Committee rejected the offer and called a Special Conference on 21st October to consider a recommendation that an overtime ban should be imposed from 1st November and that simultaneously a ballot vote should be held on the issue of strike action. As an additional indication of their anger the N.E.C. recommended that the union should withdraw completely from all levels of the consultative machinery and that the members should refuse to take and read *Coal News*.

The N.E.C. recommendations were accepted by the Special Conference. It is usually the case that delegates in conference can be persuaded to be militant so whenever the left-wing members of the N.E.C. were obstructed by its right-wing majority on matters requiring national action they tried to get them referred to a delegate conference. This conference confirmed such a belief. The tone of the debate was set by Lawrence Daly at his best, analytical, incisive, explanatory and eloquent. His lapse in 1969 was temporarily forgotten. Here he was, like Arthur Horner or Will Paynter, combining an acute intellect with a gift of expression. The visions of that small meeting in Sheffield in 1967 when Daly began to be projected as a national leader seemed to be reaching their fulfilment. Questions were raised about the accumulation of stocks by the Central Electricity Generating Board as a cushion against a possible strike, about the extent to which an overtime ban would reduce coal stocks, about coal imports, about whether, if a strike was called, it should be before or after Christmas, about the possible effect of the Industrial Relations Act on the strike. Definitive answers were not given because the Union was not able to chart its own course. No one knew how the various parties in the dispute, including miners, would react to the overtime ban. The delegates did not know what measures the Government would adopt and what response there would be from other unions. All that they could say categorically was that they were resolute.

The N.C.B. made a marginal but unacceptable improvement in its original offer. The overtime ban was applied from 1st November and the miners were balloted about the N.E.C. recommendation to strike just over three weeks later. With the customary high poll, 58.8 per cent of the miners voted in favour of strike action thus giving the N.E.C. the power to proceed with a strike if necessary. The stage was set for the first official national miners' strike since 1926. The ballot result was discussed by the N.E.C. on 9th December. In order to ensure that it met the contractual obligations of its members it gave the N.C.B. one month's notice of strike action. The strike was to start on 9th January, 1972.

Although the National Coal Board protested that it was not under Governmental pressure to resist the miners' demands there was no doubt that it was operating within financial constraints set by the Government to match its pay policy. The Prime Minister, Mr. Heath, had made it clear that the Government would exercise its authority where it possessed it, namely in the public services and the publicly-owned enterprises including the coal industry. Nonetheless the Government acted out a 'low-profile' by encouraging the pretense that the dispute was between the miners and the N.C.B. In this way it tried to give the impression that the outcome would be determined by market forces and that crude and cruel as it might be it was inevitable. Flush with the defeat of the postmen it believed that the miners would suffer the same fate.

The left-wing leaders in the N.U.M. were, as I suggested earlier, still influenced in their assessment of the prospect of a strike victory by the experiences and explanations of the 1960s. Whatever their public utterances, in private each one had reservations about the

176

miners' ability to respond to the strike call, maintain solidarity, withstand widespread criticism and weather privation. There were many questions in their minds which could only be answered through the experience of the strike itself. These leaders were not the only ones to think in this way. Politicians, both in and out of Government, leader writers of newspapers and radio and television commentators were victims of the same explanations and propaganda. Their minds were dominated by generalisations which were either half-truths or hid the reality. The coal industry was in decline, coal was without a future, coal was unimportant in the economy, miners were disillusioned, miners had no strength, the N.U.M. had lost its prestige in the trade union movement, a strike would accelerate the decline of coal. *The Times,* for instance, in a leading article 3 days before the strike stated: "coal stocks away from the pits are large enough to withstand a strike for weeks, if it does not spread, with only marginal disruption to industry and commerce as a whole. Almost all gas is now from the North Sea, many coal-fired power stations can switch to oil at a pinch, and the National Union of Mineworkers is much less of a power in the councils of the labour movement than it was. Miners have steadily abandoned the strike habit. . ."

The Overtime Ban

There were three different views about the purpose of the overtime ban amongst members of the National Executive Committee and these views were reflected amongst other officials. They were not altogether mutually exclusive. The first one, shared by the majority, was that the overtime ban was an act in its own right, an alternative to strike action, less disruptive, less costly and less likely to arouse establishment hostility. Those who held this view hoped that the ban would have a sufficient impact on the N.C.B. to induce it to improve its offer or at the least to show an interest in re-opening negotiations. When the Chairman of the N.C.B. made what was interpreted as an overture in *Coal News* the adherents of this view responded quickly. On the day the National Executive Committee met to discuss the timing and organization of the strike it also decided to respond to any intiative Derek Ezra might make. Few on the N.E.C. felt they could oppose such a resolution though a number of them thought it was a waste of time.

The second view was that the intention of the ban was to reduce coal stocks so that a strike, if it followed, would have more chance of success. It was possible of course to see the overtime ban as an alternative to strike action whilst recognizing its value as an aid to a strike. This second view was an official one; it went out in circulars to members; it was a plausible one which was consistent with the spirit of a decision to strike. A circular from the Area Office in Yorkshire on 25th October, 1971, stated: "The whole exercise of the ban is to eliminate all coal production that has previously been won by overtime, e.g. working through snap time, overtime during 5 normal days for coal production, overtime outside normal 5 days for coal production, preparatory work, ripping, etc. . . ." As the intention was to reduce production and not to disrupt production the ban was a partial one and continual circulars went out to members in Yorkshire reminding them of what was and was not permissable.

The third view was that the ban was ineffective on its own, that it was a delaying tactic, giving time to campaign and to assess and alter if necessary the real mood of the miners through pit-head meetings, delegate conferences and informal meetings. As an isolated method it was thought that the ban might be counter-productive because it was divisive - not all miners worked overtime and not all, therefore lost pay when it ceased. In the main the left-wing members saw the ban in this third light.

The overtime ban did reduce coal stocks though the extent of this was disputed. The Central Electricity Generating Board stated two days before the strike was due to begin that coal stocks had never been higher at that time of the year. The British Steel Corporation which was the second biggest consumer of coal in Britain, also claimed to have adequate stocks. There had been a mild winter and coal had been imported from the United States and Australia. While coal stocks in general were down, those of the biggest consumers were not. There was not, moreover, any panic buying by coal merchants. The long notice of the strike had, it seemed, enabled consumers, domestic and industrial, to build up their stocks without undue haste. Lawrence Daly, however, claimed that the Coal Board was much too optimistic about the supply of coal and that, in any case, the coal was not located where it was needed most. The arguments were inconclusive until experience proved one thing or the other.

The effect of the ban on the attitudes of the miners was not inconclusive. Daly sent out a circular to all Areas setting out six guidelines, including the stipulation that " No work of any kind to be carried out in overtime except that required for the safety of the men and the immediate preservation of the mine or plant." The miners themselves, however, frequently had their own ideas about the purpose of the ban and intensified their action to make it more effective. Sometimes maintenance and repairs were not carried out and safety cover was not provided. A Special Council Meeting of Yorkshire delegates met on 9th November to consider breaches of the guidelines and condemned "misplaced loyalty or indiscipline." It resolved to give no assistance to branches which acted contrary to the guidelines. There were similar difficulties in other Areas. Occasionally miners were not able to work during normal hours. If they were sent home they usually walked out on strike. Difficulties arose because managements had to re-arrange work schedules to maintain production. In a pit it requires only small extra injustices to reach the level of the intolerable and the manner in which managements reacted to the ban pushed many miners above that level. They saw management in a sharp, clear perspective striving for lower labour costs, extra effort, increased production. This was all the more obvious because overtime, contrary to the general impression that it occurs only because workers seek extra pay, is inefficient management's escape valve. Management resorts to overtime to achieve what it should reasonably have achieved in normal working hours. When it cannot rely on overtime the deficiencies become obvious and managerial attitudes emerge transparently as intolerant. The overime ban stripped away the collaborationist image to reveal starkly the conflict nature of relationships in the coal industry.

The ban did more than this. It made miners dependent upon their basic wages. The vast majority of miners were engaged on fixed shift rates. Their only opportunity of increasing their earnings above the basic wage lay in working overtime. When overtime was stopped miners realized both how low their basic wages were and how important the basic rate was. Thus the overtime ban focussed the miners' attention on the wages question and put them in the frame of mind to struggle. It had an enormous politicizing influence which no one really foresaw. Shortly after the ban started a majority of the miners voted for strike action but at the end of it they were all of a mind to strike hard and effectively. The attitudes of many of the 41.2 per cent who had voted against the strike were transformed. Areas, such as Durham and Nottingham, which had just failed to get a majority for the strike, swung in its favour. If the strike vote had been taken at the end of the ban the percentage against would have been derisory.

Intransigence

The growing hostility of the ordinary miners towards the National Coal Board and the Government was reflected in the intransigence of the negotiators. The National Executive Committee met on 9th December to hear that the national officials had been informed by the Board representatives that they were willing to raise their offer to £2.00 a week minimum for surface workers and £1.90 a week for all other grades. This represented an improvement on their original offer of 29p a week for the lowest paid surface workers and 15p for all others. The N.C.B. wanted to work out a productivity deal with the Union over the next year. It emphasized that this revised offer was conditional upon the N.E.C. recommending its acceptance to the members. This increase came nowhere near to bridging the gap

179

between what the miners demanded and what they were offered and was rejected. The N.E.C. then asked for a full meeting between itself and the National Coal Board.

The full meeting took place on 21st December, 1971, and went over ground that was familiar, added nothing that was new and acted out a sort of charade, parading reason and intellect when all that mattered at that stage was power. The arguments were to be heard again before the business was settled. As the deadline for the strike drew near the N.C.B. produced a revised package deal giving average wages rises of 7.9 per cent, fractionally below the Government's pay line. When the N.U.M. leaders rejected this response the N.C.B. withdrew all the pay offers it had made since this series of negotiations had begun, thus cancelling the backdating provisions in the offers. This was a petty, irritating gesture but then, the National Coal Board was still living in the unreal world of its own creation.

The Government emerged temporarily from its hideout almost on the eve of the strike when the national officials of the N.U.M. were invited to meet conciliation officers of the Department of Employment at the Government offices. Joe Gormley and Lawrence Daly refused to attend, saying that they would be glad to see the Government officials at the Union's head office but the Government would not allow this. This game ended on 9th January, 1972, when the strike began.

CHAPTER 15

SOLIDARITY

Class Conflict

Striking is never a game, never trivial no matter how superficial the issue might seem. It arises out of the tremendous gulf between people who sell labour power and people who buy it, out of the differences between them in incomes, in wealth, in education, in status, in authority and the exercise of power in society in general. It is an act against the facility of someone to buy the skill or effort of someone else and to utilize it as if it were a piece of coal or a machine tool and decide when it should be used, how, with whom or what, at what pace and, if it is not up to standard, to scrap it without any obligation to it. In a sense the analogy with a machine tool is not a good one for machines are tended by employers, maintained carefully with provision for their replacement. This is not so with labour power. The ignominy, the humiliation, the great insult in this transaction comes from the fact that the labour power which is sold cannot be detached from the people who sell it. So it is people, including children, old people, sick people, deprived people who are directed here and there in the struggle for profit.

Having to sell labour power under these conditions is a serious business for it causes people to combine together for protection and to struggle against employers with the bitterness and intensity of war. It evokes passions which are reminiscent of battle. There can be no other explanation which can make sense of the two centuries of industrial conflicts involving violence, deaths, injury, recriminations, starvation and deprivation. How else can one explain the desperation of employers who have used all the agencies of state power, laws, the police, the army, to protect themselves?

In this conflict the workers have to pay particular attention to their own ranks, to building durable organizations, extending their influence and maintaining solidarity. And, because they are not playing games, solidarity is sought by compulsion as well as persuasion; it is enforced if it does not come voluntarily. Historically the violence in industrial relations has occurred through efforts both to enforce solidarity and to break it. In the early stages of trade union history in Britain the greatest attention was attached to membership of organizations. Those who stood outside were designated traitors to their group: they were scabs and they were punished by ostracism, humiliation, by having their tools smashed or their homes destroyed, sometimes by death. The significance of such reactions lay in the depth of feelings which led ordinary men and women to engage in them. Later, the same reactions were invoked by strike breaking. They still are. Men and women who attempt to break strikes must

181

expect the direst consequences that organizations without any statutory powers can enforce.

The solidarity position during a strike rarely turns out to be quite so bad as is at first sight thought because a strike generates its own cohesion. A strike is an influential recruiting medium. Workers opposed to strikes tend to join them once they have started; workers opposed to unions tend to join them during strikes. There are strong compelling pressures on workers to close their ranks during periods of conflict. Some of these pressures arise not only from a desire to win a strike but also from fear of the penalties from not joining it.

The pressures making for collective solidarity are intense in the mining industry for the ones which are derived from the class position of miners are reinforced by the nature of the work situation and the neighbourhood relationship between work and home. Because of the inherent dangers in mining, workers are forced into interdependent relationships and through the relatively close proximity of work and home and the physical isolation of mining neighbourhoods this interdependence spills over into kinship and social relationships. A strike with small beginnings in a section of a face in a pit usually spreads quickly to involve the whole pit and evokes responses from the various sections of the neighbourhood. Adjoining pits tend to respond to each other's difficulties. Miners assume that there should be solidarity over whatever area relates to their dispute. They, therefore, expect sympathetic action from other Areas and other unions. When it does not occur they ask why and set out to get it.

Strike Strategy

Once the miners' strike had started on 9th January, 1972 the 41.2 per cent of the members who had opposed it melted away and instead there existed simply the N.U.M. conducting a national strike with unanimity. There was no need for pickets to keep miners on strike. The strike elicited its own support and enforced its own penalties. Pickets were posted at pit heads but largely as a token to deter non-miners from breaking or interfering with the miners' solidarity. But this was not enough. The post office workers had discovered early in 1971 that a strike could not be won simply by staying at home. The commodity or service withheld has to be exceptionally irreplaceable and indispensible for its absence to be sufficient in itself to win a strike. In many cases there are substitute commodities and services or make-shift arrangements can be made. In the case of the post office workers, undisturbed telephone communications and private postal distribution arrangements had enabled consumers to overcome the absence of postal services. In the coal industry the facility to switch to oil or to consume accumulated coal stocks were equally possible weaknesses in the defences of miners.

182

The prerequisite for winning the strike was a collective determination to win. This involved more than a majority vote in its favour; that had been simply a decision to strike. It was a mood generated by a growing awareness of being exploited and this came about through the overtime ban. The determination, however, remained merely talk without a strategy. As soon as the strike began Lawrence Daly spelled out the manner in which the Union's resources should be deployed. The interpretation and application of this advice, however, could not be stipulated from the head office. Very quickly the details of a strategy in application emerged in the Areas, forming a neatly logical pattern of activities of which any army commander would have been proud.

A number of important tactical decisions had to be taken once the strike began. The first and most immediate of these concerned the issue of safety cover for the pits. The national policy of the N.U.M. was formulated before the strike actually started. A circular to local strike liaison committees stated:

"The only men to be allowed to work are:-
(i) Pumpmen, Winding Enginemen, Fan Attendants and Telephone Operators where necessary, together with those required for the safe operation of pumping, winding and ventilation machinery, apparatus and equipment.
"In the event of an emergency affecting the safety of the men and/or colliery, it should be the duty of the Liaison Committee concerned to allow such additional men as required to work in order to deal effectively with the situation.
"Care should be taken by Liaison Committees to ensure that only the minimum of men are employed on any shift, commensurate with the necessary degree of safety."

National strike instructions had two functions: one was to provide guidelines for action and the other was to project a public image about the conduct of the strike. Every circular issued from the Union national office was scrutinized by the press. Seen in this light the national officials had no alternative to saying that the mines should be protected. If there was no safety cover there could be flooding or fire and explosions from accumulated fire damp. Without mechanical inspections there could be roof falls destroying roadways and coal faces. There were a number of small ways in which neglected maintenance could lead to the destruction of parts, even the whole, of pits. The public image of miners might have taken a severe knock if they had decided on a destruction of property course.

Safety Cover
A strike is an intensely collective affair. It can be guided by instructions but its prosecution must lie in the actions of small groups, interpreting and initiating in the light of their own experiences and

183

intentions. These groups, in this strike, had to reflect the feelings of ordinary miners for they were the ones who benefited or suffered during the course of the strike. It became clear at the outset that from the point of view of the ordinary miners the issue of safety cover was highly contentious. The left-wing leaders had no consistent policy. In fact they reflected almost every conceivable attitude to safety cover: that the mines belonged to the miners and should not be jeopardized; that they had to be saved to create a favourable public image; that there had to be unity behind the N.E.C instructions as a matter of strike policy; that the decisions should be left to branches; that if the mines could not provide decent wages then they were not worth saving. In the main they were ambivalent about the preservation of the pits and this was reflected in the actual local responses to demands for safety cover. No one really wanted to destroy the chances of future employment but safety cover was a tool of some importance and it had to be used in the interest of the strike. It was this second factor which predominated.

The character of safety cover had changed since the last official national miners strike in 1926. In 1972, due to the high level of mechanization, it was possible for colliery officials to take some safety precautions without depending on the miners. The N.C.B. did not regard this as fully adequate but in some situations it was sufficient. The colliery officials, organized in the National Association of Colliery Oversmen, Deputies and Shotfirers, were not on strike so that when they went down pits they had to cross picket lines. This aroused resentment and hostility and in some cases the officials were physically prevented from crossing the lines. The effect was to harden attitudes about safety cover.

It was known by the 15th January that the N.E.C. guidelines on safety cover were being widely disregarded. This was confirmed on 24th January when the N.C.B. complained to the N.U.M. that there were 148 pits without any N.U.M. safety cover at all, 53 pits with only winders, 54 pits with partial cover and only 34 with full cover. In addition it was claimed that miners from 15 pits in Nottingham, Yorkshire and the Midlands were preventing colliery officials from working. The Derbyshire Area executive committee banned all underground safety work from the outset. Delegates at a Yorkshire Area Council meeting tried to reach a similar decision but the meeting ended in uproar. Despite repeated pleas from the N.E.C. and much press publicity about the possibility of mines having to close permanently through inadequate maintenance, the miners' attitude began to consolidate around one point. It was that if the N.C.B. seriously wanted to protect pits then the solution was simple: pay decent wages to the miners. In any case, as Tommy Mullany from Yorkshire remarked, the term "safety" was being misused. The N.C.B. wanted to save property not men for men were safest out of the pits.

Picketing

The miners recognized at the beginning that they had to prevent the use of the existing stocks of coal as well as to prevent further production in order to make the strike successful. It was estimated that the total stocks at the beginning of the strike amounted to more than 21 million tons. The power stations alone had stocks of more than 16 million tons. Stocks were higher in 1972 than the previous year, despite the overtime ban, because the winter in 1971 was mild, 3.5 million tons were imported from America and Australia and because there had been a determined effort by the major coal users to stockpile it. There was enough coal around to keep industry supplied for about eight weeks.

The Union's only way of controlling the use of the coal stocks was through picketing with the collaboration of other unions. The national officials sent out detailed picketing instructions early in the strike which formed the basis for the strategy pursued throughout the strike. The Areas were to picket all major coal users and depots within their formal jurisdiction. In addition, each Area was allocated the responsibility for picketing particular non-mining districts; for instance, Yorkshire had the task of controlling the movement and consumption of coal in East Anglia while Kent was responsible for London and the South East of England. The pickets received instructions about the treatment of categories of users. They were told to allow coal to be moved only for use in schools, hospitals and for infirm people. The main transport unions, the Associated Society of Locomotive Engineers and Firemen, the National Union of Railwaymen and the Transport and General Workers' Union, instructed their members not to cross N.U.M. picket lines. The formal tactics of the union can best be seen by reading the instruction circulars distributed to the Areas. The main ones are reproduced at the end of this chapter.

Leadership

The N.E.C. instructions, on this occasion, were carried out in the spirit and the letter. There can have been no other strike by miners in which picketing was utilized like the deployment of troops in battle. Local strike liaison committees, branches themselves and even individual miners treated the strike as if they were living out their heritage as workers, obtaining redemption for decades of exploitation and revenge for 1926. Few of the miners had experienced the painful, humiliating defeat in 1926 yet it was often referred to. No one anticipated such an aggressively committed response, least of all the leader-writers of the national newspapers. The strike was seen as a costly grind to defeat for the miners. After all, the N.C.B.

was dependent upon the Government for financial support and the Government had shown it could turn a blind eye to the sufferings of workers as it had done in the case of the postal workers. What made the intense participation more difficult to explain was that the miners themselves could not anticipate victory for they did not know their own collective strength.

The left-wing leaders did not talk amongst themselves of victory until it appeared in their grasp. In the early stages they simply discussed strategy, emphasized that there was to be no compromise, that there had to be the closest collaboration with other unions, that pickets should be on 24 hour duty, that supplies of coal had to be located, that oil supplies to power stations had to be controlled, that miners should be involved in picketing on a mass scale to politicize them and to retain their commitment.

The strategy of the left-wing leaders became the strategy of the whole Union though they were not the only ones to operate the strike in those terms. An important characteristic of the strike was the generality and consistency of determination to win it. The miners of Nottingham and Durham were in some respects even more aggressive and uncompromising than those of Scotland and South Wales. The left-wing, however, was distinguished from the rest in terms of the quality of its leadership. There were no persons in leadership positions who could match the intellectual capacity and political integrity of those on the left-wing. The left-wing leaders were not so good at devious intrigues, at masking their intentions and they could, therefore, be out-manoeuvred. They had too many scruples to win constant in-fights. With them, one had to stand up and be counted and only when a majority were prepared to expose themselves in this way did they win. But they had the ability to see situations in their political totality, to be able to distinguish between wood and trees and, therefore, to give guidance towards the ends of trade unionism rather than away from them. This ability was vital in a struggle in which the principal device of the employer was to divide and divert.

The leadership of the left was both collective and personalized. Because the structure of the N.U.M. was federalized each Area had its leaders who were not subordinate to national ones or, indeed, to any other . When they met it was as leaders of the Scottish, South Wales or Kent miners, not as secretaries or presidents of Areas. Nor was the size of an Area a determinant of the status of an Area official. Jack Dunn, as the leader of the Kent miners, expressed no inferiority when he was discussing or arguing with officials of Areas many times larger in membership. Nor was he assessed because he represented a tiny Area. He argued from a basis of equality as did all the others. It was an unwritten rule, diligently followed, that no one told miners what to do in their own Areas, or criticized them for not following one course or another. Each Area had to be convinced of the merits of a policy and left to decide on its application. In general, there was, if anything, an inverted reaction to size. The leaders of the larger Areas had to argue their cases exceptionally persuasively to carry those from the smaller ones with them. When the officials returned to their own Areas it was as if they were crossing frontiers. Once across they were responsible only to their own members.

Yet despite this there was a leadership within the left-wing. There were men who carried more weight in argument than others; who could argue more effectively, who knew with clarity what they wanted and worked to get it, who had, in greater measure than others, those qualities usually described as leadership ones. Michael McGahey fitted this description in 1972. His defeat for the presidency in 1971 had not affected his stature in 1972. More than anyone else he had moved around the coalfields speaking at meetings, rallies, demonstrations. He was always present by invitation from inside the Area. He never trespassed in other Areas nor did he try to interfere in any way in Area problems. Whatever influence he exercised was confined to his ability to mould miners' opinions. The translation of these opinions into policy and then into action was the responsibility of miners in their respective Areas and branches. Once the strike had started Michael McGahey's arenas of action were the Scottish coalfields, the N.E.C. and the British Communist Party.

When the strike began 6 of the 26 members of the N.U.M. National Executive Committee were Communists. They formed the bulk of the left-wing vote on the N.E.C. which at its best numbered only eight. The six were united, of course, by the fact of being Communists. Solidarity figured high amongst their priorities. They were also united on the main issues confronting the Union. But they were far from being a solid political core. They argued fiercely amongst themselves about tactics and sometimes were divided when votes were taken. Contrary to the popular conception of Communists they never took unthinking action; each was an individualist who prided himself on his own analysis of a particular situation. They would rarely vote without first arguing. Indeed it was the right wing members of the N.E.C. who usually acted as an electoral machine, simply putting their hands up without first presenting their cases. If there had been no left-wing dissenters the Executive meetings would have been very brief, boring occasions. The Communists had to take into account the interests of their respective Areas. Joe Whelan, for example, who had joined the N.E.C in April, 1971 as an addition to the left-wing strength, was sometimes constrained by the conservative policies of the Nottingham Area. He could only vote with the left-wing if he had sound arguments

Jack Collins, on the left, with John Moyle during the strike in February, 1981. Jack Collins represented the Kent Area on the N.E.C. of the Union from 1971-1981. He was elected secretary of the Area in succession to Jack Dunn in 1980. John Moyle from Betteshanger Colliery became the Area president in

to justify his action to his members in Nottingham when he returned from London. The Communists reflected Area differences over such matters as concessionary coal allowances. There were, moreover, personality differences. Both Dai Francis of South Wales and Jack Collins of Kent tended on occasions to pursue their own particular interpretations of issues and to vote accordingly. Jack Collins had been elected to the N.E.C. in July, 1971, replacing Jack Dunn and becoming one of its two rank and file members.

There is always scope during a strike for new leaders to emerge. Strikers who analyze incisively, give direction and express themselves eloquently, can gain recognition as leaders even though they may not hold official union posts. In order for this transition from relative obscurity to be possible, however, there has to be a fluid leadership position. Newcomers find it difficult to emerge when the official leadership is actively in control. Yorkshire was one of the few Areas in 1972 where it was possible for new leaders to establish themselves.

When the strike began the president of the Yorkshire Area was ill, while the general secretary, Sid Schofield, had been ill but had re-emerged in a limited capacity. The full-time vice-president, Jack Leigh, did not possess the qualities to impose himself in the leadership vacuum. Sammy Taylor, the full-time Compensation Agent, had died just over a month before the strike began, leaving Jock Kane, the Financial Secretary, as the only full-time Area official with the capacity to lead. Kane too, was approaching retirement and felt the physical strain of constant campaigning. The rank and file left-wing miners in Yorkshire, however, had both the personnel and the organization to fill the vacuum and to give direction during the strike. And this they did by virtually taking over the organization of the strike in Yorkshire and picketing operations in East Anglia. Arthur Scargill, the delegate from Woolley colliery, was prominent amongst this group. After Sammy Taylor died he had been chosen to be the left-wing candidate for the post of Compensation Agent which Taylor had held. The strike gave Scargill an opportunity to display his undoubted qualities and, through his work on the committee dealing with the control of pickets, he achieved a prominence which extended well beyond Yorkshire. Within the space of the seven weeks campaign Scargill established himself not as the leading contender for the post caused by Taylor's death but as the only serious contender.

Flying and Mass Pickets

The scale and intensity of the miners' participation in the strike distinguished it from all other strikes in recent trade union history. Pickets were deployed rapidly, called flying pickets, for surveillance purposes, to obtain intelligence, to get confirmation and to make

189

Pickets outside Cockenzie Power Station, Scotland, on 20th January, 1972.

quick impacts where weaknesses in solidarity might be detected. Pickets were used in large numbers in order to create confrontation situations with coal distributors, industrial users and members of other unions which would result in satisfactory solutions for the miners. Between these two forms of picketing there were shades and combinations depending upon the needs of particular situations. In fact, a clever use was made of secondary picketing. There was only a limited amount of primary picketing to prevent the transport of coal from pit heads and to restrict the incidence of strike breaking by clerks and supervisory management. No pickets were required to prevent miners from strike-breaking.

Flying pickets had been characteristic of the unofficial strikes in Yorkshire since 1955. They came, of course, with the advent of the car as a common commodity. In 1955 relatively few miners had cars but enough could be collected to take strike leaders into other Areas. There were enough cars available in 1972 to enable flying pickets to be moved on a wider scale. Sometimes large numbers of miners moved about rapidly. Teams of up to 300 miners disrupted coal supplies to the Scottish power stations at Kincardine, Longannet and Cockenzie on the third day of the strike. They switched from one plant to another as they heard of coal supplies being moved. On the same day 300 miners tried to prevent lorries from moving fuel from a smokeless fuel preparation plant at Grimethorpe in Yorkshire. One miner was injured when a lorry drove through the picket line. The following morning the Grimethorpe miners, searching for the driver of the lorry, reinforced pickets at a coal depot at Barrow, near Barnsley. Arthur Scargill assumed the leadership of these pickets and forced the closure of the depot.

Afterwards he and other pickets with time on their hands discussed how best to deploy themselves and decided to search for coal stocks in the Yorkshire Area as well as keeping an eye open for the lorry driver who had been involved in the Grimethorpe incident. A picketing strategy began to emerge in Yorkshire through a series of *ad hoc* decisions arising out of practical problems as they cropped up. Pickets sped around in cars checking on coal movements then called upon mass support to stop them where necessary. They put no industrial limits on their action but pursued coal wherever it was used to the point where it was finally consumed. Because miners faced similar situations in other Areas and had the same determination to win the strike there was a simultaneous development of strategies in different Areas which were remarkably similar. Malcolm Pitt has described in a graphic, detailed way how the Kent miners met the responsibility of providing picket cover for the largest concentration of power stations, docks and railway depots in Britain.*

---

* *The World on our Backs: The Kent Miners and the 1972 Miners' Strike* by Malcolm Pitt, Lawrence and Wishart, London, 1979, pp. 217.

191

The story was similar in Scotland, South Wales, Derbyshire and Yorkshire.

The miners, at first, had little information about coal stocks or movements. The central office provided the Areas with details of the location of power stations taken from a Central Electricity Generating Board Year Book map. For the rest they had to rely on scanty bits of information, hunches and gossip. There was some delay, for instance, in sending pickets from Kent to London because the Union had inadequate information about coal movements. Malcolm Pitt has described the build-up of action. "Two carloads of miners," he stated, " were sent out to the London area and along the south-east coast to locate coal stocks. . . Branch officials had to organize lists of volunteers for picket duty, and a system of communications with the men once they had dispersed from the pits into the villages and towns. In the pit villages, the welfare clubs and working men's clubs were obvious centres. . . In the towns. . . certain pubs and clubs frequented by miners were nominated by the branches and visited daily by union officials."*

By the second week of the strike the Kent miners had set up an operations room in the Union head office; they controlled up to 300 pickets on round the clock duties at power stations, monitoring the movement of coal ships up the Thames estuary from its marshy banks and patrolling coal wharves from launches supplied by sympathisers. South Wales miners travelled as far as Southampton and Plymouth to contain the movement of coal at the docks there. Miners throughout the Midlands picketed a dozen large power stations in Nottinghamshire, Derbyshire and Leicestershire. The Yorkshire miners not only controlled the movement of coal at the power stations and coal depots in their Area but placed pickets at the Humberside ports and sent altogether about 1000 miners to East Anglia where they picketed 15 ports and 7 power stations including the main one at Ipswich.

There was no part of Britian where coal was stored or used which was not, after a time, supervised by miners, often aided and abetted by members of other unions. The N.U.M. failed to get anything more than sympathy from the T.U.C. at the outset. The Finance and General Purposes Committee of the T.U.C. General Council refused to summon a conference of transport unions to organize aid for the miners. The leaders of the transport unions, however, directed their members not to cross picket lines. The Clerical and Administrative Workers' Union refused to bring out on strike those members who worked for the National Coal Board but advised them to perform only normal duties and not to cross picket lines where hostility to them was shown. The reality of support, however, was not determined by national union directives, but by face to face confrontations where picketing took place. This, in turn, was influenced by the extent and determination of the picketing.

* ibid, p. 122

Pickets and police at Longannet Power Station, Scotland, during the 1972 strike.

Solidarity through Force

The miners were constantly urged by their officials to engage in peaceful picketing only. During the actual operation of the strike, however, this was a meaningless exhortation for in so far as the miners were determined to win their strike violence was implicit in it. Whether violence actually occurred depended upon the potential for strike breaking for this was the main provocation. The support given by railwaymen, particularly the train driver members of the Associated Society of Locomotive Engineers and Firemen, was immediate and complete. One solitary picket on a railway bridge was sufficient to inform train drivers where they should or should not move their trains. Their solidarity was simple, uncomplicated. Many transport drivers responded in a similar manner but in the field of road transport there was no unity amongst drivers themselves. There were many small firms, highly competitive, and willing to utilize any situation to add to their share of the market. Mostly the sheer force of numbers with the risk of violence to themselves persuaded road transport drivers to respect picket lines. Some lorry drivers, however, were paid by their employers to break picket lines and others, with a feckless disregard for human safety, and for reasons known only to themselves, ignored them. In consequence there were provocative incidents and violence in all of the coalfields. Local branches of the Transport and General Workers' Union were often compelled to collaborate with the miners because they knew that their members and their lorries were at risk if they attempted to strike-break.

Local union re-assessments about collaboration were made whenever workers crossed picket lines, such as in the case of Coal Board clerks and colliery deputies. When the miners directed their attention to oil supplies power workers were confronted with the problem of deciding on their allegiances. Bill McLean announced on 17th January that the Scottish miners would attempt to stop oil supplies to oil-fired power stations. In Yorkshire the miners curtailed the supply of black oil used to spray on coal to prevent it deteriorating. Whilst the strike was on, power station workers mounted their own campaign for a wage increase, threatened an overtime ban and identified themselves with the miners. Solidarity between the miners and workers in related activities increased as the strike wore on but it was often a fragile thing, forged out of violent, disruptive circumstances. It was, however, always used successfully. Managements used every conceivable device to break or avoid picket lines. At Longannet power station in Fife at the end of January oil was slipped passed pickets in what appeared to be a "cloak and dagger" operation. Managements frequently claimed that the picketing was ineffective or that the miners' intentions were

194

a bluff. By the end of January, however, it was plain that the denial of essential supplies other than coal to power stations, such as hydrogen, chemicals and lighting up oil, was having an immediate effect. Thorpe Marsh power station in Yorkshire, for instance, was closed because of the lack of hydrogen while stations in South Wales were closed because lighting-up oil was not getting through.

The strike was replete with incidents which indicated a unique commitment to it. There was the case of the train driver who stopped at a station to discharge his goods, looked back and saw a solitary picket standing on a bridge over the railway lines and, on realizing he had crossed a picket line, backed his train to the other side of the bridge. At Southwick in Sussex two of the miners who had been trying to stop coal being taken out of a coal merchant's yard in Albion Street jumped on the back of a lorry and scattered bags of coal along two miles of road. The miners later agreed to allow the company to distribute bagged coal provided it did not send bulk supplies for industrial use. There was the case of miners sitting in a launch patrolling the Thames with one of them using a loud hailer to cajole dockers and Battersea power stations workers to support them. There were arrests as the police clashed with pickets in the endeavour to protect strike-breakers. Miners sieged the N.C.B. regional headquarters in Doncaster, trapping night workers and preventing day workers from replacing them. The police there fought with pickets to form a cordon along which young female strike breakers could pass. Four of these pickets were arrested. On most days there were arrests in one coalfield or another though the extent of police retaliation varied considerably from one constabulary to another as the policies of Chief Constables varied. In general, considering the scale and manner of the picketing, there were relatively few arrests.

As the pattern of action emerged it was so unlike other and earlier strikes. The miners were not left to sit at home amidst domestic pressures to return to work. They were all on call for picket duty, likely to be instructed to move to one strategic point or another. Large numbers of them became involved in the planning and execution of the campaign, interested in locating supplies of coal and willing to risk arrest to stop them being moved, denying supplies to some consumers whilst allowing them to go to others. There were, of course, hardship cases resulting in hospitals being without fuel, schools having to close and old people being left without heat, for some essential users were caught up in the general struggle to blockade coal. Exceptional movements of coal were determined by the local strike committees which often did not have full knowledge of either the priority needs in their localities or the implication of their decisions. They could not, moreover, always be sure that coal which was allowed to move would go to its scheduled

A group of pickets after a meeting with Dennis Skinner, M.P., at Birdwell Working Men's Club, Yorkshire at the conclusion of the 1972 strike. Left to right: Eric Roberts, seated (Woolley colliery); unknown, standing; unknown, sitting; Colin Pickering, standing (Rockingham colliery); Don

destination so they tended to be cautious and this sometimes created hardship cases. But the ability to create hardship, like that to endanger the safety of pits, was a weapon in the struggle and it was used when the strike situation became tense or desperate.

It would be wrong, however, to emphasize too much the extent to which solidarity was produced through force. Relatively little of the force was explicit anyway. It was present frequently, simply because mass picketing conveyed an impression of force. There was much uninvited, spontaneous solidarity from unions and other groups of people. The isolation and loneliness of the miners was never present in 1972 as it had been in the 1926 coal lockout. Miners' officials were invited to speak before a wide range of local organizations in industry and communities. Often money was raised for the miners after one of them had spoken at a meeting. Students in higher education were especially active in supporting the strike. Speakers were invited to student society meetings in Universities and Polytechnics. Some students' unions assisted with the organizing of pickets by raising money and arranging accommodation. Pickets from Yorkshire were billeted in student accommodation at the University of Essex, despite opposition from the University administration. Similarly students at the London School of Economics and Goldsmiths' College housed Kent miners in London. Ruskin College students, organized by former miners, worked closely with pickets from the Midlands. The part the students played in general was the very reverse of the strike-breaking services they had provided in the 1926 General Strike. The relationships which miners and students formed had value for each group. Many miners saw students in a different, more positive light afterwards.

Saltley Gasworks

The strike position altered as it moved into its second month. For two weeks or more the miners had the hope that the electricity power workers would join them by enforcing an overtime ban. This hope disappeared when power station workers accepted a pay offer on 7th February. The miners from then on were dependent on their own resources. For a month they closed one coal depot after another though they were mainly the small ones. By the fifth week they were tackling the big depots in Saltley, Birmingham and the Longannet power station in Scotland but for these they needed pickets in greater numbers than before. The feeling of solidarity was strengthened by a march of 20,000 miners and other trade unionists in London at the beginning of the fifth week. A few days later, Fred Matthews, the Yorkshire miner who was killed by a lorry whilst on picket duty at Keadby power station near Scunthorpe, was buried at his home village of Dunscroft near Doncaster in the presence of 10,000 people. Printing trade unionists in London and the Provinces

197

held one-hour token strikes as a mark of respect for the dead picket. The climate of conflict became more pervasive and overbearing. The pickets at Warsop Main colliery in Derbyshire refused to release coal for hospitals and old people's homes. The miners became more aware of police collusion with strike breakers and interference with pickets. The Scottish miners complained about the behaviour of six police forces in their Area. Firms were having to lay-off employees as the electricity power situation deteriorated. The effects of the strike became more generally experienced. Profit-making as well as old people's homes began to suffer. The Government declared a State of Emergency on Wednesday, 9th February at just about the time that Fred Matthews was being buried. The coke depot at Saltley Gasworks in Birmingham was the last big fuel depot to remain open in the Midlands. It had 100,000 tons of domestic coke and was serving lorry drivers from all over the country. The lorries were queueing up to be loaded. 200 pickets were sent there on 4th February and the Birmingham region of the Transport and General Workers' Union warned that any lorry driver crossing the picket line would be expelled from the union. Each day the number of pickets increased. There were 1000 of them by Monday, 7th February. Each day the intensity of the confrontation increased as drivers attempted to cross picket lines and the police endeavoured to protect them. On the day that there were 1000 pickets there were also 500 policemen and 21 arrests. The N.U.M. wanted the coke in the depot to be distributed on a permit basis so that it went only to essential users but the chairman of the West Midlands Gas Board would not agree.

The Saltley depot became the centre of a symbolic struggle. The coke which was being distributed from there had virtually no effect on the total power situation; it could not alleviate the increasing difficulties being confronted by industry. Nonetheless it represented a trial of strength which each side felt it had to win. The national office of the N.U.M. appealed for all available pickets to go to Saltley. The secretary of the Birmingham Trades Council also appealed for pickets to assist the miners. On Tuesday, 8th February 1800 Midland car delivery workers struck in sympathy with the miners and on the following day about 200 shop stewards in the Midland engineering industry called for a solidarity stoppage by 40,000 engineering workers and a march to Saltley on Thursday, 10th February. The West Birmingham district secretary of the Amalgamated Union of Engineering and Foundry Workers, Mr. Norman Cartwright, expressed the feelings of the shop stewards when he said that, "This plant will be closed until the West Midland Gas Board accepts the conditions laid down by the miners union — that coke can only go to essential users. If any lorries from our well-organized factories try to cross the picket lines tomorrow, they can forget about coming to those factories in future." He added, according to a report in the *Financial Times* on 10th February, that "We saw what happened to the postal workers last year. We are not going to let it happen to the miners."

There was a coincidence of events as the confrontation at Saltley came to a head. The State of Emergency had been declared. Power cuts were enforced throughout the country affecting about one-third of the domestic, commercial and industrial users of electricity. There were unpredictable blackouts. Industrial workers were being laid off or put on short-time in increasing numbers. The British Steel Corporation, Courtaulds and Tate and Lyle in particular were affected. There was talk in Parliament about using troops.

Thursday, 10th February, was the day of mass action at Saltley. Almost 40,000 workers in the Birmingham area went on strike and 10,000 of them marched to Saltley to join the 2000 miners who were already there from South Wales, Yorkshire and the central coal-fields. This was mass picketing on such a massive scale that the 1000 police on duty were insufficient to control the situation in the interests of the coke consumers. The Chief Constable of Birmingham ordered the gates of the Saltley depot to be closed. This was done reluctantly and hesitantly by the Gas Board. It was only after two of the organizers of the pickets, Arthur Scargill and Alan Law from the Transport and General Workers' Union threatened further intensified action against the depot that the Gas Board agreed to implement the miners' terms and operate a permit system.

The closure of Saltley was proclaimed a victory by the trade union movement and Arthur Scargill who had been given much publicity during the struggle emerged as a potential miners' leader. There was no question after this that Scargill would soon be a full-time official in Yorkshire. There was, of course, much discussion in the press and by politicians about the intimidating character of mass picketing and about legislation to control and weaken picketing. The national officials of the N.U.M. also reacted fearfully and advised the Area Secretaries "to review the position so as to ensure that only the minimum number of men should be involved essential for effective picketing." This exhortation was ignored. The miners would have been negligent of their own interests if they had dropped their most effective weapon at a time when they could sense victory.

Many Saltleys

In each Area of the Union there was at least one power station or coke or coal depot which was like that at Saltley, large, crucial and symbolic, requiring mass picketing activities in order to neutralize it. Each Area had its own 'Battle of Saltley Gate,' not of course on the same scale as Saltley, but nonetheless as important in the total struggle. Longannet power station was the Scottish equivalent of

Saltley. There had been mass picketing at Longannet power station throughout the strike but after the closure of the Saltley depot the Scottish miners increased their pressure. More than 2000 miners turned out on 14th February and 13 trade unionists, including a full-time agent of the N.U.M., Graham Steel, were arrested. When the 13 men appeared in court the following day they were remanded in custody, handcuffed and fingerprinted. This incident provoked even greater expressions of solidarity in Scotland than had occurred before. The executive of the Scottish Area called on the trade union movement to demand the release of the arrested men and to take industrial action for this purpose if necessary. The cases against the pickets were eventually dismissed.

The miners' determination to win induced solidarity within the trade union movement as a whole. As the power stations closed so unions rallied closer to the miners, contributed money to their funds, joined them in mass demonstrations and reinforced the picket lines. Miners in their thousands rallied and marched in each of the main coalfields. When an official enquiry into the dispute opened on Monday, 15th February, 10,000 miners and other workers marched to the House of Commons to lobby their Members of Parliament and virtually forced their way into Parliament. With a few remarkable exceptions the national unions gave support in the wake of action by their members in mining areas. For this reason solidarity was real; it was not decreed from central offices but imposed on them. The Trades Union Congress played no part of any significance because the General Secretary, Victor Feather, offered its services as a mediator when they should have been given to achieve victory.

It is difficult to calculate the scale of the participation of miners in the dispute but it was large. It was estimated that 500 establishments were picketed on a 24 hour basis by an average of 40,000 miners each day. Altogether 200,000 miners had been involved in strike duties. The Government, in a House of Commons statement on 21st February declared that 263 people had been arrested for offences connected with picketing. Not all of these people were miners and about one-quarter were arrested at Saltley. The picketing undoubtedly intimidated possible strike-breakers but it induced a relatively small amount of actual violence. The complaint against it was not specifically its mass scale, or its mobility or, as *Labour Research* aptly commented in April 1972, its legality, but its effectiveness. Victory could not have been achieved in any other way in 1972.

APPENDIX II

NATIONAL UNION OF MINEWORKERS
222 EUSTON ROAD, LONDON NW1 2BX

President J. GORMLEY, O.B.E.   *Secretary* L. DALY

Telephone 387 7631-8

CTB/ES.   11th January 1972

Circular No. A.S. 17/72

To: AREA SECRETARIES

Dear Sirs,   PEACEFUL PICKETING

The support for the Miners' Strike offered by other
Unions at National level has already been given practical
interpretation by some transport workers at Local level. A
further assurance has been received from the T.U.C. that
the Unions whose Members are engaged in the distribution
of coal will issue firm instructions that their Members
should not cross N.U.M. picket lines.

You should, therefore, take immediate steps to place
pickets at such places as coal stock yards, open cast sites,
Docks and Power Stations. The National Office will be
seeking assistance to cover those places which are not in
or adjacent to Mining Areas.

Please keep this Office fully informed of developments.

This instruction does not in any way effect the service
which we have offered to Hospitals, etc.

Other Unions with whom you are already co-operating
should be made aware of the picketing arrangements which
you make.

                    Yours sincerely,

                    L. DALY
                    Secretary

NATIONAL UNION OF MINEWORKERS
222 EUSTON ROAD, LONDON NW1 2BX

President J. GORMLEY, O.B.E.

Telephone 387 7631-8

Secretary L. DALY

JW/NS/2

Instructions to Pickets

12th January 1972

The aim of the NUM picket is to prevent the movement of coal and alternative fuels between power stations, coal depots and other coal consumers.

Most fuel is normally moved either by rail or lorry. The organising unions, ASLEF, NUR and TGWU have instructed their members not to cross NUM picket lines. These picket lines should therefore be placed at strategic rail and road access points to prevent the movement of coal or alternative fuels.

Pickets should not attempt to prevent workers other than those transporting fuel entering plants. All picketing must be peaceful and it would be advisable for pickets to inform local trade union officials of other unions that the picketing will be taking place.

Pickets should not enter private property.

NATIONAL UNION OF MINEWORKERS
222 EUSTON ROAD, LONDON NW1 2BX

President J. GORMLEY, O.B.E. *Telephone* 387 7631-8 *Secretary* L. DALY

JW/NS/2

Area Circular No 19/72

To Area Secretaries

12th January 1972

Dear Sir,

NUM Pickets - Power Stations

Enclosed is a list of power stations in your geographical area.

Pickets must be arranged at the major power stations and at other power stations where manpower is available.

At oil fired power stations fuel in excess of normal deliveries should be halted where possible. It would be advisable to co-ordinate with local trade union officials to determine normal deliveries.

Area Secretaries are advised to contact local officials of other trade unions to inform them of the proposed picket lines. The chief picket should also contact officials of trade union branches at the picket line.

Not all coal/dual fired power stations will be in operation, particularly the smaller stations and the necessity to picket these should be determined by coal stocks and the possibility of operating the stations (again local trade union advice could be useful). Pickets should always be posted at sites where coal stocks are held.

All picketing must be peaceful and the National Officials of transport unions have instructed their members not to cross NUM picket lines during the course of this dispute.

Letters of authority for chief pickets have been enclosed together with instructions for pickets. These should only be given to your chief pickets.

Yours sincerely,

L. DALY

Secretary

NATIONAL UNION OF MINEWORKERS
222 EUSTON ROAD, LONDON NW1 2BX

President J. GORMLEY, O.B.E.

Telephone 387 7631-8

Secretary L. DALY

JW/NS/2

Area Circular No 22/72

To Area Secretaries

13th January 1972

Dear Sir,

Non-Colliery Picketing

All pits are already being picketed throughout the country.

Some Areas are also picketing non-colliery establishments. If this strike is to be fully effective and of as short a duration as possible all major coal users and depots must be picketed in view of the assurance given by other unions that their members will not cross NUM picket lines.

As stated in Area Circular No 19/72, and the NEC decision of today, all power stations, steel works, ports, coal depots etc in the country must be picketed. This exercise will only be possible with the co-operation of other trade unions and Area Secretaries are requested to contact the relevant local trade union officials to ascertain the location etc of the points to be picketed.

A list of power stations and also a list of ports which have imported coal have been sent to you (Area Circular Nos 19/72 and 3/72). Your liaison with local trade unions could lead to the adjustment of this list in your Area in view of information received.

Outside the coalfields it will be necessary for pickets to be arranged from NUM Areas. The NEC has today allocated responsibility as follows: -

South East England and London	Kent and Midlands
South West Area	South Wales
East Anglia	Yorkshire
Scotland (non-mining areas)	Scotland, Northumberland, Durham, Group No 2

Area Secretaries must liaise with bordering NUM Area Secretaries to prevent the duplication of pickets at border cases. Areas should also liaise with COSA in their Areas for pickets. The present strike committee machinery may be helpful for liaison.

All pickets must be peaceful and abide by the decisions of the NEC regarding picketing and the movement of coal in special cases.

Further copies of picketing instructions and authorisations are available from Head Office. Picketing authorisations should be stamped with the Area stamp where possible.

NOTE: The NEC decision today regarding expenses for pickets operating outside mining areas was that Areas should provide transport, food and accomodation for these pickets. Area Circular No 20/72 should therefore be amended accordingly. (The Reference to £2 in that circular should be deleted)

Yours sincerely,

L. DALY

Secretary

NATIONAL UNION OF MINEWORKERS

222 EUSTON ROAD, LONDON NW1 2BX

President J. GORMLEY, O.B.E.   *Secretary* L. DALY

Telephone 387 7631-8

TO WHOM IT MAY CONCERN

      _ _ _ _ _ _ _ _ _ _ _ has been authorised by the National Union of Mineworkers to co-ordinate picketing at this plant.

    The aim of the National Union of Mineworkers picket is to prevent the movement of coal and alternative fuels during the course of the current miners' dispute.

    Members of trade unions affiliated to the Trades Union Congress have been instructed by their national leadership not to facilitate the movement of coal or possible alternative fuels by crossing NUM picket lines.

                L. DALY
                Secretary
                National Union of Mineworkers

205

NATIONAL UNION OF MINEWORKERS
222 EUSTON ROAD, LONDON NW1 2BX

President J. GORMLEY, O.B.E.

Telephone 387 7631-8

Secretary L. DALY

JW/NS/2

Area Circular No 35/72

To Area Secretaries

21st January 1972

Dear Sir,

Instructions to Pickets

Many Areas have requested Head Office rulings and guidelines to men on picket duty. A summary of the national guidelines are given below.

1. Collieries - all movements of coal and stocks at collieries should be stopped (except for deliveries to pensioners, hospitals, schools and the infirm). Members of COSA and NUM men on safety duties should be allowed through gates if they carry the authority of the local NUM liaison committee.

2. Power Stations - all movement of fuel and stocks at power stations should be stopped. Oil fired power stations are now taking extra loads as the result of coal fired closures and supplies should also be stopped. Oil tanker drivers in the TGWU have been told not to cross our picket lines. All attempts should be made to ensure that equipment, especially safety equipment, is allowed through picket lines.

3. Coal Depots - the only coal that may leave depots will be for pensioners, hospitals, schools and infirm people. All other coal movements should be stopped as supplies for the permitted customers could otherwise be exhausted.

4. Steel Works - coke supplies from coking ovens for steel works should be stopped. Where NUM Cokemen are working at coke ovens, supplies of coking coal consistent with the requirements of the cokemen should be supplied.

5. Casual helpers - in many Areas, members of the public are offering help on picket lines. This help should be accepted but there must be at least one NUM member in charge of the line at all times.

6. General - Reports have been received about fuel deliveries to power stations when NUM pickets have been away. A 24 hour picket line must be maintained unless the other local unions give firm assurances that they will contact the NUM should fuel be moved. In such cases checks should still be made to ensure that there are no fuel movements.

   Where coal is allowed through picket lines for the special cases mentioned in 1 and 3, a picket should, where possible, accompany the lorry to ensure correct delivery. Where escorts are not available. lorries should be followed from time to time to ensure correct delivery.

   ALL PICKETING MUST BE PEACEFUL AND AT NO TIME SHOULD THERE BE ANY PROVOCATION FOR ANY REASON ON THE PART OF OUR PICKETS.

   As picketing becomes more effective, there will be less for the pickets to do, but the lines must be maintained throughout the strike. Areas should endeavour to make pickets as comfortable as possible whilst on duty.

   If, regardless of our peaceful picketing, coal is moved, details should be taken of the merchant and lorry and these details forwarded to Head Office in due course.

   The above guidelines may have to be varied according to the local situation. In such cases Areas should inform Head Office (Jim Wheeler) of any necessary alterations. A written picket report should be posted to Head Office daily except in emergencies.

Yours sincerely,
L DALY
Secretary

CHAPTER 16
VICTORY
Forecasts of Doom

At the beginning of the strike editorial comments in all of the national newspapers except the *Morning Star* forecast defeat or at the most a pyrrhic victory for the miners. On Friday, 7th January, 1972, the *Daily Express* declared that "A colliery shutdown will mean the death-warrent for more of the nation's uneconomic pits. The major victims of the miners' strike will be the miners themselves." The *Financial Times* commented that "It is extremely difficult to see what the miners hope to gain out of the national strike they are bent on starting this weekend. Mr. Joe Gormley . . . has explained that they are fighting a battle with the Government over its wages strategy on behalf of the trade union movement . . . The last union leader to speak in similar emotive terms was Mr. Tom Jackson of the Union of Post Office Workers early last year. But the union movement learnt a salutary lesson from his long and unproductive strike both about the futility of taking on a determined Government and about the apparent inability of the unions to unite together in a battle . . ." The *Daily Mail* believed that "It will hurt them more than it hurts us . . . There's plenty of coal in stock. And few believe that the miners will stay out long enough to inconvenience the public . . . A fight to the bitter finish would not only end in a defeat for the miners as abject as their last official strike in 1926. It would also cripple morale, increase absenteeism and make it even more difficult . . . to find young men to go down the pits to refresh the ageing labour force." Mr. Woodrow Wyatt, writing in the *Daily Mirror* stated that "The coming coal strike billed for Sunday is the saddest industrial cock-up since the war. Rarely have strikers advanced to the barricades with less enthusiasm or hope of success . . . Even if the strike lasts two and a half months, it would have little effect on electricity supplies." *The Times* believed that the strike would be likely to accelerate pit closures while *The Guardian* urged the miners "to think again, and settle" because "they are likely to be defeated after a long stoppage, damaging to them and their industry."

These prophets of doom continued to emphasize the obstacles, the difficulties, the casualties, the impossibility of winning. Hardly a headline was printed which did not anticipate defeat. *The Glasgow Herald* proclaimed on 11th January that "Miners fail to gain support from union colleagues" while the following day the *Scotsman* declared in large type "Pickets stop coal from moving but cause few worries." With apparant increasing satisfaction the *Glasgow Herald* headed their strike report on 13th January with the statement that "Clerks strike means miners will soon run short of cash." *The Daily*

207

Telegraph reminded readers on 17th January: "Power supplies not hit by picketing." Then, as the strike moved into its second week the emphases began to alter.

These early press predictions no doubt confirmed Mr. Heath in his belief that the miners could be beaten without any obvious display of Governmental power. So, although it was generally recognised that the miners were attacking the Government's pay policy the Cabinet continued the pretence that it was not involved. It could not, however, keep the matter off the floor of the House of Commons for long. A debate on the strike took place on Tuesday, 18th January. In anticipation of the occasion the National Coal Board circularized all M.P.s with details of its case. And, as if in anticipation of a Government move the N.C.B. chairman declared that the Board would be willing to participate in a Court of Inquiry. The miners' M.P.s were briefed by the Union.

When Mr. John Davies, the Secretary of State for Trade and Industry, opened the debate he gave no hint that the Government was party to the dispute. He simply reiterated the gist of the many editorial forecasts of defeat for the miners: the N.C.B. will be pushed into an increased deficit, the critical importance of coal was being reduced, North Sea oil had been discovered, natural gas had virtually displaced coal, nuclear power was settling down to a sustained improvement, the bitterness caused by the strike would adversely affect productivity. The suggestion, he said, that the Government should compensate the N.C.B for making an increased pay offer was "manifestly irresponsible." The Secretary of State for Employment, Mr. Carr, criticized proposals for miners to be treated as a special case. The Government, he stated, was not seeking a showdown with the miners. The door of his office was wide open tor either the Union or the Board to enter. But he made no move to ask them in. The Government had an incomes policy, described as N-1 which had so far been applied relatively successfully. Mr. Carr put the Government's view on this: "A major de-escalation of pay settlements and prices was going on," he stated. "The rate of increase in prices had been falling sharply. This was the basis of further advance and was the basis which any government had the duty to maintain because it was in the underlying interest not only of the whole country but of the miners as much as anybody." Unless the Government won the struggle with the miners its policy of successively reducing wage demands would crumble. In the absence of Government initiatives it was left for the General Secretary of the T.U.C., Mr. Feather, to busy himself as a mediator, flitting between the N.U.M., the N.C.B. and the Cabinet, trying to get a resumption of negotiations. On the day after the debate he succeeded in bringing the two sides together for 3 hours for talks about talks but nothing materialized from them.

The Miners' Resolve

The beginning of a strike is always a difficult period for strikers. It is the time of doubts, of questions about the wisdom of incurring the financial problems a strike inevitably brings, of family stresses, of tensions in social relationships and competing loyalties. In all strikes it is during the first week or so that the strikers are vulnerable. After this they adjust to the exigencies and become harder to move, though there is, of course, a limit to the endurance of strikers and a point beyond which they cannot go.

In this strike there was undoubtedly an early spell of adjustment by individual strikers. The union was not paying strike pay. Some miners received income tax rebates; their wives and childern were eligible for social security payments; single miners received no benefits. Personal savings, if they existed at all, quickly disappeared. But whatever problems individual miners experienced they were not given a collective expression. Miners identify closely with their Union and there was no indication that the Union, or sections of it, was hesitant about the strike once it had started.

The press and politicians, in their inevitable translation of deep social problems into personality matters, fastened on Michael McGahey as the prime instigator of the strike. His movements were watched, his words were recorded and his thoughts were anticipated. He was caricatured in the mould of a stereotypical blend of Scotsman, Communist and miner. For those who were hostile to the strike he became the embodiment of evil. He was threatened to the extent that the Scottish miners wanted to provide him with a bodyguard. He refused. His family was abused by letters and telephone calls. The Special Branch, doubtless with a dual purpose in mind, kept a watch over him, his family and home.

In one sense the attention given to Mr. McGahey was warranted. He had not instigated the strike as the earlier parts of this book explain. He was not *the leader* of the strikers. If there was *a leader* it was in the person of the President of the N.U.M., Mr. Gormley. Nor was Mr. McGahey *the leader* in an unofficial capacity. The union had many leaders separated by the distances between the coalfields. But he was, during the strike, representative of the stubborn, uncompromising feelings which miners in the various coalfields were experiencing. When he said that we want no compromise it was a representative statement. His steel hard unwillingness to make concessions was, therefore, a guide which the Government should have studied rather than castigated.

As the weeks went by and the miners and their families had fallen into a routine for coping with the exigencies of the strike, their attitudes hardened, their strategy became more explicit and intentional and their determination to win increased. They went beyond the point where they could contemplate cutting their costs by unilaterally ending the strike. This kind of understanding, however, was beyond the Government and the N.C.B. The ineptness of the N.C.B. and the implacability of the Government would not have mattered, of course, if the miners had been collectively weak. As it was, they were important in influencing the direction of the strike.

Once the miners' pattern of resistance was set then the Government alone was left with the initiatives. It had to be aware of the changing impact of the strike and of the possibilities of ending it. A Cabinet emergency committee under the chairmanship of the Home Secretary, Mr. Reginald Maudling, was given the task of assessing the power situation but it was the mass media which assumed the responsibility for suggesting how the strike should be ended. As the strike bit harder, power cuts were enforced, workers were laid off, the pressures on the Government to come out of hiding, face up to realities and to end the strike intensified. The most commonly suggested solution was to make a concession to the miners by treating them as a special case. But how could this be done without persuading other unions to desist from following the miners' example? If they refused, the miners case could quickly become a general one. There was, moreover, the question for the Government of 'face-saving.' Its incomes policy was at risk and preserving it was a major priority.

The House of Commons discussed the strike again on 4th February in an emotional atmosphere following the death of Fred Matthews. Mr. Carr still maintained that the time was not ripe for the Government to intervene. He refused to admit that the Government was a party to the dispute and projected it as a mediatior. The Government, he stated, could not intervene while the gap between the two sides was so wide. But the pressures were on. The power workers had threatened an overime ban for 7th February, confrontations at Saltley were intensifying, trade unionists generally were displaying their solidarity with the miners as the mass rally in London on 6th February showed and, despite the increasing inconvenience of the strike's effects, people in general appeared to support the miners. In this context the declaration of a State of Emergency on 9th February was a panic reaction, unlikely even to alleviate the problems let alone resolve them.

Earlier that day the Minister of Employment had met the national officials of the Union. He said that the National Coal Board might be able to improve its offer if the Union would consider a settlement of longer than 12 months but he would not say how better the offer would be or for how long the settlement should last. He asked whether or not the T.U.C. would use the case of the miners in other negotiations if they were given special treatment. He also enquired about their attitude to arbitration or a Court of Inquiry. The N.U.M. negotiators, Joe Gormley, Sid Schofield and Lawrence Daly, made it clear that they could only discuss the miners case and not the attitude of other trade unions towards it and that they did not want either arbitration or a Court of Inquiry. They were supported by the National Executive Committee but which agreed nonetheless, to have exploratory talks with the National Coal Board.

The N.U.M. maintained a consistent negotiating position. In negotiating parlance it was always "willing to talk," even though the N.C.B. continued to make unsatisfactory offers. The anticipated revised offer was made on Thursday, 10th February but it was largely a permutation of an earlier one spread over 18 months instead of 12 and failed to meet the Union demands. More important than this the offer failed to induce the right wing members of the Union executive to break with the militant ones and seek a quick settlement. All executive members, of course, were constrained by the obvious determination of their members but there were some who would have justified ending the strike as it moved into its second month if the Government, through the Coal Board, had made an offer with divisive qualities. The Government did not do that because it continued to believe that confrontation tactics would succeed and the Coal Board's failure even to try was a measure of its ineptness. In consequence, the running continued to be made by the Union militants until it was too late to try to divide.

The Wilberforce Inquiry

On the 33rd day of the strike, the 10th February, the Government, following the breakdown of the exploratory talks, announced that a Court of Inquiry would be set up. The Union agreed to participate in the Inquiry, though not unanimously. Four executive members voted against this proposal. The Minister for Employment had suggested that the miners should return to work on the basis of the N.C.B.'s latest offer on the understanding that any improvement which might be suggested by the Court of Inquiry would be applied retrospectively to the date on which the miners returned to work. The Union executive rejected this proposal and added, moreover, that it would not necessarily be bound by the Court findings. Implicit in the Government's decision to initiate an Inquiry, however, was a willingness to accept its terms. But, as if to ensure an outcome it would like, the Government, through the Prime Minister, intervened with gloomy prognostications the very next day. Mr. Heath, in a speech at Liverpool, attacked the unions and announced "massive restrictions" on the use of electricity. Millions, he said, were likely to be put out of work. Mr. John Davies predicted on television that industry would come to a halt if the crisis continued for another 10 to 14 days. He said it would be unwise to move in the troops but that the time would come when this would be necessary. On the following Monday much of industry was on half-time working. Electricity for

211

heating was banned in offices, shops, public halls, restaurants and premises used for recreation, entertainment and sport. Large industrial plants were prohibited from using electricity on Sundays and three weekdays. A contravention of these regulations could result in three months imprisonment or a fine of up to £100. Householders were urged to heat only one room in a house. The Government, after hesitating for so long, had jumped in with both feet. It inserted full page notices in the daily press about its regulations.

The background of gloom and crisis was filled in with reports of continued deterioration in the pits. Equipment was being ruined, it was stated in the press, through the impact of the moving physical environment on machinery. Powered roof supports were becoming embedded in rock. Water was rusting machinery. Damp was penetrating electrical equipment. The National Coal Board announced that 17 coal faces would not be re-opened because of their deteriorating condition.

The Government having been criticized for not intervening was now criticized, even by its own supporters, for a late, panic intervention, for not giving prior warning of the seriousness of the crisis. The reply was that the Government had not realized that the picketing of the electricity supply industry could be so effective. It was a genuine reply for not even the miners' leaders anticipated that consequence. Mr. Heath was accused of making a fetish of non-intervention, of underestimating the strength of the miners and, in any case, of not trying to divide the Union leadership. To these accusations he had no reply.

The Court of Inquiry, consisting of Lord Wilberforce who had headed the inquiry into the pay dispute involving the power workers the year before, John Garnett, the director of the Industrial Society and Professor Lawrence Hunter from Glasgow University, met in an atmosphere of competing pressures. The firms' shut-downs, rising unemployment, talk of the possible use of the troops and of accelerated pit closures were intended, from the Government's point of view, to warn the public of the damage the action of the miners was causing the economy. It was projected as evidence in support of the Government's stand against the miners. Each day the Inquiry met the numbers of unemployed workers was highlighted in the press. By Tuesday, 15th February, the day the Inquiry began sitting in public, 1,200,000 workers had been laid off. This was one-twentieth of the total working population. Cold weather was forecast. On the following day, the one on which the Inquiry ended, 1,400,000 workers were out of work and 12 power stations were closed.

None of this information was intended to re-inforce the miners action but in effect this is what it did for it was daily increasing evidence of their own power. It also helped to consolidate the support they were receiving from other workers. There was a lobby of Parliament on Tuesday, 15th February, by more than 12,000 workers, conducted peacefully and in the manner of a pageant. The General Council of the Trades Union Congress rejected a call from the Government that the miners should relax their picketing. There was no evidence then that the miners were weakening. When the Inquiry opened in public about half of the 4.8 million tons of coal in stock was immobilized by pickets. Gradually the predictions of a full blackout, a complete shutdown and mass lay-offs were becoming reality.

The Court of Inquiry could not abstract itself from this situation. It had been thrust into a power struggle not a national debate about competing needs. The Government was in a dilemma for whilst it wanted to avoid the humiliation of a defeat by the miners, it could not shrug off the responsibility it had for avoiding the ecomonic and social consequenses of attempting to avoid defeat. It was the implicit task of the Inquiry to resolve this dilemma, leaving the Government with as much credibility as possible.

The Inquiry, of course, did not conduct itself as if it were implicated in a power struggle. It had published terms of reference 'to inquire into the causes and circumstances of the present dispute between the National Coal Board and members of the National Union of Mineworkers and to report' which made no reference to the Government. Nor did it require the Government to give evidence of its case. During the two days if its sitting it concentrated on the submissions of the N.U.M. and the N.C.B. though it also heard the case of the Confederation of British Industry. The Trades Union Congress did not think it was necessary for it to appear before the Court.

The Court behaved as other courts of inquiry before it had done. It sat formally, heard lengthy submissions and questioned the main presenters; it allowed witnesses for each side and cross-examined them. It was like a court of law but without the power to subpoena. Its proceedings were wholly devoted to hearing evidence, eliciting facts, clarifying points, confirming attitudes with great seriousness and sincerity. Both parties identified themselves with this decorum.

Lawrence Daly, although he had expressed doubts about the freedom of the Court from Government pressure, nonetheless tried to show the logic and reasonableness of the miners' case in a lengthy submission. He received the help of the Ruskin College Trade Union Research Unit in preparing the Union case. It consisted of the following nine sections: the years of decline, declining earnings, the special case of mining, productivity proceeds and earnings, the debt structure of the N.C.B., the question of markets, what miners were offered, what the miners want and the miners' job. It was a comprehensive argument backed by statistical evidence where it

213

was necessary.* Daly excelled in his presentation of the case and in his ability to defend it against criticisms from the N.C.B., and questions from the Court. He began with a pertinent statement about the role of the Government. He said:

"When we tried to argue our case with (the N.C.B.) we found we were confronted by men whose minds had been made up for them. They were men who had no power to settle. They had been instructed to keep within limits that necessarily meant that they could not listen to a single one of our arguments. The men who gave them those instructions have not, in their turn, come forward to bargain with us.

In speaking to this Court of Inquiry we are also speaking to millions of people beyond these four walls. We are speaking to, we are appealing to, the conscience of the Nation; we are appealing to the conscience above all of the working people of this country.

Many of these people have now got caught up in the effects of this dispute. The Government that has so disastrously denied us any channels of fair-dealing, that has denied us any genuine process of conciliation, that same Government has now moved on towards a general lock-out of the working people of this country.

The Government has said that they have had to act now because of the effectiveness of our 60,000 pickets. What they mean is that they would have let this affair drag on even longer if we had not, through our picketing, brought forward the economic impact of the miners' strike. We are entitled to ask whether it would have been to the benefit of the coal industry of this country to have had this dispute drag on for several more weeks because we had not picketed? We asked the N.C.B. would that have improved the state of the pits or the Coal Board's finances? We ask our miners' wives, would that have helped to feed our kids? And there need be no doubt that this appalling Government, the worst Government the miners' have experienced in this century, would have done for weeks more what it did for the previous five weeks. It would have done nothing. It would have continued its futile primitive nonsense of trying to create the suffering that might break men's wills . . ."

If the Court of Inquiry had any doubt about its task then this statement must have had a clarifying effect. The dispute was between miners and the Government.

The National Coal Board case was similarly diligently prepared. It was longer and more detailed than the Union case mainly because it had continuing access to research facilities. The N.C.B. usefully provided a diary of events from the passing of the wages resolution at the 1971 N.U.M. Annual Conference. It described the operation and effect of the overtime ban and the strike. It presented the Union's wage claim and the arguments used in support of it; described the problem of recruiting and retaining miners and then put the Board's case. The gist of the case was that the N.C.B. could not satisfy the Union demands and at the same time fulfil its responsibilities under the Coal Industry Nationalization Act of 1946 "to secure the efficient development of the coal-mining industry, and to make supplies of coal available of such qualities and sizes, in such quantities and at such prices, as may seem to them best calculated to further

* The full case, including the Report of the Wilberforce Court of Inquiry, has been reprinted in *A Special Case,* edited by John Hughes and Roy Moore, Penguin Books, 1972.

the public interest in all respects" and to ensure "that their reserves shall not be less than sufficient for meeting all their outgoings properly chargeable to revenue account on an average of good and bad years." It explained, through a discussion of the markets for coal, particularly the electricity generating industry, the Board's strategy for wages, hours of work and holidays, and referred to comparable jobs in other industries. The case was completed by a list of appendices useful to the historians of the dispute.

The N.U.M. presented statements from two expert witnesses. Michael Meacher, M.P. discussed the "poverty trap" while Professor Hugh Clegg made out a case for 'exceptional pay settlements.' It called seven witnesses to testify about the life of a miner. This was done in the style of Ernest Bevin when he represented dockers at the Shaw Inquiry in 1920. Bevin had earned the description of the Dockers' K.C. through the dramatic and graphic way he described the conditions of life of dockers. The witnesses on this occasion were working miners from different Areas and different jobs. There were three underground workers, a craftsman, two surface workers who had previously been face workers but who had been compelled to move to the surface because of illness and one other surface worker who had never worked underground. Two of these surface workers, including one who had worked underground, qualified for the whole range of government means-tested family income supplements. Their stories amounted to a composite picture of a miner.

A matter which particularly interested the members of the Court of Inquiry was the effect which the National Power Loading Agreement of 1966 and the Third Day Wages Structure Agreement of 1971 had had on relative earnings for here they could detect a source of legitimate grievances apart from other factors. The evidence of the face workers highlighted this matter. The National Power Loading Agreement, as was stated in an earlier chapter, was phased in over a period of five years. It had introduced a national rate for workers on mechanized coal faces. The Nottingham rate which was the second highest was taken as the standard rate and other Areas had to be brought into line with it by 31st December, 1971. During this five year period the higher rated districts received smaller increases than the lower rated ones of Scotland, Durham and South Wales. The Wilberforce Inquiry reported that even the lowest Area received increases which involved some decline in real earnings while the higher paid Areas, such as Kent, suffered substantial reductions not merely in relative earnings but also in absolute money terms.

The negative effects of introducing a national agreement for workers on power loaded faces were felt by other workers when the Third Day Wages Structure Agreement was applied. This Agreement had had a chequered course for it had involved grading a variety of workers not covered by the National Power Loading Agreement

215

and subjecting them to national rates. All tasks underground had to be defined and allocated a grade and, therefore, a rate of pay. The rates of workers on hand-filled faces, pieceworkers and taskworkers presented particularly difficult problems and it proved to be impossible to iron-out anomalies without a cost to some groups of workers. It was unfortunate for miners that the real earnings of miners in general had fallen during the negotiation and application of these two major national wages agreements.

The Court of Inquiry, though it sat for only 10½ hours, was impressive as it sifted through the evidence. It gave the impression of a victory for reason over force and when it published its findings it appeared to be a victory for justice, too. The conclusions of the Report showed sympathy and understanding for the miners. The Court had considered a number of aspects concerning miners, the coal industry and society at large and, it stated, had "tried impartially, independently and urgently to bring these considerations into balance." It listed the factors which convinced its members "that the miners' claim should be given exceptional national treatment."

"1. The surface workers who are on the minimum rate of £18 are among the lower paid. Their opportunities for alternative work are limited because they may well live in isolated communities. In a number of cases they have suffered sickness and injury in the service of the mines.
2. The large group of men underground but not at the face do work which is heavy, dirty, hot and frequently cramped. In this day and age when physical conditions in other jobs have improved greatly the relative discomforts of working below ground become greater. Other occupations have their dangers and inconveniences, but we know of none in which there is such a combination of danger, health hazard, discomfort in working conditions, social inconvenience and community isolation.
3. The men working on the face and associated with the face, who are in key jobs winning coal, not only suffer the problems of other people below ground but they may need to work in dust masks and suffer considerable noise and are at maximum danger risk.
4. There has been quite exceptional co-operation shown by miners in the last few years in moving from piecework schemes to day working schemes in the interest of greater efficiency. This co-operation has been a model to industry as a whole. The consequence of this change in pay structure has been to hold back the pay of most face workers in relation to the rest of the industry, and to hold back the pay of some groups of face workers far more than others to the extent that some miners are now earning less than they were five years ago. It is normal in such cases elsewhere in industry at the time of major changes to the wage structure to inject a significant overall increase. No such injection has taken place in the case of the miners.
5. Shift payments are minimal or non-existent, which has advantages in terms of efficiency by giving greater flexibility in the organization of work."

It then added "We are convinced, from the arguments we have stated that the present is a time when a definite and substantial adjustment in wage levels is called for in the coal industry." This, in terms of cash, was spelled out as follows:

	Wilberforce Award		N.U.M. Demand
	Minimum Rate	Actual Increase	Minimum Rate
Surface workers	£23	£5	£26
Underground workers	£25	£6	£28
Face Workers	£34.50	£4.50	£35
(N.P.L.A. and Grades			
A, B & C of the Third Day			
Wages Structure)			

It was recommended that all these increases should be back-dated to 1st November, 1971 and should run for a period of 16 months, that is until 28th February, 1973. The N.U.M. and the N.C.B. were urged to give their attention to increasing productivity for only in that way could any long-term increases in real wages be obtained. "In this industry," the Report stated, " for reasons which the Court entirely supports, piecework earnings and other forms of fluctuating incentives have been removed, and there is therefore a particular need to improve face to face communication and leadership of the working group. The N.C.B. has recognised this need . . . We have heard from both the N.C.B. and the N.U.M. of their efforts to evolve a productivity payments scheme which would avoid returning to the disadvantage of piecework type payments . . . The N.C.B. and the N.U.M. should commence discussion before the end of March to agree a scheme by September, which would reflect increases in productivity. The scheme should be agreed nationally, and could be based on increases in productivity nationally or by individual pits, or by a combination of the two."

The Report is Rejected

The National Executive Committee of the N.U.M. had been summoned to London in anticipation of the publication of the Report of the Court of Inquiry on Friday, 18th February. It met on that morning. There was a general feeling that the findings of the Report represented a defeat for the Government but there was dissatisfaction with its terms. A number of members thought the amounts recommended were too low, particularly as they were to be spread over 16 months rather than 12. There were other issues, too, they wanted clarified. The officials of the N.E.C. went off to see the Secretary of State for Employment, Robert Carr, and then the N.C.B. for improvements but they received none. The Executive then rejected the Wilberforce recommendations by 13 votes to 12. The view of the majority was succinctly expressed by the Yorkshire representative, Jock Kane, who stated "we have the Government on the run so let us keep it running."

The dominant view of those N.E.C. members who rejected the Wilberforce award was that it did not represent a victory for reason but was the result of the exercise of miners' power. If they had not

217

gone on strike, they argued, there would have been no Court of Inquiry; if the economic consequences of the strike had not been mounting and severe there would have been less compulsion to meet the miners' demands. The miners' case was well known and had been so even before the strike. Why had not reason prevailed before action had been taken which was costly for miners, their families and millions of other workers to varying extents? The miners' case had not improved, or even changed at all, with time. Why, therefore, was it so reasonable to accede to it on 18th February and not on 9th January? There had been talk about the impressive, compelling manner with which Lawrence Daly had presented the miners' case and the firm intellectual grasp which he had exercised over the Inquiry. But if the intellectual ability of miners' leaders won cases then the earlier general secretaries, Arthur Horner and Will Paynter, would never have lost a case since 1947. The logic of the situation for those who saw the dispute in power terms was that they should continue using a weapon which was being so effective. Why, they argued, should they not get other grievances settled along with the pay issue?

So, with a fragile majority of one, the miners' national officials were instructed to resume negotiations with the N.C.B. "on the basis that the Union would be prepared to settle and recommend a return to work for increases of £6.00 on the surface, £7.00 underground and £4.50 at the face." At this stage the N.C.B. sought refuge in the Wilberforce Report stating that if it went beyond the recommended increases then it would make nonsense of arbitration procedures in the future. The N.C.B. agreed, however, to settle a number of outstanding issues which were due to be the subject of negotiations later on. There were 15 of these fringe issues, including the payment of adult wages to miners from the age of 18 years within the next two years, extra holidays, the consolidation of the bonus shift into shift rates, a new wage structure for lorry drivers and extra pay for winding enginemen. Miners were to be protected from some of the financial effects of the strike.

The National Executive Committee saw the Secretary of State for Employment and then went on to 10, Downing Street to see Mr. Edward Heath who informed them that the Cabinet had decided it could not improve the recommendations of the Court of Inquiry but that the N.C.B. would be as generous as it could be within the terms specified by the Wilberforce Report. In effect this simply meant the implementation of the fringe offers which the Board had already made, amounting to about £10 million in all. Mr. Heath convinced the officials that this offer was final and, in doing so, settled the dispute. The marginal supporters of the strike on the executive swung behind Mr. Gormley and converted the 13 votes to 12 majority for continuing the strike into a 16 votes to 9 majority for ending it.

The final settlement included a rather bald declaration that discussions were "to be commenced forthwith on a productivity scheme with a view to its introduction by the end of September, 1972" in response to the cautious conditional support given to incentives in the Wilberforce Report.

An Untidy Ending.

The end of the strike was untidy and confusing. At the same meeting as the Executive decided to accept the "package deal" and recommend to the miners that they should end the strike it pre-empted a ballot decision by voting by 14 votes to 11 to call off the pickets. This information was interpreted through the press, radio and television as a decision to call off the strike before the deal had been ratified by the members. In any event, without pickets the strike could not continue. Some miners heard the news while others did not hear it. Employers were quick to assume that the strike had ended and informed picketing miners to this effect. So instead of a disciplined decision about whether to return to work or not, following a debate about the Government's offer and a ballot of the members, there was an undignified, unorganized and, in some cases, acrimonious ending.

The decision to call off the pickets before officially ending the strike destroyed any opposition there might have been to the Government's offer. The Kent Area Council, for instance, recommended the Kent miners to reject the offer but quickly reversed its stance when it realised that the strike could not be re-started. It was for this reason that officials in the other left-wing Areas advised their members to accept the offer, thus isolating the Kent Area in its opposition.* The miners decided overwhelmingly to accept the offer with only 3.5 per cent voting to reject it and returned to work on Monday, 28th February, after being on strike for seven weeks.

The strike was an historic one in important respects despite its rather inglorious ending. It had effectively destroyed the Government's N-1 incomes policy and was perceived as a defeat for the Government. The final offer represented a 27.75 per cent increase for surface workers, a 31.6 per cent increase for underground workers and a 15 per cent increase for face workers. Many weaker groups of workers used the miners as price leaders and made similar demands on employers. The strike, moreover, provided an extremely rare example in British trade union history of a union knowingly opposing the Government with strike action and maintaining its determination to win in the face of pervasive ideological pressures to give way. It showed how a disillusioned, demoralized labour force could be transformed by a strike which directly involved the strikers in its organization. For miners with long memories or a sense of history it was sweet revenge for the heartless, humiliating

*Pitt, op. sit.

219

defeat of 1926. Seen in this context, the financial aspects of the strike were unimportant. The miners suddenly became confident, proud and aggressive.

CHAPTER 17

CONTRADICTIONS

The Political Setting

The miners' strike had taken place within a period of intensifying political action by trade unions. The struggle against the Industrial Relations Act and the Upper Clyde Shipbuilders' dispute with the Government continued throughout the strike and afterwards. There was a mounting campaign by the Trade Union Movement against entry into the European Economic Community. So, although the miners' victory was an historic one in that it was a purposeful use of industrial action against the Government, it was not the only such act. The country was alive with them.

When the strike ended, therefore, the raised consciousness of the miners was not allowed to collapse through a mixture of euphoria and exhaustion. The miners had broken the Government's incomes policy but they had not stood alone, isolated, as the great disruptors of political convention. Hardly before they had got their breath back they were involved at local and national levels in various challenges against the Government. At the time it seemed to many participants that great changes were afoot and that politics would never be the same again.

The trade unions were reacting strongly to the impact of the high and rising level of unemployment, the sharply rising prices and the attempts of the Government to impose a consensus in industrial relations through the constraints of the Industrial Relations Act. Unemployment in the first half of 1972 was at its highest level since the end of the Second World War. At the same time the Government was withdrawing the financial support for ailing firms which the previous Labour Government had provided. The combination of these factors had sparked off the occupation of four shipbuilding yards on the Clyde which under the direction of the shipyard shop stewards caused the Government to reverse its industrial policy in May, 1972.

Meanwhile the campaign against the Industrial Relations Act was intensified largely as a reaction to its application. The Act, which was not fully operative during the miners' strike, was used in April, 1972, to impose a 14 day cooling off period during a railway dispute. When the cooling-off period ended without agreement the Government applied to the National Industrial Relations Court for a compulsory ballot of all railwaymen. The result, announced on 31st May, showed that 90 per cent of all railwaymen voted and that 85 per cent of these were in favour of industrial action. The Act, in effect, had transformed an industrial dispute into a question of loyalty to trade unions.

221

The political momentum of trade union action was maintained by the actions of dockers in Liverpool and London in refusing to handle containerized cargo. In March, 1972 a transport firm operating in Liverpool reported the dispute as an unfair industrial act to the National Industrial Relations Court thus bringing the Act, which the Trades Union Congress and unions in general refused to acknowledge, let alone operate, on to the industrial scene. The Court ruled against the dockers, placed the responsibility for their action on to the Transport and General Workers' Union and fined it. The reality was different. Dockers continued their dispute as if nothing to the contrary had happened — but transferred their attention to the Midland Coal Storage Company in London. The Liverpool proceedings were repeated but this time 5 London dockers were imprisoned for contempt of court. The union reactions were immediate. On Friday, 21st July, the day of the arrests, a strike movement began to roll starting with the dockers, then printers on national newspapers. By Monday, 24th July, it included miners and engineering workers. Two days later the General Council of the T.U.C. called for a one-day general strike to be held on Monday, 31st July. That same evening the court ordered the release of the dockers, without conditions. The sympathetic strikes, which were illegal under the Act, ended the next day. The general strike was cancelled.

The Industrial Relations Act continued to be applied and equally defied, mainly by the Amalgamated Union of Engineering Workers. There were strikes against the Act right through to the end of the year but during 1973 it tended to be ignored with impunity.

The Wages Claim and Government Policy

In the midst of this political excitement the miners went through their annual ritual of formulating their Area motions early in the year and debating them at the Annual Conference in July. The difficulty this time was that the Areas could not frame their wages motions until after the end of the strike for they had no idea what figures to put in. Right at the deadline for the submission of motions for the Annual Conference the Kent Area put one in with figures: £30 for surface workers, £32 for underground workers and £40 for face workers. This amounted to a 16 per cent increase for face workers. There were no divisions in the Conference over it. The National Executive Committee added its support and the motion was accepted unanimously. The emphasis was not wholly on wages. Both the Scottish and the Yorkshire Areas attempted to start a movement for shorter working hours, pointing out that underground workers worked longer hours in 1972 than they had in 1919. The two Areas wanted a 30 hour week underground and this too was endorsed by the Conference. It was difficult, however, to distract the miners

222

from wage increases. There had never been a concerted militant campaign for a reduction in working hours. Wages had always been regarded as the primary subsistence issue. When the N.U.M. negotiating committee met in October, 1972, it decided to make a package demand to the N.C.B. comprising wages, a narrowing of wage differentials and hours of work.

The Union's claim was politely turned down by the National Coal Board. The Board thought that the Union's objectives were commendable but beyond its capability. The costs were too great and it provided figures as proof. The negotiations were allowed to drag on for neither the Union nor the Board negotiators wanted to hurry into a second strike. The Board's final offer was put to the Union N.E.C. on 16th March, 1973 and rejected as being unsatisfactory. In accordance with the terms of the Conference decision arrangements were made for a national ballot vote of the members "to ascertain whether they were in favour of the National Executive Committee being given authority to call a national strike or other industrial action . . ." At this stage the impression was that there was going to be a repetition of the action experienced in the autumn of 1971.

The Government had discarded its policy of trying to contain wage demands through confrontation between employers and unions after the miners' strike. For some months afterwards unions which could not have succeeded through confrontations with the Government benefited from the miners' success, for the Government had no policy. Then, in complete contradiction with its declared means for tackling economic problems, the Government introduced a statutory wages policy in November, 1972. The Counter-Inflation (Temporary Provisions) Act enabled the Government to freeze wages, prices, rents and dividends for an interim period of 90 days. As with all counter-inflation policies since 1947 it affected wages substantially but influenced prices and profits only marginally at the most. The Government had no mechanism for regulating prices and, in any event, pursued budgetary policies which ensured that prices and profits would rise. From the April, 1972 budget the Government embarked on a policy of substantial economic expansion. The growth rate of the economy rose to 6 per cent from the middle of 1972 to the spring of 1973. Profits rose so that on average they were 25 per cent higher in 1973 than they had been in 1972. The expansion, however, could not be met by home production and induced, therefore, a sharp increase in imports which pushed up the cost of imported goods and raw materials and created a large balance of payments deficit. The Government had simply added another dimension to its problems, without reducing the rate of inflation.

The Government's interim measures of November were replaced

in January, 1973 by a Counter-Inflation Act which established a Pay Board and a Price Commission to regulate pay and prices according to a Pay and Prices Code. The Act set out the details of Stage Two of the Government's pay policy. In this Stage the total annual increases for any one group of workers was not allowed to exceed the sum which would result from the payment of £1 a week plus 4 per cent of the current wage bill of that group, excluding overtime. Negotiators could decide on the manner of distributing the sum but no individual could obtain an increase of more than £250 in the year. Wage settlements were not to be made more frequently than every 12 months. The N.U.M. negotiations with the Coal Board were conducted during the period of Stage I of the Government's pay policy and whilst discussions about Stage II were taking place. The National Coal Board's final offer remained within the limits of Stage Two and amounted to an average increase of £2.29 a week.

There was pronounced hostility in the trade union movement to the Government's policy. The General Council of the T.U.C. refused to discuss the details of the policy with the Government or to put its representatives on the Pay Board and the Price Commission. A special Congress of the T.U.C. was held on 5th March to discuss the Government's policy. It called on the General Council "to organize and lead co-ordinated action in support of affiliated unions in dispute and who request such support" and to organize as quickly as possible a day of national protest and stoppage against the wage control policy and increases in food prices. The continuing hostility towards the Industrial Relations Act was reinforcing opposition in other areas of Government policy.

The Spread of Left Wing Influence

The ballot of the miners was held during the heat of the campaign against the Government, just after the Special T.U.C. Congress and before the 1st May day of action. There were conflicting reports about the miners' willingness to repeat the 1972 confrontation. The left wing leaders campaigned but found it difficult to influence the mood of their members because there was not an upsurge of hostility towards the Government's policy. The influence of Union leaders at all levels was always expressed through tapping and moulding feelings already felt by the ordinary members. They never created those feelings.

Yet despite an uncertainty about the miners' attitude towards the Government's policy there was a marked swing towards the left in the election of full-time officials in the N.U.M. The first election in Yorkshire after the strike was to fill the post of Compensation Agent left vacant by the death of Sammy Taylor. Arthur Scargill had already been selected as the sole left-wing candidate and was the best known miner in Yorkshire in March,1972. He had a natural

Hemsworth colliery, Yorkshire, in 1973.

flair for attracting publicity and, because of his confident and intelligent commentaries, he appeared regularly on television in Yorkshire. He had achieved national notoriety for his part in the Saltley Gate affair. He had not been the only possible left wing candidate before the strike but after it he stood out on his own and easily won the election. The National Executive Committee position which became vacant with Sammy Taylor's death was filled by Owen Briscoe, the left wing candidate. Jock Kane retired in June, 1972 and was replaced on the N.E.C. by Arthur Scargill in September. Thus Scargill had a national platform for the first time. His influence in Yorkshire increased because there was a leadership vacuum due to the illness of both the president and general secretary of the Area. For a time Scargill became the acting general secretary.

There were growing tensions amongst left wing miners in the Yorkshire Area as opportunities for official positions increased and potential candidates competed with each other. Long arguments took place about the rights of succession. Personality problems also emerged because Scargill's popularity enabled him to pick and choose posts and others resented this. When Sam Bullough, the Area president died in January 1973 his position was taken by Scargill who received 26,362 votes compared with 15,007 votes for the other two candidates combined. The vice-president, who normally would have succeeded the president, came at the bottom of the poll. Despite the tensions, however, the Yorkshire Area had a left wing president. There were other changes in the Area later in 1973 when Peter Tait, a Communist Party member, succeeded a right wing representative on the N.E.C. and Owen Briscoe, the left wing candidate became the Area general secretary in place of Sid Schofield who resigned through ill-health. The transformation of the Yorkshire Area which a small number of left wing miners had aimed for in 1967 was virtually completed in 1973. Pits began to elect left wing delegates to the Yorkshire Area Council and as representatives on the Area executive committee. For Arthur Scargill, Owen Briscoe, Peter Tait, Johnny Weaver, Martin Redman, Ian Ferguson, Don Baines, Ron Rigby and others, it was a success story. The militancy of the working miners began to be matched by the politics of their representatives and officials.

There were important changes at national level and in two Areas. Michael McGahey was elected as vice-president of the national Union in July, 1973. This position was the only national one elected by the Conference. It was held for two years at a time and was preceded by intensive canvassing. In 1973 the decision of the normally right-wing Midlands Area to support McGahey gained him the election. The vice-president of the Union, though a part-time national official, confers with the president and general secretary on matters delegated by the N.E.C. in between meetings. He can, if he wishes,

Peter Heathfield, who had been elected Secretary of the Derbyshire Area of the N.U.M. in 1973, second from the right at the Scottish Miners' Gala in Edinburgh, June 1977. Also in the picture are Betty Heathfield, flanked by Michael McGahey on her right and Ray Buckton, General Secretary of the Associated Society of Locomotive Engineers and Firemen, on her left. Tony Benn is just behind Ray Buckton. At the far end of the picture is Bill McLean in a light raincoat while at the near end is David Bolton, then the Vice-President of the Scottish Area of the N.U.M.

assume many of the responsibilities which go with the other national positions. He can engage in exploratory talks with the N.C.B. and the Government, lead delegations, and in many ways participate in the activities of the president and general secretary. McGahey intended to do all of these things. His election, therefore, was of material as well as symbolic significance for the left wing.

The commitment of the South Wales and Derbyshire Areas to progressive trade unionism was re-inforced during 1973 by the election of Emlyn Williams as the South Wales Area president and of Peter Heathfield as the secretary of the Derbyshire Area. Emlyn Williams had been active since 1967 in the campaign to raise the consciousness of the miners. Derbyshire, partly because of its proximity to Nottingham, had constantly to be won over to progressive policies so that Peter Heathfield had a difficult, continuing task of persuasion.

These changes in personnel altered the political composition of the National Executive Committee. The rump of left wing members during 1972 came within striking distance of a majority by the end of 1973. They commanded a fairly consistent core of 11 votes and intensified the struggle for the waverers on the N.E.C. The left-wing was almost in a dominant position in the Union as a whole at this stage. Its main drawback was that it did not control the presidency and this, as is shown later, was a crucial stumbling block.

Contradictions in Miners' Attitudes

When the national ballot was held on the wages issue on the 27th and 28th March, 1973, the balance of the evidence pointed to a majority for strike action. The miners, with the 1972 victory still fresh in their minds, had no need to fear the consequences of striking; they were confronted by the same Conservative Government as before and were subjected to a restrictive incomes policy which allowed them much less than they demanded and which the National Executive Committee recommended them to reject. This evidence seemed to overshadow that from individual officials who found little enthusiasm for a strike amongst the ordinary miners.

The result of the ballot was an emphatic rejection of the call for strike action with 63.38 per cent voting against it. There were small majorities for strike action in Yorkshire and Scotland but in all other Areas the majorities were for compliance with the Government's policy. Immediately following this the wages offer from the Coal Board was accepted and Government's incomes policy was left intact. The Phase I 90 day freeze lasted for nearly five months and ended on 31st March. The miners' ballot result on 3rd April came at just the right time to enable the Government to embark with some confidence on Phase II of its policy. During the pay freeze few of the major unions were involved in claims. There were substantial strikes against the conditions of Phase II by gas workers, civil servants and hospital ancillary workers but none of the traditionally militant groups such as the miners, dockers and car workers, opposed it. This Phase was replaced by a third one on 7th November, 1973, by which time the miners were processing another wages claim in a changed context.

The right wing members of the National Executive Committee welcomed the result of the ballot even though they had recommended the opposite. They had not campaigned in their Areas to get their members to support the N.E.C. Their militancy, if such it can be called, began and ended at the monthly meetings of the N.E.C. They had been given directions by the Annual Conference and felt obliged by the rules of the Union to follow them to the letter. They were, for a time, in a constitutional straightjacket. But this was not the case with the representatives from Scotland, South Wales, Yorkshire, Kent and Derbyshire, plus Joe Whelan from Nottingham who were utilizing the constitution and expanding their influence through it. For them the ballot result posed a serious contradiction.

Just what had happened to the consciousness of the miners? Where was the political awareness which had been visible in 1972? Why was there this apparent contradiction between increasing left wing influence and the attitude of the miners as expressed through the ballot? Perhaps something somewhere had been misjudged. What was it? These questions dogged the minds of Michael McGahey and others in the months following the April ballot vote. They were not answered definitively but enough was learned about the make-up of miners to recognize what the campaign had lacked. The deficiencies were repaired in the next round of negotiations.

There had been a tendency to view the behaviour of miners in 1972 as a sign of a real, profound alteration in their attitudes rather than as a response to a particular situation. This was encouraged by the fact that when the miners and their officials recognized that in order to obtain their demands they would have to force concessions from the Government, even change its policy, they did not get cold feet and start scheming to retreat. That appeared to be a new and ominous sign for the Government. The miners showed through the 1973 ballot, however, that they did not have political motives. They simply wanted wage increases. They were entirely pragmatic in their approach. In this respect their attitude was as it had always been. So, on the one hand they were willing to strike and, if necessary to strike against the Government while on the other hand they were simply interested in securing an incremental improvement in their living standards. They did not make any correlation between the manner in which they struggled for subsistence and the capitalist system.

This did not mean that the miners' actions were not political. The extent and nature of the intervention of the Government made every attempt to increase labour costs above the limit set by its policies a political act. In the same way every breach of its complex Industrial Relations Act was a political act. In other words, despite themselves the miners were using industrial action for political ends. So what had been seen during the 1972 strike was not a raised political awareness so much as the imposition of political consequences upon ordinary economic demands. The crisis in the capitalist system which required the intervention of the Government to ensure its temporary survival brought its own contradiction by creating political consequences which threatened that survival.

When the next wage demand came round after the 1972 strike the miners were interested only in that demand and not in taking on the Government. Indeed, it is likely that they consciously did not want to take on the Government again. The refusal of trade unionists to use industrial action for political ends was historically determined, deeply ingrained and constantly reinforced by propaganda. That attitude would only be discarded if the precise conditions of the moment were favourable and quite clearly they were not so in 1973.

The miners in 1973, in fact, were not sure what they were fighting for. Their wage demand had become submerged in a basket of demands and it was this basket which was rejected by the National Coal Board. When the miners voted it was not just about wages but also about pensions, concessionary smokeless fuel, redundancy pay, sick pay, working hours, holidays and a productivity scheme. This claim was destined to created confusion. It was a well-worn tactic that in order to defuse one issue it should be related to others which could be more or less satisfactorily settled.

Lastly, it was unreal to expect miners to commit themselves to a major confrontation without some actual evidence that the issue was worth it. They had to have evidence which would over-ride the intense ideological pressures not to strike. There had, therefore, to be a campaign in the pits. From the time of the 1972 Annual Conference until March 16th the following year the Union claim, its extent and character were the property of the National Executive Committee. In the left wing Areas there was some debate but it was overshadowed by rumour. In the other Areas the issue was hidden except in so far as miners read references to it in *The Miner* or *Coal News*. The only time provided for active campaigning in preparation for the ballot was during the 10 days in between the day when the Executive decided to reject the Coal Board's offer and the date of the ballot. The left wing members of the N.E.C. tried to persuade it to hold a delegate conference before the ballot but they were unsuccessful. A delegate conference would have expressed an opinion about the issue more forcibly than the N.E.C. and it would have provided delegates with facts and arguments to put to their branches.

The real evidence which was lacking, however, was an awareness of the actual rate they were being given for their labour power. Many miners worked overtime which created an illusory and inflated impression of their earning capacity. In this respect, the experience of 1971 should have been remembered for the overtime ban then showed how niggardly was the base rate, how divisive overtime payments were and how hostile management was when it could not use overtime to cover its own deficiencies.

The Overtime Ban

In 1973 the branches and Areas of the N.U.M. had to discuss and formulate their ideas about wage increases before the negotiations over the 1972 wages demand had been completed and prior to the ballot vote which rejected strike action. The motions which went forward then from the Areas to the Union Annual Conference in July, 1973, were based on the previous year's claim and not on what was finally negotiated. The one which was accepted, demanding £35 a week for surface workers, £40 for underground workers and £45 for face workers, therefore, involved relatively high percentage increases. The delegates, however, were not interested in moderating their demands. They lived in a rapidly deteriorating economic environment due to Britain's entry into the European Economic Community and the rises in the price of oil which, they felt, necessitated a large proportionate increase in wages.

The possibility of taking industrial action of some kind was raised during the debate at the Conference even though there had been such a momentous NO to strike action just three months before. This was not anomalous for although the refusal of the miners to engage in strike action was explicable in March it seemed irrelevant in July. Miners in a number of ways had begun to show signs of militancy following the ballot vote. The General Council of the T.U.C. organized a day of national protest on 1st May, 1973 as part of a nation-wide campaign against the Government's pay and prices policy. The N.U.M. nationally declined to take part in the protest because its rules forbade it to engage in national strike action without previously balloting its members but the Areas did participate and 113 of the National Coal Board's 281 pits went on strike. In South Wales, where there had not been a sufficient majority for a strike in the ballot, the whole coalfield stopped work. Altogether 70,000 out of 280,000 miners took part in the stoppage.

Later on the traditionally moderate Nottingham miners began to show signs of unease. The Nottingham miners, with the exception of those in one pit, had rejected the T.U.C. call for action. But they had a grievance which could not be settled within the terms of the Government's policy, so early in September, 1973, they and the Derbyshire miners decided to ban night-shift working from 1st

November in order to get improved shift-payments. In both Areas the pressure for action came from the pits and not from the officials.

When Michael McGahey led the wages debate at the Annual Conference he raised the question of banning overtime, adding "let us start thinking in terms of various forms of industrial action." He was supported in this by many left wing delegates who began agitating for an overtime ban to start on 1st November, the traditional completion date for wage claims before the Wilberforce Award had altered it. After the summer holidays the demand escalated as the Yorkshire Area, then South Wales and Scotland joined with other Areas in lobbying the Union N.E.C. in October in order to get a ban. In some Areas individual pits began using the overime ban as a device for their own particular grievances, as did Dawdon colliery, one of the biggest pits in the north east coalfield, at the end of September. Miners adjusted to the idea of banning overtime before a national decision was taken to enforce one.

The wages claim was rejected by the Board in October. The National Executive Committee took its case to the Prime Minister who, obviously influenced by the rank and file rejection of strike action earlier, made no concessions to it. Two days after this meeting, on 25th October, the Executive recommended a complete ban on all overtime. The next day a Special Conference of the Union put the issue to the branches, some of which, in Durham for example, began operating the ban as soon as they had voted in favour of it. There was an eagerness for action in the traditionally moderate areas such as Northumberland, Durham and Nottingham. When the Areas voted on the issue there was no opposition. The ban was imposed "with effect from the first production shift on Monday, 12th November, 1973."

The Oil Crisis

There was talk about an impending oil crisis throughout 1973 arising from a growing world shortage and the ability of the main oil producing nations to exploit it by pushing up oil prices. The drastic contraction of the coal industries in Western capitalist countries during the 1960s had increased the demand for imported oil. In 1973 about 64 per cent of energy requirements of the European Economic Community was satisfied by oil and 95 per cent of this was imported from the Middle East and Nigeria. The U.S.A. had changed from being self-sufficient in oil to become a major importer. The oil needs of Japan, which was entirely dependent upon foreign sources, had grown with its industrial expansion. As each capitalist country anticipated an energy crisis in the 1980s, its attempts to protect its own interests in competition with others made the crisis more likely to be sooner than later. There was no coordinated response to the problem by capitalist countries nor was there one between the members of the European Economic Community. In Britain there was not even an energy policy which related and integrated the different sources and uses of energy. There was just a discussion about possible solutions, including the expansion of the coal industry.

The crisis began to be real and immediate during the spring of 1973 when the Organization of Petroleum Exporting Countries (OPEC) issued an ultimatum to the oil companies to produce a "positive" price offer or face counter measures. The reaction of the oil companies, accustomed to negotiating from a power base of imperialism, was typified by the chief company negotiator for British Petroleum who said that B.P. had no plans to contact O.P.E.C. for "We have been confronted with this kind of thing before."* But the power base had been eroded. The oil exporting countries had lost an estimated 11.11 per cent of their revenue due to the devaluation of the dollar in February, 1973 and, under pressure from Libya, were seeking compensation and a new system for fixing crude oil prices. For this purpose, and the growing recognition that they could use oil as a weapon in their conflict with Israel, the Arab countries raised the price of oil and cut back on supplies. The Arab war with Israel which broke out on 6th October, 1973 was a catalyst for action over oil. The Gulf States took unilateral action to fix crude oil prices and raised them by 66 per cent on 16th October. They then banned supplies to the U.S.A. and planned to cut exports by 5 per cent a month. The increased prices accelerated existing inflationary pressures while the cutback in supplies intensified existing shortages. The oil consuming countries in the West were forced to take emergency measures to economise in the use of fuel. This was the situation when the miners' ban on overtime began on Monday, 12th November, 1973.

The Government's Reaction

It is difficult to state whether the Government's reactions to the ban were the result of a conscious plan to discredit the miners by turning public opinion against them or were caused by hysteria. They were, in any event, drastic and immediate. The Government declared a State of Emergency the day following the start of the ban, before any of its effect could be seen. On this occasion, in contrast to 1971 and 1972, it entered the dispute as a prime participant. On Thursday, 15th November, the Prime Minister spoke on television about the miners' dispute. He mentioned that petrol rationing might be a possible consequence and raised a question which was to loom larger later concerning the political motives of the miners. If the miners' action was political, he said, then they would be confronting Parliament. Having sown this seed in the minds of people the Government went on assiduously to cultivate it.

* *The Guardian*, 25th April, 1973.

The Government took further steps the following week when it ordered oil companies to cut their fuel deliveries to petrol stations and industrial and private consumers by 10 per cent. It became illegal to buy petrol in cans and motorists were urged to observe a voluntary speed limit of 50 miles per hour. The Government embarked on a widespread press and television campaign about the need to conserve fuel. About three weeks later, new, drastic, unprecedented restrictions were imposed. It was estimated that by then coal supplies had fallen to 40 per cent below the normal level. The new measures were:

(a) Further savings of 20 per cent of overall electricity consumption but without rota cuts.

(b) Industry and commerce to be limited to a total of five days working over the two weeks from Monday, 17th December till 31st December.

(c) In the New Year the working week was to be limited to three specified days, either Monday, Tuesday and Wednesday, or Thursday, Friday and Saturday.

(d) The working days were to be specified in advance by the Electricity Boards. The number of working hours was not to be increased.

(e) Penalties for infringing the regulations by industrial users were to be a £400 fine or three months' imprisonment.

(f) Shops and offices were allowed to open on no power days but were forbidden to use electricity for heating and lighting.

(g) It was permissible to use electricity for all types of office machinery, communications equipment and lifts.

(h) Continuous process production was exempt from these restrictions, except that it was limited to 65 per cent of normal electricity consumption.

(i) Essential industry and services, such as food manufacture, fuel, newspapers, railways, ports and water supply were also exempt.

(j) Food shops, restaurants and premises used for sport and entertainment were excluded from the restrictions.

(k) Television was to close down not later than 10.30 p.m. each evening, except over Christmas and on New Year's Eve.

(l) Voluntary savings were urged on domestic users. Electric space heating should be confined to one room per house, for restricted periods and with lower temperatures.

These measures were applied from 1st January, 1974. They affected the profitibility of firms, reduced earnings and caused numerous inconveniences to people at large. They provided all the signs of a crisis.

The Miners' Response

The miners' first response to the Government's reactions was one of amazement. They were perplexed by the speed with which the

Emergency Powers Act had been promulgated. The amazement turned to suspicion as different restrictions were introduced. The officials in the right wing Areas were particularly affected by the Government's behaviour for after all, they said, they were only applying an overtime ban. The miners were still working a normal week. As the suspicion developed so attitudes hardened and miners began to see the measures as a means of defeating them rather than as a way of protecting community interests. The solidarity-making factors which had worked in 1971 also worked this time so that a widespread determination to win the dispute evolved as the weeks went by. A willingness to ban overtime but an ambivalence towards strike action was transformed into a willingness to strike which was far more general and determined than in 1971.

Phase III of the Government's pay policy permitted an increase of 7 per cent on basic rates or £2.27 a week, whichever was the greater. The National Coal Board had offered the miners terms which were consistent with the Government's policy but which exploited the flexibility it contained so that the offer really represented about a 13 per cent increase. The actual terms contained an increase of £2.25 a week for surface workers and £2.50 a week for underground workers plus an improved shift allowance, an extra statutory holiday, a threshold agreement, a productivity scheme which would yield up to 50 per cent of the wage increase and a sum equalling 1 per cent of the wages bill to be used for one or other of a variety of small anomolies. The terms were to apply from 1st March, 1974. The rejection of them led to the overtime ban.

Subsequent negotiations rejigged the offer so that increases of between 7 per cent for face workers and 9.4 per cent for non-craft daywage men underground became possible. This too was rejected on 21st November. Then the National Executive Committee met the Prime Minister and members of the Cabinet on 28th November. At this stage it was clear that the N.C.B. was merely a messenger for the Government. The Prime Minister tried to persuade the N.E.C. to accept the latest offer by reminding its members of the problems the Government faced and the policies it was pursuing. There was no question, he stated of Phase III being abandoned, altered or sidestepped. Mr. Heath explained that the Government recognized the importance of the coal industry and had taken on heavy financial commitments to secure its future. But nothing was said by either side which was fresh. There were no new persuasive elements present. The left wing members were unaffected by the status and glamour of No. 10 Downing Street, where the meeting was held. Some had been there in 1972 and they adopted the same attitude of cynical detachment to their surroundings and the same irreverent approach to members of the Cabinet which had protected them from seduction before. They made outspoken comments.

Mr. McGahey said that he wanted to see the Government fall while Lawrence Daly insisted that the Union was determined to force the withdrawal of the prices and incomes legislation. This meeting, because it involved no negotiations, was counter-productive for the Government. The N.E.C. reaffirmed the overtime ban and also decided not to hold a ballot vote on the question of strike action at that time.

There was much backstage activity after the meeting with the Prime Minister in order to try and find a formula which would satisfy the miners' leaders. A lot of attention was given to the suggestion that miners should be paid for unpaid time spent in the pits, that is for the period when a miner is preparing for descent and getting bathed and changed after the shift. It was also suggested that European Coal and Steel Community funds might be used to provide a State payment for underground workers or to help to recruit and stabilize labour. The Coal Board was willing to negotiate terms for waiting and bathing time provided they satisfied the Pay Board but this depended on whether or not they fell within the terms of Phase III. This particular issue was dropped early in January when the Pay Board ruled that waiting-time payments would infringe the Pay Code. No formulas were found which could provide both extra cash and a plausible reason for contemplating ending the dispute. The stumbling block each time was the Phase III Code. Although the Prime Minister and the Secretary of State for Employment admitted that the Phase III policy was designed to meet the needs of the miners its restrictive conditions consistently prevented a settlement of the dispute being reached. Of course, it may have been that the working miners were not interested in trimmings but simply wanted their base rate raised substantially. This point was being made in the left-wing Areas.

There were some pressures within the Union to ballot the members about the Coal Board offer and to call off the overtime ban. When a motion to hold a ballot in order to test the miners' attitudes towards the overtime ban was put at an N.E.C. meeting on 13th December only 5 members supported it. These men represented the white collar workers and four of the smallest Areas in the Union, namely Cumberland, Group 1, the Power Group and Power Group No. 2. The Chairman of the N.C.B. found it increasingly difficult to understand why a ballot was not being held. The feeling amongst the majority of the N.E.C., however, was why ballot for a strike when the overtime ban was having the effect of a strike without the loss of wages to the miners concerned. There were other factors such as an unwillingness to take a step which might lead to a strike or a feeling that the strike call might be rejected. There was a public demonstration of the attitude of some miners towards the ban when Mr. Frank Smith, the secretary of the Leicestershire Area, called for an

236

end to it early in January and provoked unofficial strikes in his own pits against himself. After this there were only isolated and unimportant objections, such as a demand to end the ban from members of the Colliery Officials and Staffs' Association at Ashington pit in Northumberland. The strongest pressures on the N.E.C. were to strengthen the ban.

Some doubts about the continued usefulness of the ban began to affect the attitudes of Union leaders during the course of January. There was the coal stocks position. Although the overtime ban had caused coal production to fall from 2.4 million tons a week to 1.7 million tons by the 10th January, 1974, the three day working week had reduced coal consumption by roughly the same proportion so that coal stocks were being maintained. There was, moreover, no sign of a break in the determination of the Prime Minister to preserve the Government pay policy. He had rejected a unique initiative from the General Council of the T.U.C. The General Council had intervened mainly because of its concern about the effect of the Government measures on trade unionists. More than 1 million workers had been laid off by the middle of January. Its Economic Committee announced on 9th January that:

"The General Council accept that there is a distinctive and exceptional situation in the mining industry. If the Government are prepared to give an assurance that they will make possible a settlement between the miners and the N.C.B., other unions will not use that as an argument in negotiations for their own settlement."

This offer to treat the miners as a special case was put to the Government at a meeting of the National Economic Development Council. The Chancellor of the Exchequer, who was present, reacted by stating that the T.U.C. had no power over individual unions to enforce its offer. This attitude of disbelief was repeated by a Government spokesman in the House of Commons. The T.U.C. held a conference of union presidents and general secretaries on 16th January which endorsed the initiative yet five days later the Prime Minister informed the T.U.C. that he was unable to respond to it. The Government had the power to deal with a wage claim on an exceptional basis under its Counter Inflation Act but it would not say under what conditions it would use the power. Following this, Mr. Heath appealed to the N.E.C. to accept the offer and then discuss the future with the N.C.B. and the Government. It was a situation of stalemate.

The Ballot Vote

Feelings of exasperation at the lack of progress began to be expressed in the coalfields. Area delegate meetings were demanding an escalation of the struggle. Left wing members of the N.E.C. came out openly in favour of strike action. For instance, Bill McLean, the general secretary of the Scottish Area, declared that the overtime ban had served its purpose and that a full-scale stoppage should take its place.* Miners in many Areas reacted to the frustrations caused by the ban by striking over managerial attempts to overcome its consequences. Their situations politicized them. They became exasperated and frustrated but not disillusioned. When the National Executive Committee met on 24th January its members were already convinced that the time was suitable for a ballot. The day before the meeting, the president, Mr. Gormley, had made his views clear. "My opinion is," he said, "that the members are ripe to strengthen the industrial action . . . I shall be suggesting that we should now have a ballot for a national strike . . . I feel we would get a vote in the region of 70 per cent in support . . . "** The N.E.C. accepted his advice and arranged for a national ballot on 31st January and 1st February.

The miners' leaders' attitudes hardened. They refused to meet the Prime Minister again unless he came prepared to improve on the wages offer and they condemned the Government for not responding to the T.U.C. initiative. The days leading up to the ballot were dominated by political controversy. A few days before the ballot Mr. Heath accused the miners' leaders of pursuing a political confrontation designed to defeat the Conservative Government rather than trying to get a satisfactory wage settlement. He singled out Mr. McGahey, in particular, for wanting to smash Phase III, adding "that I mean smashing what is accepted as fair now by five million people and approved by Parliament, and to get rid of the elected government of the day . . ."** This theme was taken up by Conservative politicians and political commentators generally so that when the ballot was held the choice before the miners was between loyalty to their Union and loyalty to the elected Government. The matter of wages was submerged.

Mr. Heath's tactic was to transform the dispute into a constitutional issue by separating the Communist miners from the rest and accusing them of anti-democratic intentions. He hoped, it seemed, to split the miners into a large social democratic majority and a small but influential Communist rump and have them attack each other. The Prime Minister was helped by some remarks made by Mr. McGahey concerning the use of troops in the event of a strike. Mr. McGahey had said at a meeting in Scotland that if troops were used then miners would speak to them and explain their case to them. This was interpreted as attempting to subvert the armed forces and he was attacked widely. Union officials in some right wing Areas dissociated themselves from Mr. McGahey's views; the Union president emphasized that he alone spoke for the Union and

*   *Glasgow Herald*, 21st January, 1974.
**   *The Times*, 23rd January, 1974.
*** *The Times*, 29th January, 1974.

not those "people who are using the miners' dispute for political motives;" the Parliamentary Labour Party Shadow Cabinet tabled a motion repudiating the statements made by Mr. McGahey and persuaded many Members of Parliament to support it. For a time Mr. McGahey became the butt for political denigration and, though he insisted that his words had been distorted and taken out of their context, he remained as a justification for a powerful press campaign to isolate and condemn Communist miners.

The Prime Minister's tactic succeeded in so far as public attention was drawn to Communist miners and members of the Labour Movement attacked each other over them. The important question, however, was how much all of this influenced ordinary miners. What significance did the mass media have in moulding the attitudes of miners about their dispute compared with the influence of their conditions of work and the expressions of the Union? The issue of the constitution was not dodged by the left wing Union officials. A Yorkshire leaflet, for example, distributed on the eve of the ballot, quite plainly marked it out and urged miners to vote for solidarity with their Union. Very few miners voted in ignorance of the political implications of their decisions.

The result of the ballot astounded even the most optimistic militant members of the Union for 80.99 per cent of the 232,614 miners who had recorded valid votes were in favour of calling a national strike. There were majorities for strike action in every Area except C.O.S.A. which organized white collar workers. High majorities were expected in South Wales, where it was 93.15 per cent, Yorkshire, where it was 90.30 per cent, Scotland and Kent where it approached 90 per cent. The surprise lay in the voting figures for Durham which showed an 85.70 per cent majority, Nottingham with a 77.08 per cent majority and Lancashire (which had attacked Mr. McGahey) with an 82.02 per cent majority. There were large majorities in favour of strike action in all the small Areas represented by the N.E.C. members who had wanted to end the overtime ban. Under the circumstances of free elections it is difficult to imagine a greater expression of solidarity with a union than the miners showed on this occasion.

When the national officials of the Union met representatives of the Coal Board a few days before the ballot vote they anticipated a majority in favour of strike action and gave notice of a strike from midnight, 9th February. This was done, they said, to ensure that they complied with the minimum legal notice required of them. The N.E.C. endorsed this action on 5th February, 1974, and laid down conditions for the conduct of the strike.

CHAPTER 18

HISTORIC

A General Election

The miners' leaders made preparations for the strike with the memory of the 1972 national strike fresh in their minds, with the knowledge of its organization and the preconditions of its success. No miners' official in 1972 had benefited from experience of that kind. Some had never been involved in a widespread strike before 1972. Those who approached the 1974 strike cautiously knew what they wanted to avoid. It was clear that on this occasion they wanted to avoid the spontaneity of 1972, the relative autonomy of local strike committees and the confrontations. This time they wanted to control the strike from the national centre so that they could determine tactics and regulate its scope. They planned from the outset to contain the strike and, in so far as it was possible, to give it a respectable image. The national officials wanted the success of 1972 but none of its abrasive tactics which so obviously made that success possible. It is likely that if the conditions of 1972 had prevailed the strike would have been planned into failure. Things, however, were different in 1974. New conditions were present which tended to make the actual conduct of the strike less relevant for its success or failure than in 1972. In the end it really did not matter very much how the strikers behaved themselves, except that by containing the strike, keeping a low profile and showing some degree of conventional respectability they projected an image which did not invite so much retaliation and which made life easier for all concerned. Striking as they did in 1972 was a great emotional and physical strain. That, at any rate, was avoided in 1974.

The National Executive Committee of the N.U.M. laid plans for the strike a few days before it was due to begin but on the 7th February as its Strike Committee was meeting to add details to them, the Prime Minister announced that Parliament would be dissolved the following day and that a General Election would be held on 28th February, 1974. Thus what had been rumour for so long suddenly became fact. The Prime Minister immediately tried to get the strike called off. He wrote to Mr. Gormley stating "It is clearly desirable that during the General Election campaign the people should be able to concentrate their attention, in an atmosphere as undisturbed as possible, on the issue upon which they will be asked to cast their votes. In these circumstances, I ask the Executive Committee of the N.U.M. in the national interest very seriously to consider suspending the national coal strike during the period of the Election Campaign."

Mr. Gormley sympathised with the view of the Prime Minister

and argued for the suspension of the strike at a specially summoned meeting of the N.E.C. on Friday, 8th February. The case he put was recorded in the following minute of that meeting: "The purpose of the strike was to support the claim for an improvement in the present wages offer and this could only be forthcoming if the Government took the necessary action or changed its point of view. As a consequence of dissolution of Parliament there would be no effective Government for the next four weeks and therefore little or no authority to enable anyone to make the necessary money available to meet our claim. It was suggested that in these circumstances there was little point in commencing the strike as planned. It was true that the N.U.M. had the support of other unions, but everyone's activities would be concentrated in support of the Labour Party in the forthcoming Election. The Government it was reported had referred the miners' case to the Relativities Board; the Labour Party had called for an interim cash settlement and nothing more positive could be forthcoming during the Election. It was therefore proposed that the strike should be suspended so that the members would not be asked to strike during a period when no progress could be made."*

Mr. Gormley had little support from the N.E.C. which agreed by 20 votes to 6 to continue with the strike. Delegates and officials in South Wales, Scotland, Kent, Yorkshire and Nottingham had already made known their opposition to any move to delay the strike. Their reasons made sense to ordinary members. Both the overtime ban and the strike, the majority on the N.E.C. contended, were about wages and were not politically motivated. Although some of the left wing leaders had said that they would like to see the Conservative Government fall, none envisaged the strike as a means of achieving this aim. Emlyn Williams, the newly elected president of the South Wales Area, made this point when he stated: "For us to accept the letter of the Prime Minister that we withdraw strike action during the election campaign would be an acceptance by us that it is a political issue. We are not involved in political blackmail, but merely trying to bring to the attention of the public the deplorable wages of the miners." The political intentions attributed to miners' leaders by the Government and most of the media were calculated to swing opinion against the miners. But not even in the Scottish Area where there was a solidly based left wing leadership could a campaign have been waged in the coalfield which made political capital out of the wages struggle. In the view of most miners, the General Election and the political complexion of the Government had no direct relevance for the strike. Arthur Scargill represented the extreme spectrum of this view when he stated that "a general election will not solve anything."** The National Executive

* Minutes of a Special Meeting of the National Executive Committee held at 222 Euston Road, London N.W.1 on Friday, 8th February, 1974.
** *Morning Star*, 8th February, 1974.

Committee simply wanted a Government which would accede to its demands and that could be achieved without an election.

It was thought, moreover, that it would be impractical to interfere with the strike. In the first place it would be difficult to call the strike off because there had been such a large majority in favour of it. The Yorkshire Area secretary, Owen Briscoe, put this point when he said before the special N.E.C. meeting "that if the strike was called off the lads themselves would carry it on." When the miners voted for the strike in such large numbers they were aware of the possibility of an election for they knew about the election rumours. Secondly, if the strike were postponed it would tend to lose its momentum and would be difficult to restart. And lastly the Government and the National Coal Board could use the period of the election to build up coal stocks so that miners would be strategically weaker at the end of the election than they were at its beginning.

The decision to continue with the strike was interpreted by the Prime Minister as another example of the influence of subversive forces in the N.U.M. This was made clear in a statement from No. 10 Downing Street on Saturday, 9th February in which he thanked Mr. Gormley and some of his moderate colleagues for trying to prevent the strike from starting and then added: "It is a matter for deep regret that their arguments have been overruled and that we are now prevented from holding the election in an atmosphere of industrial peace.

"We have lost the opportunity to go back immediately to a five-day working week, and as a result jobs, industrial production and exports will all be put in jeopardy . . .

"I know that the miners themselves are democrats. It is therefore especially disappointing that the politically motivated arguments of some of their leaders should have prevailed."

Mr. Heath hoped that the Executive would review its decision before it was too late. But no review took place. The last minute cancellation of a strike has rarely been received with relief by workers whose usual reactions have been of indignation, let-down, even of betrayal. The collapse of the Triple Alliance strike, involving miners, railwaymen and transport workers on the day it was due to begin, Friday, 15th April, 1921, and described as 'Black Friday' in the annals of trade union history, still figured in the folklore of miners. If the strike had been cancelled or suspended Mr. Joe Gormley might easily have entered the records with the reputation of J. H. Thomas who led the National Union of Railwaymen out of the Triple Alliance strike and was never, for the remainder of his life, allowed to forget the consequences. As it was, Mr. Gormley supported the N.E.C. decision and denounced Mr. Heath's appeal as a "political ploy." The strike began as scheduled.

Who Governs Britain?
The strike was not a politically motivated one in the sense meant by
Mr. Heath but it was political. As I showed earlier the political
content of industrial action was the creation of Government intervention rather than the changing political consciousness of the
workers. The 1974 miners' strike was highly political for this reason.
Once the election was called the National Union of Mineworkers
took sides in it and supported the Labour Party but then it had done
this in previous general elections irrespective of the reasons for
calling them. The Labour Party supported the miners in their dispute
but it had done so before an election seemed likely to be held.

The difference about this election was that it was called as a
means of resolving the miners' dispute. The scenario for it was
anticipated by political commentators as early as December, 1973.
On 21st of that month Alan Watkins, a political writer in the *New
Statesman,* wrote: "Let us have a look, to begin with, at the apoca-
lyptic thesis. According to this, Mr. Heath would appeal for a
'doctor's mandate' to carry out various unspecified measures of
'strong government' chiefly directed at 'militants' and 'trouble-
makers.' Who governs Britain? he would resoundingly ask. The
elected government? Or the brothers from the branches? This
setting was favoured by many Tory M.P.s and Ministers who wanted
to electioneer over the issue of the "Communist Conspiracy."

By the middle of January there were Conservative forecasts that
an election would result in a landslide victory in their favour and
pressures were put on the Prime Minister to call a quick, single issue
election. He was faced, he was advised, with two alternatives, either
sit out the strike in the hope of a capitulation by the miners or call an
election to give the Government the authority to take whatever
measures it thought necessary to resolve the dispute. The question
of going outside the limits of Phase III for a settlement was not
considered for the constitutional danger of this was seen by Conservatives as being too great. *The Times* spelled out this danger to its
readers on 9th January. "Mr. Heath's Government cannot survive if
they are seen to be defeated by the National Union of Mineworkers.
Such a defeat would not only destroy the authority of the Conservative
Government . . . (but) would involve damage to the constitutional
principle on which the authority of all governments in Britain is
based."* As the miners continued to hold out, intensified their
action and then voted so overwhelmingly for a strike, this kind of
reasoning persuaded those Cabinet Ministers who favoured a
negotiated settlement to opt for an election as a way out of the
impasse. There were some members of Mr. Heath's Cabinet, however, who had consistently pressed for a general election, who had
never been willing to compromise with the miners and who favoured

* *The Times,* 9th January, 1974.

a confrontation. If the Government had given way to the miners then Mr. Heath would most likely have been faced with resignations from some of these and his Government might have foundered through internal dissention.

The Government was in an untenable position. It intervened in the running of the economy on a large scale and in such a way as to touch the subsistence interests of workers at every important point so that trade unions could not take up even marginal matters concerning wages, hours of work and working conditions without offending Government policy. Yet, whenever this happened the Government cried 'constitutional crisis.' It used the authority of Parliament to give credibility to its policies of intervention thus transforming conventional trade union action to improve the living standards of their members into challenges to the authority of Parliament. Under these conditions the attitude that Parliamentary authority must take precedence over all other matters led inevitably to demands that the Government should be insulated from extra-parliamentary protests.

Where free trade unionism exists such insulation is not possible. In fact, historically, the ability of a Government to assert its absolute superiority and to get licence to do whatever it wishes has always depended on its ability to control, even suppress trade unions in the first instance. This was the case in fascist Italy in the 1920's, in Nazi Germany in the 1930's, in Franco's Spain and Salazar's Portugal. The Conservative Government in Britain from 1970 had tried to contain trade unions through its Industrial Relations Act but by 1974 it was as clear as daylight that the Act had failed.

The Conservative Government either had to live with militant trade unionism or suppress civil liberties. But it was not a real choice because it could not suppress civil liberties without first controlling trade unions. The only real option open to the Government in 1974 was to play according to the rules of Parliamentary Democracy in the hope that they would operate as they had done previously by intimidating trade unions. This meant calling an election over the issue of Parliamentary authority, winning it and hoping that the result would persuade miners in particular and trade unions in general into retreat for fear of offending the 'constitution.'

It is difficult to see what else the Government could have done. What it needed was a fresh mandate to govern as it wished. But the question then arose as to how it could interpret a fresh mandate to govern. Would this mean that the miners could be coerced into compliance if they refused to retract voluntarily? But how could coercive methods be applied in a way which would ensure that coal would be produced? Moreover, even if such methods could be devised, how could the rest of the trade union movement be prevented from retaliating on behalf of the miners without massive oppressive

Left to right: Bill McLean (Scotland), Joe Whelan (Notts), Michael McGahey (Vice-President), Eric Clarke (Scotland), on their way to an N.E.C. meeting in London during the 1974 miners' strike. Eric Clarke had joined the N.E.C. in November, 1973, to fill the vacancy caused by Michael McGahey's election as Vice-President. He subsequently became General Secretary of the Scottish Area after Bill McLean's death in 1977.

measures? And lastly how could the Government succeed in a new confrontation with the trade union movement when it had failed so miserably in the last one? The truth was that the Government was being forced into an election by circumstances it did not control and without any idea about how it should proceed if it won it.

Throughout most of December and the whole of January rumour pursued rumour. By the end of the third week of January, 1974 there was virtually an election fever with the Prime Minister being pressed in the House of Commons for a decision, one way or the other. The three day week persisted; the economic situation was deteriorating and it seemed likely that a drastic Easter budget would have to be introduced. The Government could not sit out a long strike. Mr. Heath had indicated that an early election was his last option but it was obvious by the end of January that it was his only option. His only influence was over timing and even that was limited. He needed a united Cabinet behind him in that the doves, such as Mr. Whitelaw, and the hawks, such as Lord Carrington, had to agree with each other. But the issue really had little to do with personalities, or with the idiosyncrasies of Mr. Heath. He just happened to be around at the time and gave it flavour.

In much the same way the scenario for the election was provided by the character of the crisis, namely the contradiction between the freedom implicit in social democracy and the need of Capitalism for a compliant labour force which employers could control with an authoritarian rule. The Government was obviously in dispute with all miners and it needed to be able to dictate their behaviour. But it could not blame or attack all miners, their wives and families, for this would have offended the ethics of social democracy. On the contrary, such a large and formidable group of workers had to be commended as 'democrats,' reminded of their 'common citizenship' with other people in Britain, praised for their 'basic moderation' and 'essential decency.' The Government could only account publicly for the uncompromising behaviour of the miners by claiming that they were being misled by their leaders. The miners leaders, however, were not of one kind as Mr. Heath made clear when he praised Mr. Gormley for attempting to get the strike called off. Some were opposed to industrial action, others favoured its use but were prepared to compromise, while a third section saw industrial action as a means of fulfilling the policy aims of the Union. The Government's target had to be the third section amongst whom was a recognizable group of Communists with an ideological commitment to changing the structure and character of British society. By highlighting this minority group as the main enemy the Government was able to maintain the pretence that there was a consensus in the society, an identity of interests between workers and employers, provided disruptive Communist elements could be controlled.

So it was that Michael McGahey, Bill McLean, Jack Collins, Peter Tait, Dai Francis and Joe Whelan with the Labour Party members, Eric Clarke, Arthur Scargill and Emlyn Williams, prominently bracketed with them, became the objects of an election campaign. The Prime Minister went on television on the day the election was announced to try to set the terms for the campaign. He said that a vote for the Conservative Party was a vote against the militants who wanted to disrupt industry, that some of the people in the miners' dispute had made it clear they wanted to bring down the elected Government and to change Britain's whole way of life. He added that "the great majority of you are fed up to the teeth with them and the disruption they cause. The election gives you a chance to make it clear to these people how you feel."

The Labour Party, on the other hand, committed itself to allowing the miners and the National Coal Board to negotiate freely if it won the election which, in effect, meant satisfying the miners' wages demand. But it refused to confine the election to one issue. Indeed the leader of the Labour Party, Mr. Harold Wilson, regarded the miners' dispute as a smokescreen behind which the Government wanted to make a "desperate run" for re-election. In a television broadcast on 8th February, he broadened the campaign to cover the economic incompetence of the Government. In the electioneering which followed a whole range of issues such as unemployment, inflation, the Industrial Relations Act and the European Economic Community, was raised by the Labour Party. The miners' dispute lingered in the experiences of everyone for the three-day week and power cuts continued but it did not dominate the election as Mr. Heath hoped it would.

The Strike Organization

The National Executive Committee of the N.U.M. made formal arrangements for the strike at its meeting on 5th February. In the first instance, it tried to make sure that the control of the strike would be centralized in its own hands. It stated that the administration of the strike should not be controlled by pit level liaison committees but by Area Liaison Committees comprising all sections of the Union in consultation with the National Strike Committee. It stipulated that if an emergency arose at a pit then it should be dealt with by the Area Liaison Committee after taking advice from the National Strike Committee. It also laid down that picketing should only take place after it had been authorized by the National Strike Committee. These regulations were aimed at curbing spontaneous picketing decisions involving the use of flying pickets and secondary picketing activities.

The detailed formalities for conducting the strike were made by the National Strike Committee on the day the general election was announced. This Committee, with a powerful coordinating function, was weighted in favour of the right-wing and contained two out of the seven members who had been consistently against the strike. Its three left wing members were Communists. The Committee prescribed picketing practice as follows:

"That selected targets would be picketed with cover provided 24 hours per day; there would be no more than six pickets at any site at any one time.

Targets would be:-

(a) Sizeable coal dumps, not interfering with domestic supplies.

(b)   Pits and open-cast sites to be given nominal coverage.

(c)   Power stations would be covered to prevent deliveries of supplies but workmen would be admitted.

(d)   Ports, Docks, Steel Works would be covered in the light of information received.

(e)   Deliveries to coking plants, wherever situated, would be controlled and any exceptions would be considered when emergency situations were reported.

(f)   Non-mining areas would be covered when the National Strike Committee considered it necessary. Areas would be informed from National Level when and how their assistance would be required. Responsibility for providing pickets would be on the following basis:-

South East England	— Kent Area
London	— Kent, Midlands and other Areas as decided by the National Committee.
East Anglia	— Yorkshire, Nottingham and Derbyshire.
South West England	— South Wales.

AREAS MUST CLEAR ALL THEIR PICKETING PROPOSALS WITH NATIONAL OFFICE."

The National Executive Committee had already decided that fuel supplies should continue to be supplied to hospitals, schools, the old, sick and the needy. It had also set up a National Strike Fund into which Areas were required to transfer all the donations they received. The expenses of picketing were to be met by the National Office and common rates throughout the coalfields were set for subsistence and travel. The Areas were asked to submit weekly accounts in order to be re-imbursed for picketing expenses.

In general the National Strike Committee tried to identify the various contingencies which might arise and to specify regulations for them so that it would retain control of the strike. It wanted an effective but low key strike but before it could discover whether these aims were contradictory the general election commenced.

The Strike Practice

The general election prevented the strike from running a normal course so it is not possible to assess the effectiveness of the strike plans. The ordinary miners would have been very difficult to constrain if the success of their strike had depended entirely upon their own efforts as in 1972. Miners tend to react to emergencies or crises at pit level. Whatever discipline they have exercised has usually

248

stemmed from feelings of solidarity rather than centrally imposed rules. Moreover, in a strike as volatile as a miners' one, the behaviour of strikers depends largely upon the extent and character of provocation by management, other workers, the police and the Government. It has always been the case that violence in strikes has not occurred because the strikers wanted to be violent but because attempts were being made to break their solidarity. Neither the National Strike Committee nor the miners themselves could predict the future in this respect.

The development of picketing practice depended in part upon the kind of collaboration given by other unions in the mining industry and those which organized related activities. The General Council of the Trades Union Congress asked all unions and trades councils to instruct their members not to cross the miners' picket lines but the most effective constraints came from bilateral arrangements. The N.U.M. differentiated between the two management unions in the mining industry. It quickly reached an agreement with the British Association of Colliery Management which organizes management above the level of deputy and allowed its members to undertake some duties during the strike. It wanted the other union, the National Association of Colliery Overmen, Deputies and Shotfirers, however, to call an official strike either in support of the miners' claim or on behalf of its own wages demand. N.A.C.O.D.S. refused to call its members out on strike and requested that some of its members should be allowed to cross the picket lines. The extent of solidarity between the N.U.M. and N.A.C.O.D.S. varied between the Areas but the lack of general solidarity caused cases of friction throughout the strike. There were a number of instances where confrontations occurred at picket lines as deputies tried to get to work.

Formal agreements with unions outside of the mining industry were reached fairly quickly. As in 1972 there was a quick, unequivocal response from the railway unions, especially the Associated Society of Locomotive Engineers and Firemen and the National Union of Railwaymen. The control of the transport of coal by rail presented no problems. The Transport and General Workers' Union issued a circular to its members advising them how to behave in relation to the strike and urging them to avoid damaging the miners' campaign but this union had problems controlling transport drivers who had contractual relations with their employers. The National Union of Students, with the excitement of the 1972 strike still lingering, offered to help in any way possible. Miners' leaders were invited to speak at students' meetings and solidarity committees were set up in a number of Universities and Polytechnics to assist pickets and to raise finance.

The strike was called within the context of the Industrial Relations

Act which, though virtually a dead letter, was used at the outset as a threat to the miners unless they conformed to the Government's code of practice. A couple of days before the strike began the Attorney-General, Sir Peter Rawlinson, warned unions that their funds could be at risk if legal action was taken against them for interfering with contracted supplies. "Pickets," he stated, "are not above the law of the land." The warning was directed not only at the N.U.M. but at unions which were willing to take sympathetic action in support of it. None of the unions involved was registered under the Act. Without registration they all lacked protection in law from the consequences of their acts. Any aggrieved person or organization could claim to the National Industrial Relations Court that the N.U.M. was guilty of an unfair industrial practice and expose it to a large fine. The Central Electricity Generating Board was quick to follow the Attorney-General's admonition with letters to the N.U.M. and three unions which had agreed to ban the movement of coal and extra supplies of alternative fuels, warning that it could be entitled to compensation if deliveries to power stations were interrupted. Neither the Attorney-General's statement nor the warning letter had any effect on the behaviour of the strikers and their supporters. The letter was dismissed by the N.U.M. as a "political ploy." The Industrial Relations Act was barely mentioned afterwards.

The main effect of the Act was in the way in which it influenced the use of union funds for financing the strike. The N.U.M. met picketing expenses from an Industrial Action Fund out of which it made allocations to the Areas. This money was almost exhausted within a week so that some Areas were compelled to stop making payments for picket duty except to cover travelling expenses. This financial constraint on picketing coincided, however, with a decrease in the need for extensive picketing because of the the widening support the N.U.M. was given from other unions.

The strike was real for miners and their families despite the overshadowing influence of the general election. They were not making a token gesture nor were they just sitting tight, waiting for a favourable election result. As in 1972 they had to make financial sacrifices. The only financial assistance most miners got was in the form of the social security payments made to miners' wives and dependents. Single miners were not eligible for social security and received nothing except occasional grants from branch hardship funds. In this respect the strike bit as deeply into the social fabric of miners' lives as the 1972 one had done.

Each branch carried responsibility for caring for the welfare of its own members and their families; for organizing credit, providing food and generally coping with hardship cases. There was not a uniform pattern of branch activities for much depended upon the commitment and capabilities of branch officials and upon the involvement of the local communities. The union branch at the large Kellingley pit in North Yorkshire, operating from the spacious miners' club in Knottingley, had a complex strike organization which tried to meet all the needs of its members. At Lochgelly in Fife the strikers were given a free meal each day at the Miners' Social and Recreational Club. The food was prepared and served by miners' wives, friends and supporters The local provost was a member of the strike committee and the local council donated money to help buy the food. In the traditional mining areas where whole communities were dependent upon the coal industry very few groups could remain dispassionate and uninvolved. In such places there was an interaction between the striking miners and the rest of the community which involved miners in accepting responsibility for maintaining fuel supplies to needy cases. For instance, in South Wales the miners moved coal from stock to enable classrooms to be heated in schools which had been closed through the lack of fuel. They also provided coal for hospitals and old people's homes. The South Wales miners refused to collect payment for coal delivered to needy families. Those who did this work were not paid and received only 75p a day as a subsistence allowance. There were illustrations in every coalfield of miners establishing their own services in response to the social welfare problems caused by the strike.

The strike had its own dynamism which could be dampened but not smothered by national regulations or national concerns. Many miners I met on picket duty in Yorkshire showed little interest in the election campaign or its outcome. Their approach was clear and simple. They wanted a Government which would meet their wage demands and they did not really care how it emerged. They reflected a degree of cynicism about party politics which was new in the coalfields and which showed signs of a distrust in the Parliamentary system itself. What kind of system is it, they said, which suffers a constitutional crisis simply because miners are demanding a living wage? They had detected a symptom of inherent instability in British capitalism. Workers had experienced a succession of Government wages policies since 1947, each one promising to be the last, each one launched as a panacea for the country's economic ailments, yet each one failing miserably to improve things and having, after a breathing space, to be replaced by another, usually more stringent and punitive. Despite the numerous wages policies the system was moving into rather than out of a crisis. There was no dispute among workers about the meaning of crisis. It was an increasing inability to alleviate the perpetual struggle of most workers to maintain, let alone improve, their living standards.

So, distrustful of the system, the miners drew themselves in, realizing that they could trust their affairs with no other organizations but their own, and concentrated on making their own solidarity effective. This took them into spheres of activity which had been common in 1972. The Yorkshire miners, for example, tightened up their picketing of steel plants at the end of the first week to counter management attempts to find ways of getting supplies of coal. They were threatened with legal action by the police when they intensified their picketing of railway bridges and level crossings to prevent the movement of coal into power stations and steel plants. In some instances the police physically prevented miners from picketing. In such cases the two main railway unions agreed to act as if pickets were present and not to run fuel carrying trains across the symbolic picket lines.

As the strike got under way the Scottish miners demanded a stricter control over the movement of oil. The Transport and General Workers' Union had instructed its members to convey only normal quantities of oil to power stations and steel plants but managements had devised ways of getting extra supplies in. There were problems in Durham because oil tanker drivers were crossing picket lines with abnormal loads. Local N.U.M. officials on Teesside urged tanker drivers to observe the Transport and General Workers' Union instruction to do nothing to harm the miners' case and to cooperate with the N.U.M. over solidarity action. The branch officials at Easington colliery in Durham threatened to organize mass pickets unless the tanker drivers agreed to cooperate with them.

Incidents of this kind occurred thoughout the strike but in the main they were confined as local issues and attracted little publicity. Area officials generally tried to defuse potentially difficult situations in keeping with the increasing desire of the National Executive Committee simply to keep the strike ticking over. Arthur Scargill intervened at Grimethorpe in Yorkshire at the end of February in order to prevent miners from harrassing office staff who were going to work at the N.C.B. area offices there. The relations between miners and supervisory management, particularly concerning the provision of safety cover in the pits, were smoothed out as the strike proceeded. The National Association of Colliery Overmen, Deputies and Shotfirers, with 22,000 members, decided on 27th February to hold a strike ballot but the miners' strike was finished before it could be held. In any case, the Pay Board had ruled that the overmen were entitled to a differential of 10 per cent more than the highest paid coal miners they supervised. The members of N.A.C.O.D.S. simply had to sit tight in the hope that the miners would win a subtantial pay increase. As the strike was nearing its close the National Executive Committee of the N.U.M. was justifiably in a self-congratulatory mood about the use and conduct of pickets.

The Relativities Report
The general election campaign prevented the resumption of nego-

252

tiations between the N.U.M. on the one side and the N.C.B. and the Government on the other for if a settlement had been reached it would have defeated the purpose of the election. Another factor which prevented the resumption of negotiations was that the Government had referred the question of the relative pay of miners to the Pay Board just before the strike began in order to decide whether miners should receive payments outside of what they were entitled to under Phase III of the Government policy. It was expected that a report would be produced by the end of February. The N.E.C. was formally informed of the reference on 12th February when it decided that provided the T.U.C. had no objections the Union would give evidence to the Pay Board but that it would not commit the Union to accept the Board's findings. The Pay Board began to collect evidence from Monday, 18th February. Thus, apart from the election, the impasse could not be broken before the Pay Board had reported.

The only attempt to end the strike before the general election and prior to the publication of the Relativities Report on miners' pay, was when a group of anonymous industrialists, represented by the London Mercantile Corporation, offered a single contribution of £2,470,000 to miners if they returned to work. The money, it was claimed, would be paid direct to miners and would be both tax free and in addition to anything the Pay Board might offer. The offer received much publicity and was discussed at a specially convened meeting of the Union's N.E.C. on 12th February. The left-wing members of the N.E.C. regarded the intervention with some suspicion and scepticism. It was indicative of the way in which industrialists perceived workers, as mechanistically motivated economic units, that they should believe that miners could be bought off because all that mattered for them was cash in the hand. The miners' leaders, of course, had consistently maintained that no progress in negotiations could be made unless there was a "cash on the table offer." But this was said in the context of a struggle to get the rate for the job. the dispute was more about exploitation than actual amounts of money but industrialists could not acknowledge this even if they were able to recognize it. Judging from the attitude of the industrialists they did not recognize any element of indignation, of resentment, of pride in the attitude of the miners. The National Executive Committee predictably, but politely, declined the offer from the London Mercantile Corporation, emphasizing that if the industrialists had wanted to stop the strike they should have put pressure on the Government before it started.

There was little rational public discussion about the merits of the miners' case before the beginning of the Pay Board's inquiry. In the first place there was not in 1974 the same general feeling of injustice about miners' wages as there had been in 1972. The relative position of miners in the industrial wages table had deteriorated since the Wilberforce award but it was not perceived as being near the level of 1971. Secondly, so many things had been said so convincingly prior to 1974 that people just believed that miners were poorly paid in relation to the kind of work they did. It had almost reached the stage where miners simply had to protest to get their case recognized in public.

Lawrence Daly gave evidence to the Pay Board on the opening day of its inquiry, when the strike was a week old. It was less dramatic and emotive than the case had been in 1972 but this was of little consequence. But it was stronger because of the impact of the oil crisis. The argument for higher pay was based on the need to recruit and retain labour for an expanding coal industry. In Daly's words, "wages levels are the key to solving the manpower problem." Miners had to be compensated, he claimed, for the risks to their health from injury and disease; they had to be rewarded so that they would not be induced to leave for other industries and the rewards had to be sufficiently attractive to induce young men to choose mining as a career.

Mr. Daly provided data about the incidence of injury and disease including a testimony from Dr. Hugh Faulkner, the Medical Secretary of the Medical Practitioners Union, emphasizing that "in terms of death and permanent disability from accidents, occupational chest disease, sickness and stress, (miners) carry greater all-round risk than any other group in our community — except, perhaps, deep sea fisherman." He showed that in years of increased economic activity outside of mining there was a drift of manpower out of the pits into more congenial, safer and better paid jobs. The case was particularly concerned with the deterioration in the manpower situation after the Wilberforce award. The voluntary wastage of labour was twice as high in 1973 as in 1972 and was higher than in 1971, before the Wilberforce award rectified some of the imbalance in the relative pay of miners. Moreover, because of the high wastage rate and the difficulty of recruiting young miners the mining labour force was ageing. The cause of this was attributed to low relative wages.

The effect of the Wilberforce award had been to place the wage rate for face workers about 10 per cent above the average earnings of manual workers in manufacturing industries. By the time of the Inquiry it was estimated that the wages of face workers needed to be raised by 24.2 per cent to £45.70p in order to maintain the 10 per cent margin. This was in line with the union demand for a £45 a week wage for face workers. Lawrence Daly made other comparisons and concluded that "miners' pay, relative to average pay in manufacturing industries, has fallen even lower than the levels which the Wilberforce Report set out to remedy."

An unusual feature of the Inquiry was that the Department of Energy and the National Coal Board both submitted evidence which supported the miners' case. The Department of Energy, in a brief but concise memorandum, described the importance of coal in overcoming the fuel crisis. It stated: "About two years ago it became clear that the balance (between oil and coal) might be changing. The Government took steps, through the Coal Industry Act 1973, to stop the industry's decline and thereby to hold open the possibility of retaining for the future a larger coal industry than had hitherto been thought viable . . . In the event, oil prices rose earlier and more sharply than had been expected. By the end of 1973, the price of crude oil had quadrupled compared with its cost in 1972, with severe effects on the balance of payments. As a result of this increase, indigenous coal (even if repriced at its true costs, with present subsidies eliminated) is now competitive overall with oil." It concluded that the coal industry had the prospect of an assured market for many years to come but that it would require a substantial increase in investment even to maintain existing levels of production. The N.U.M. case really carried on from there.

The evidence of the National Coal Board supplemented that of the N.U.M. because its own interest lay in supporting the case for an expanded coal industry. The N.C.B. had dutifully contracted the industry when instructed but self-decimation could not have been its natural inclination. Now it saw an opportunity for expansion and it took it. The Board was not constrained as an adversary in the struggle for it had not been allowed by the Government to participate. Perhaps for the first time in its history it was allowed to act in the manner perceived for it by miners at the inception of nationalization. It remained concerned about cost, of course, and in consequence with productivity, but in a manner which took account of the interests and expectations of the miners.

The N.C.B. repeated the assessment of the fuel crisis made by the Department of Energy, though in greater detail. It stated that:

"To meet the changed energy situation, the Board are now planning to halt the contraction of the industry by
(a)   maximising the utilization of existing capacity;
(b)   major investments at existing mines either to extend their life or to increase output levels.
(c)   opening new mines;
(d)   maximising opencast production.
The implementation of this programme will require both a substantial increase in investment, and measures to ensure that the necessary manpower is available. It is clear that the relative importance of coalmining to the U.K. economy has increased and that it will continue to hold its new importance in the future. Because of this it is the Board's view that corresponding improvements in the wages and conditions of service of the work-force are vital so that the challenge of this new role can be met successfully."

255

The National Coal Board did not make specific recommendations to the Inquiry about pay but its evidence supported the claim. With so much agreement between the main witnesses and with such a mountain of evidence supporting the miners, the Pay Board, with an eye on its own credibility, had no alternative but to fall in line and support the claim. Its only scope for independent judgement lay in determining amounts at the margin and differentials between grades.

The Pay Board ended its formal deliberations in public on 22nd February. It had been agreed amongst its members, however, that it would not publish its report until after the election and a new Government had been formed. The election campaign ended, therefore, amidst speculation about the Board's findings and uncertainty about the importance it would be given for the Labour Party had pledged to abolish the Pay Board if it was returned to power.

The Government Loses

The election campaign ended for the Conservative Party as it began by concentrating on political extremists in the National union of Mineworkers. On the evening before the poll Mr. Heath appealed to the electorate to support the Conservatives so that "the extremist will see that they have been defeated." He stated from his Bexley constituency: "Do you want a strong Government which has clear authority for the future to take the decisions which will be needed? Do you want Parliament and the elected Government to continue to fight strenuously against inflation? Or do you want a Government which will abandon the struggle against rising prices under pressure from one particular powerful group of workers? . . . Let us show beyond contradiction that the decision of the British Parliament is not to be overthrown by industrial force . . ."

The electorate responded indecisively on Friday, 1st March by not giving any party an absolute majority.* The two party system was fractured by the Welsh and Scottish nationalist parties and the uncertain allegiance of the Northern Ireland political parties. Neither of the major political parties could govern without the support of the Parliamentary Liberal Party and it was some days before it was decided whether the Conservative or Labour Party would get it. After an initial attempt by Mr. Heath to remain in Government the Liberals gave their support to the Labour Party which formed a minority Government under the leadership of Mr. Harold Wilson.

Mr. Michael Foot became the new Secretary of State for Employment and promptly received the Pay Board's Report. It recommended that miners should be given "exceptional increases"

* The election results were as follows:

Labour	301	seats
Tories	296	seats
Liberals	14	seats
Others	23	seats

worth an estimated £57.5 million a year and that the money should be allocated as an underground shift allowance of £1.20, as an allowance of half of that amount for surface workers who had served a qualifying priod underground and as a contribution, amounting to £4 million, to the existing offer of the N.C.B. in order to make further adjustments in the internal wages structure. The Pay Board had been influenced by the argument that while underground workers might be regarded as a special case outside of mining, surface workers would not be treated in that way. Railwaymen, in particular, it was thought, might resent preferential treatment for surface workers with whom they worked on railwaysidings in pit yards.

The Report repeated the main arguments and details about mining provided by the principal witnesses. It fastened its attention, however, on the request by the National Coal Board for a productivity scheme. In its evidence the N.C.B. claimed, though without any supporting evidence, that "In industry generally there is a periodic cycle moving from time rates to incentive payments and back again over a period of years. The Board consider that the present national structures provide a firm base for the introduction of local incentive schemes and that the time is now ripe for this." It pointed out in another part of its evidence that the two parties had not been able to agree on a locally based incentive scheme so the N.C.B. had submitted a national scheme for the approval of the Pay Board. It nonetheless still preferred a scheme to be introduced which operated at local level.

The Pay Board responded by stating that a productivity scheme had implications for "the long-term ability of the mining industry to remain competitive with oil . . . We see distinct possibilities of a national scheme operated at colliery level. We envisage a national productivity payment for the achievement of a national productivity target based on targets set for each pit taking into account its particular circumstances . . ." The Pay Board believed that this suggestion would avoid the divisive effects of previous piecework systems.

The impact of the Report on the dispute was undermined by the result of the election for when the new Secretary of State for Employment met the National Officials of the N.U.M. he said that the Union and the N.C.B. could resume negotiations immediately without being constrained by previous Government policy statements or the Pay Board's Report. He stated that the Report could enter into the argument if they wished but that "it was not a governing document in the situation." It did not enter into the argument though the total amount of money involved in its proposals might have influenced the approach of the N.C.B. in the final negotiations. When the Union and Coal Board representatives met after the

257

intervention of Mr. Foot the Coal Board was informed that the N.U.M. did not accept the Report. It objected, in particular, to the proposal relating to the relative wages of underground and surface workers and to the suggestion for an underground allowance.

The negotiations were resumed in an apparent atmosphere of free collective bargaining. The Secretary of State for Employment made no comment about the outcome except to say that the cost of meeting the wages settlement, whatever that might be, was a matter for the Government and that it would be financed through increased prices or subsidies or both. With the constraints removed, the original wages demand for £45 a week for face workers, £40 for other underground workers and £35 for surface workers, re-entered the discussions. After some disagreement between the negotiators, but only a day after negotiations had been resumed, a settlement was reached, which gave face workers the rate of £45 and other underground workers and surface workers £36 and £32 respectively. Improvements were agreed in a number of fringe benefits, such as payments for unsocial hours, holiday pay, shift payments to craftsmen, death benefit and the lump sum payment to retiring miners. The package was approved by delegate conferences in the Areas and miners returned to work on the first normal shift on Monday, 11th March, 1974.

If the success of a strike is judged by the extent to which the Union's initial demand is met then this strike was won by the miners. But it would be a misinterpretation to describe it in this way for the miners action was in some ways symbolic. It was more of a holding operation than a campaign to win. There was, of course, a dynamism in the strike which compelled miners to be alert and to take initiatives but there was little of the aggression and determination to win which characterized the 1972 strike. In reality the strike was lost by the Government more than it was won by the miners. But it was a defeat which had little to do with the ineptness of Ministers and idiosyncricies of Mr. Edward Heath.

The explanation lies in the character of the crisis in British capitalism which compelled the Government to intervene in industrial relations but denied it the authority and facility to subvert union power. The strike was an illustration of the way in which the mere existence of a large, virile, responsive trade union movement is an automatic brake on authoritarian Government. It was historic because the miners knew that they were confronting the Government and, despite charges of constitutional impropriety and the overshadowing presence of an election, did not retreat.

CHAPTER 19

DEMOCRACY

Interpretations

Democracy does not have a universal meaning. It does not have a meaning which transcends different types of societies or class barriers within one society. Certainly it embodies a single principle of behaviour but how the principle is perceived and the way in which it is applied depends upon the circumstances of each case. The circumstances of a State cannot be compared with those of a trade union which differ from those of a drama club or a gardening society. The circumstances of political parties vary depending on whether they are revolutionary or not. In each separate case the distribution of power within the organization and the relationship between it and its environment stipulates how, in what manner, the principle of equal rights for all should be applied.

Democracy is about the distribution of power so that the way in which it is perceived depends upon where the perceiver stands in the power structure. What is democratic for an employer will not be democratic for a worker for they have an unequal power relationship. From the worker's point of view democracy necessarily involves altering the employer's position, perhaps even eliminating it altogether.

The different ways of interpreting democracy have been illustrated in recent years in the debate about industrial democracy, in particular the application of the Bullock Report proposals.* All parties professed to believe in industrial democracy but no agreement could be reached about what it should entail. There was disagreement even amongst trade unions. The proposals have fallen flat. The discussions between the National Coal Board and the National Union of Mineworkers about a scheme to give miners greater rights in running the industry have suffered a similar fate. Miners who opposed the scheme saw it as a means of weakening them collectively in their relations with the Coal Board while, for the Board, it was as far as it could go without damaging its power position.

In the main, democracy is seen by workers as a means of extending and asserting their rights while employers see it as a method for containing workers in their demands for greater power. The different views and intentions have been blurred and confused by ideological pressures on workers to convince them that what is democratic for employers is also democratic for themselves. There has been a profusion of prescriptions from Governments, politicians, media writers about democratic practices which has overwhelmed the central principle of equal rights and made democracy into a tool for controlling and not freeing people.

---

* Report of the Committee of Inquiry on Industrial Democracy, Cmnd 6706, H.M.S.O., January, 1977.

Trade unions have been at the centre of the debate. The main grievance against them has always been their success against employers or the Government and the aspects of their organizations which have been attributed with undemocratic tendencies have been those which have been seen to contribute most to that success. So at different times unions have been attacked for being too centralized or too decentralized, for having strong leadership or weak leadership, for having too much consultation with the members or too little, for using the block vote method of decision-making in Congresses or for not using it enough. It has always been said in the name of democracy for the outsome always determined whether a means was democratic or not. The unions could never win the argument.

The National Union of Mineworkers has been similarly criticized especially after its spectacular strike successes. The Union's Annual Conferences were democratic expressions until they began to be militant. Then referenda were deemed to be the ultimate in democratic mechanisms, until miners, through the referenda began rejecting compliance with the National Coal Board. With these two instruments maligned the National Executive was projected as the custodian of democracy in the Union. And everything was said or written without reference to what the rules of the Union intended.

It is clear that there is little point in using one yardstick, calibrated in units of democracy, with which the extent of democracy can be measured in this or that organization. Yet this is what has been done. Democracy has become a single descriptive term, with its genesis in the principle of equal rights for all, to cover a whole variety of power struggles and to serve different contradictory purposes in those struggles. But it is meaningless to ask whether or not the National Union of Mineworkers is suitably democratic for *everyone* for the answer will depend on whether the question is asked of the National Coal Board, the Government, the president of the Union, the secretary of a small Area like North Wales, one of the leaders of the left-wing Areas, a full-time official or a lay member. What can be done, however, is to give a meaning to the term and then ask whether this meaning is being fulfilled in the lives of the members of the National Union of Mineworkers.

This Union, and its constituent county unions beforehand, were formed in order to protect and improve the living conditions of miners. This task has been undertaken in a situation dominated by class struggle and in an environment which has always been hostile towards the Union's primary aim. The Union has to take it for granted that most of its activities will be regarded with suspicion or hostility by every institution which can be counted as part of the "establishment;" that is by Government, employers, churches and the mass media. Another element in the life of the National Union of Mineworkers is the historically based belief that the Union can

260

Ready to descend at Sharlston pit, Yorkshire, 1979.

Miners at Denby colliery in Derbyshire, including young boys barely tall enough to hold the 'safety bar,' about to ascend the shaft in about 1910.

best pursue its purposes through the direct involvement of its members, without discrimination between them and without prejudice to any of their particular interests. Thus the perception of equal rights for all is present but not as a value which has been introduced to miners from outside their own experiences. It is present precisely because inequality and authoritarianism have dominated their lives. Thus the negative, degrading, humiliating experiences which arise from being compelled to sell labour power under harsh conditions have produced a positive belief in their antithesis. It was through this process that early trade unionists formed organisations in which all members shared responsibility and made conscious attempts to prevent the accumulation of authority in particular persons. Through the same process of equality the payment for the same work irrespective of where it is performed or by whom, in other words the rate for the job, became one of the earliest and persistent trade union demands.

The scrambling, competitive, relentless and bitter struggles for wages under piece-work conditions which penalized the aged, the sick and the physically incompetent of the workers, thus piling muck upon muck in their lives, taught miners unforgettable lessons about the principles of living together. They did not have to read Plato or Thomas Payne to learn about democracy or the rights of man, though some of them undoubtedly did. Nor when they formed their unions did they need to copy the crude democratic methods of control used by Seventeenth Century non-conformist religious sects, though there was undoubtedly some resemblance. They simply built on the values their experiences taught them should be their ultimate goal.

The daily experiences of miners were not unique. Their basic oppressive character was shared by workers in general. The differences occurred through the miners' daily flirtation with disease, injury and death and the realization that their safety in the pit depended on solidarity. So miners placed greater emphasis on trade unionism in itself than did many other workers.

The Constitution

The constitution of the National Union of Mineworkers is rooted in the miners' perception of democracy as an ongoing process of struggle to assert themselves, to direct their own lives, to make decisions in the vital areas of their everyday experiences, to escape the iniquities of inequality and the authoritarianism which is derived from it. But it is an imperfect reflection because it is not possible to embody ideas about behaviour within institutions without modifying or, perhaps, distorting them. This institution, the miners' union, has a long history during which it has grown through mergers,

263

adapting itself to a changing environment and altering its ways of doing things. It has had to live, moreover, through a hostile environment with a constant ideological attack on its method of government and under the influence of contrary ideas about the meaning of democracy. The miners' union has not been able to immunize itself from these influences. Yet the basic conditions for democracy remain largely intact in its consitution.

The membership of the National Union of Mineworkers is "composed of workers employed in or connected with the coal mining industry of Great Britain." Each member belongs to a branch located in an Area or a constituent association and has complete freedom to engage in the activities of the Union subject only to certain membership conditions in the case of elections to official positions. There are no categories of members and there is no discrimination between them. Face workers, haulage men, craftsmen, surface workers and clerks all have the same rights under the constitution. The branches formulate policies through their respective Areas and through them determine national policies at Annual Conferences. Each Area is entitled to elect delegates to the Conferences in proportion to its membership and to submit up to three motions for debate.

The locus of power in the Union is clearly stated in the rule book. Rule 23 states: "The Conference of Delegates . . . in which the authority and government of the Union shall be vested, shall function in Annual Conference or Special Conference. The Annual Conference shall be held in each year in the first week in July, or such other time as the Conference of Delegates may resolve. The duties of the Annual Conference shall be to transact the business of the Union and to discuss matters affecting the welfare of the membership; to consider resolutions submitted to the Annual Conference by the National Executive Committee and Areas; to receive the National Executive Committee's report of its proceedings, and to receive the Auditor's report on the financial position of the Union for the previous year." In between Conferences the National Executive Committee administers the business and affairs of the Union. Rule 8 states that it shall "perform all duties laid down for it by resolution of Conference, and it shall not at any time act contrary to, or in defiance of, any resolution of Conference." Provision was made in the rules for holding ballot votes of the members but only through Conference decisions. Rules 23 went on to state that "A Special Conference may be called at any time by the National Executive Committee. Any question arising thereat (with the exception of a question of alterations and/or additions to rules or a question which in the opinion of the delegates present is one calling for immediate decision) shall be submitted to the decision of the Areas by a proxy vote or, if the Delegates present so decide, the members generally by a ballot vote . . ." There is no other provision for ballot votes except in the case of the election of officials.

The National Executive Committee consists of representatives elected by each Area according to its membership but with no Area being allowed to have more than three members. Each member holds office for two years but can then seek re-election. All officials of the Union have to be elected by members in different constituencies depending upon their status, by a transferable vote system as defined in Section 41 of the Representation of the People Act of 1918, supervised by an outside and independent electoral reform organization.* The full-time president and general secretary are elected by national ballot votes and do not at any time have to seek re-election. The remaining national official, the vice-president, is elected every two years by Annual Conference. Full-time Area officials are elected within their respective Areas, also without having to seek re-election. Lay positions on Area Councils and/or Executive Committee's and in branches are elected ones on a one or two yearly basis. Special provisions are made for colliery national strikes and altering rules. A national strike must be supported by a 55 per cent majority of the members who vote in a national ballot while an alteration of rules requires a two-thirds majority in a Conference. It is quite clear from this synopsis that power was intended to lie in the hands of the ordinary members.

The Union has had to cope with its own history. It was formed, as is described in chapter 3, in a compromise fashion through the amalgamation of the county unions. These unions, either singly or in groups, became Areas and their officials became Area officials. They retained a large degree of financial independence, maintained many of their past practices concerning the election and control of officials. In so far as the new rules referred to the activities of the Areas then they were treated as model ones, to be adopted as and when Areas thought it necessary. There are still Areas which ignore the national rules in their local activities, even in the manner in which they select their National Executive Committee representatives.

The practice which most of the county unions had followed of sending their leading officials to sit on the executive of the Miners' Federation of Great Britain continued after the amalgamation. The National Executive Committee of the N.U.M. has largely comprised full-time officials who have gone to London as hitherto, as leaders and not as representatives. Rank and file members have only occasionally sat on the N.E.C. During the 1970s only Yorkshire and Kent plus Scotland from November 1973 until July 1975 were represented by rank and file members. The elections for the N.E.C. have been carried out every two years in most, but not all, of the Areas, but they have often been formalities. There have been

* The Electoral Reform Society supervises ballot votes.

occasional cases in recent years, as in Kent and the Midlands, when the main full-time officers have not sat on the N.E.C. but in most Areas it is considered bad politics to exclude their leading officials from decision-making in London.

Unequal Representation on the N.E.C.

At the time of the amalgamation in 1944 a system of representation for the N.E.C. was worked out as follows:

> One representative from each Area (or Consolidated Group of Areas) for the first 7,500 members or fractional part thereof, and one additional representative for the next 40,000 additional members, with a further additional representative for the next 50,000 additional members; the representation to automatically rise and fall according to the increase or decrease of members provided that no Area (or Consolidated group of Areas) shall have more than three representatives on the National Executive Committee.

Thus each Area irrespective of its size had at least one National Executive Committee representative while the maximum number was three. As each member had one vote this method of representation favoured the small areas from the outset. In order to have 3 representatives an Area had to have almost 100,000 members. Yorkshire, South Wales and Durham were in this category. Yet an Area such as North Wales or Cumberland with only 7,500 members was entitled to one representative. The reason for starting off with such an inequitable system was given at the Special Conference of the M.F.G.B. on the Re-Organization of the Federation in August, 1944, when it was stated that the spheres of interest of the county unions had to continue for some time after the amagamation otherwise the amalgamation would not even materialize. Each county union demanded its own representation on the N.E.C. If a system of proportional representation had been used, allowing at least one representative for each Area then the N.E.C. would have been of inordinate size. Yorkshire, Durham and South Wales would each have had 15, 14 and 13 representatives respectively. Indeed the intention seems to have been to maintain the National Executive Committee at its pre-amalgamation size. There was no satisfactory way of reconciling the desire for continuity with that of equity.

The amalgamators envisaged changing the composition of the Areas. Rule 7 stated that "It shall be the duty of the National Executive Committee to review the organization of the Union in the various Areas, and if they consider it advisable after discussions with the Areas concerned, the National Executive Committee may recommend to Conference that Areas adjoining one another shall be combined to form one Area." A patchwork alteration followed. The Midlands Area was created out of an amalgamation of five Areas in 1948. In 1951 C.O.S.A. representing white-collar workers was formed out of seven colliery and official staffs' associations. Then, in 1958, Somerset merged with the South Wales Area. At various time winding enginemen and craftsmen were involved in minor mergers. No significant alteration in the composition of the Areas occurred after 1958 and at no time did the N.E.C. attempt to view the Union as a whole in an endeavour to remove the anomalies and undemocratic tendencies which the amalgamation compromises had left.

A number of attempts were made at Annual Conferences to alter representation on the N.E.C. Usually when motions were introduced they were remitted into the hands of the body they proposed to alter. At that point the vested interests which had been carried over from the county union days took charge and nothing was done. In any event no changes could occur without the support of the N.E.C. Two resolutions proposing changes in representation on the N.E.C. were remitted to it at the Annual Conference in 1961 on the understanding that the Executive would do something about it. Will Paynter, the General Secretary, responded by producing a memorandum which proposed a complete logical re-organization of the Union so that its Areas fitted National Coal Board Divisions. The N.E.C. refused to discuss the proposals and the existence of the memorandum was not even minuted.

The resistance to a re-organization of the Union into at least a tidier, more evenly balanced organization and at the most a highly centralized bureaucratic machine did not come only from chauvinistic Area Union officials who wanted to protect their petty domains. It came from the ordinary members who were conscious of their county identities, proud of their local traditions and jealous of their financial autonomy. The arguments for merger had to be overwhelming in order to convince these people that they should give up their relative autonomy.

This attitude continued during the contraction of the coal industry. The discrepancies in the sizes of Areas widened as some were reduced to the size of individual branches in others. The basis of representation on the N.E.C., prescribed in Rule 10, was amended in 1969 to take account of the falling membership. Every Area with less than 22,500 members was allowed one representative while Areas with 55,000 members of more were allowed the maximum of three representatives.

In 1979 there were 20 Areas of which only three had more than 22,500 members. The membership of those entitled to one representative ranged from nearly 19,000 for C.O.S.A. to 914 for Cumberland. Four Areas had less than 3,000 members each while 9 of them had less than 6,000 members each. The anomalies, as can be seen from the following table, were not only marked but ridiculous. Yorkshire with 64,060 members had three representatives while Cumberland with 914 members had one. Cumberland's members had exactly the same voting power on the N.E.C. as Scotland's

16,373 members. Voting situations could, and did, occur where a minority on the N.E.C. commanded a majority of votes in the coalfields.

Some of those special agreements which had been made in 1944 to secure the co-operation of unions organizing within the proclaimed jurisdiction of the N.U.M. had become anachronistic. The National Union of General and Municipal Workers had made an agreement over the organization of cokemen and were given one representative on the N.E.C. The number of cokemen was never very large but in 1979, under the title of Power Group No. 2 it had only 1,230 members, mostly in a couple of plants in Yorkshire. Cokemen who were not members of the N.U.G. & M.W., numbering 5,138 in 1979, organized separately in a Cokemen's Area.

TABLE A

Representation on the National Executive Committee

1979

Area	Size	No. of Members
Yorkshire	64,060	3
Nottingham	34,275	2
South Wales	26,092	2
C.O.S.A.	18,980	1
Scotland	16,373	1
Durham	16,258	1
Midlands	13,973	1
Derbyshire	11,617	1
Group No. 1	9,471	1
North Western	8,798	1
Northumberland	7,767	1
Cokemen	5,138	1
Power Group	4,982	1
Group No. 2	4,638	1
South Derbyshire	3,269	1
Leicester	3,241	1
Kent	2,759	1
Power Group No. 2	1,230	1
North Wales	1,052	1
Cumberland	914	1

As odd as it may seem this imbalanced executive representation did not cause any concern until the left-wing Areas were able to command a majority of votes in Annual Conferences but found that their intentions could be thwarted by the National Executive Committee. This situation did not become obvious until after the 1974 strike. Of course, the left-wing members on the N.E.C. always looked to the day when they could claim a solid and committed majority on all issues but they were not confronted by the stark unrepresentative character of N.E.C. voting until the constitution was flouted so that the right-wing could retain some semblance of power in the Union.

Broken Rules: Wages

As I have mentioned in an earlier chapter, until 1970, the Union functioned smoothly with its various parts operating in harmony. There was always a strong and vocal left-wing opposition but it was never sufficiently powerful to disrupt the machine. The mandarins who belonged to the National Executive Committee could act in the belief that they controlled the Union without infringing the rule book because their decisions also dominated the Annual Conferences. At each Annual Conference the majority of delegates coming from Yorkshire, Nottingham, C.O.S.A., Durham, the Midlands, North Western and Northumberland, consistently advocated and supported policies which the majority on the N.E.C. were happy to apply because they were the source of them. So although on the surface power in the Union seemed to reside in the Annual Conferences its real repository was the National Executive Committee.

This real power relationship between the National Executive Committee and the Annual Conferences was not recognized until after the Union had been through two major strikes. From 1970 when the Yorkshire vote at Annual Conferences was swung behind those of the left-wing Areas to give them a virtual majority the N.E.C. worked according to the rule book. When Conference decisions said "demand" it demanded; when they said "consult the membership" it consulted the membership; when the membership said "strike," it called a strike. There was often opposition on the N.E.C. to these instructions but for so long had they worked the rule book for their own ends that they saw no way of avoiding it when the ends were not those they wanted. They did not realize that the power structure of the Union was such that the N.E.C. could break the rule book with impunity.

The main objective factor which destroyed the constitutional compliance of the N.E.C. was the election of a minority Labour Government during the 1974 strike which could only survive with the collaboration of the trade union movement. The miners were seen as the key to that collaboration; if they could be contained then the risks were negligible. It became the dedicated task of Joe Gormley, the Union president, and the right-wing members of the N.E.C. to ensure that the miners were contained. In order to achieve that, the Annual Conference had to be neutralized by ignoring its instructions and using the N.E.C. as the prime policy-making forum. It was a gamble. At the same time the right-wing control of the N.E.C. had to be perpetuated and this entailed blocking all moves to introduce organizational changes. The occasion had its man for Gormley possessed the qualities of ingenuity, defiance, obstinacy and cockiness required to do things which were contrary to the Union rules, and to get away with them.

The first act of N.E.C. defiance occurred within a few days of the end of the 1974 Annual Conference. The Conference had rejected a Yorkshire resolution on pay but had passed a Scottish one expressing "total opposition to all forms of incomes policies, whether statutory or voluntary, so long as the capitalists' private profit-making character of British society remains unaltered . . ." At its first meeting after the Conference the N.E.C. by a majority of 12 votes to 10 decided to submit a resolution to the September T.U.C. giving "full support to the T.U.C./Labour Party Liaison Committee in the efforts they are making towards solving the economic problems facing Britain today." It was argued on the Executive that this was directly contrary to the policy which the Conference had endorsed because it implied support for the 'Social Contract' which was being drawn up between the T.U.C. and the new Labour Government. The miners' motion for the T.U.C. became part of a composite one explicitly supporting the Social Contract which was moved by Lawrence Daly, the N.U.M. general secretary. There was loud opposition from the left-wing Areas but the N.E.C. could not be disciplined until its report came before the next N.U.M. Annual Conference in 1975.

When the 1975 Annual Conference was held at Scarborough the British mass media concentrated its attention on it. The miners discussed their wages policy in a blaze of publicity and, therefore, scrutiny. The swing towards militant wage policies which began in 1970 and provided near unanimous decisions had been obstructed in some Areas as well as on the N.E.C. by the advent of the Labour Government. The officials in the right-wing Areas worked hard to contain militant tendencies and consistently co-operated together to oppose left-wing motions. In consequence, the Union became so evenly divided that the swing of a small Area could tip the balance one way or the other. A change of mind by one fairly small delegation at the 1974 Annual Conference caused the defeat of a militant Yorkshire wages motion.

The situation generated a lot of emotion. An Area which intended to vote out of pattern was put under heavy pressure to conform. In addition increased attention was given by right-wing leaders to the wording of resolutions. This, as I showed earlier in the book, was one of the means used by the left-wing to bind the N.E.C. to Conference decisions.

Before the 1975 Scarborough Conference a campaign for a £100 a week miner was launched. The £100 a week miner originated in a meeting addressed by Michael McGahey in London when he asked his audience how much they would require to work down a mine. The general response was that they would not go down a mine for £100 a week. So why, said McGahey, should miners not be paid £100 a week. The figure was taken up. It was a handy, rounded figure and had attractive propaganda features. It appeared in both the Yorkshire and the North Western resolutions for the Conference.

270

The difference between the two resolutions, however, was in the wording. The Yorkshire resolution demanded a wage of £100 a week whereas the North Western resolution stated that the "objective shall be to attain . . . a wage of £100 a week" adding that "whilst realizing that this figure may not be attainable in one round of negotiations, Conference further agrees that it should become priority number one in the Miners' Charter." The North Western Area wanted a rather leisurely progression to the £100 target.

The difference between the two resolutions emerged when an attempt was made to produce a single composite wages resolution by the Conference Business Committee. There a protracted argument took place over whether the words "demand" or "seek to achieve" should appear in the resolution. The Yorkshire delegation, led by Arthur Scargill, at first refused to remove 'demand' but, almost at the last minute, compromised and accepted a wording which instructed the N.E.C. "to seek" a £100 a week. This left the N.E.C. with the latitude to do whatever it wanted, which it did by fitting in with the Government policy.

Each Conference now became a scene for manoeuvering in one way or another by the president, the only person with the authority and opportunity to do it. The president of the Union was the chairman of each Conference. He decided how the rules and standing orders for the Conference should be interpreted. Delegates could challenge his rulings but to overturn them it required a majority of two-thirds of the delegates. Given the relatively even balance between the opposing sides in the Conference it was impossible to get this majority.

The chairman of the Annual Conference displayed his powers of discretion at the 1976 Conference in the Isle of Man. When the National Executive Committee met on 13th May, 1976, it had before it a T.U.C. Report on the Pay Guidelines which had been agreed with the Government and which were to be operative from 1st August until 31st July, 1977. These stated briefly that wage increases should amount to five per cent on total earnings for all hours worked with a cash minimum of £2.50 and an upper cash maximum of £4 per week. The Executive decided to submit the Pay Guidelines to a ballot of the members with a recommendation that they should be accepted. The ballot result, announced on 10th June, was in favour of the T.U.C./Government policy though by a small majority.* At the Annual Conference Joe Gormley ruled that because of this ballot result the six wages resolutions on the agenda were out of order. Wages were not to be discussed at all. Much time of the Conference was spent in challenging the chairman's ruling. Tommy Mullany who had played an important part in transforming the Yorkshire coalfield in 1968 and 1969, and was attending his last

* The voting was 103,506 in favour and 90,387 against.

271

Conference, protested, as did Jack Dunn from Kent and George Rees from South Wales, but unsuccessfully. Each time the chairman was challenged 145 delegates voted for him and 128 voted against him. The Government had few problems in applying its wages policy that year.

The tactic of manipulation to diffuse the militancy of the miners was altered in 1977. On that occasion there were six resolutions dealing with wages. The South Wales and Scottish Areas demanded £100 a week for face workers; the Yorkshire Area demanded £110 a week for face workers while the Nottingham Area sought "to achieve" £135 a week but without stipulating by when it should be achieved. The South Wales, Scotland and Yorkshire resolutions were composited to demand the sum of £110 a week but the composite resolution was defeated by the Conference. The delegates went on, however, to support the right-wing Nottingham Area's resolution seeking "to achieve £135 a week." Most of the left-wing Areas refused to vote for this resolution. What was done, in effect, was to discredit the wage claim in the eyes of the miners by setting an unreasonably high target. Many miners at that time, even in the left-wing Areas, thought that the figure of £110 was too high. In addition, by putting in the words "seeks to achieve," the Nottingham Area gave the N.E.C. latitude to get whatever it could without any preconditions. This resolution was as vague as the ones of the 1960s which had demanded 'substantial' increases.

By 1978 the wages resolutions passed by the Annual Conference had ceased to be of any significance. The N.E.C. had recovered its previous position of primacy. It entered into negotiations with the National Coal Board without any constraints and negotiated what was considered to be consistent with the Labour Government's policy, confident that there would be no movement of opposition in the coalfields. The left-wing Areas were in a dilemma because behind them lay a trail of unfulfilled rising wages demands yet they felt that they had to keep up their own momentum each year by adding more to the list. The demand in July 1974 which had been for £65 a week for face workers was raised to £100 in 1975 and 1976, then put up to £110 in 1977 and 1978 reaching £140 in 1979. Yet in 1979 the basic wage had not reached the figures demanded in 1975. The proposed wage rates were moving into the realm of fantasy and failed, therefore, to make sense to most miners. Even in the left-wing Areas, except for Scotland, there appeared to be an increasing unwillingness to press for large wage demands. But by 1978 there was another element concerning incentive payments through which the National Executive Committee asserted its superiority by over-ruling not simply Conference decisions but the result of a referendum.

Broken Rules: Incentive Schemes
The issue of incentive payments, raised by the Wilberforce Report,

became a subject of negotiations between the N.E.C. and the National Coal Board for two years before an agreed scheme emerged. The difficulty was that the Coal Board wanted a scheme which would directly and immediately increase productivity while the Union wanted one which would not lead to differences in earnings, disunity between miners and unofficial strikes. The N.C.B.'s scheme contained the ingredients to produce the consequences the Union wanted to avoid; the Union's scheme, on the other hand, was unlikely to increase productivity in the manner required by the N.C.B. Eventually, by September, 1974, the negotiators found common ground and submitted details of a draft agreement first to the National Executive Committee, then to a Special Delegate Conference and finally to the ordinary members through a ballot vote.

The draft agreement was based on the Coal Board proposals. It involved fixing a standard task through method study on each coalface and development face. The basic task would be 75 per cent of the standard task. The incentive lay in the fact that a miner who completed 100 per cent of the standard task would be paid an additional £2.50. It was estimated that face workers, in the main, would be able to earn £12.50 a week in addition to the basic rate of £45 a week. A proportion of the increase was to be paid to other underground workers and surface workers.

The draft agreement created deep divisions on the National Executive Committee which did not correspond to the left-right spectrum. A motion from Dai Francis to reject the agreement was narrowly defeated but a motion for acceptance was also defeated. The Executive could not make its mind up one way or the other so it decided first to call a Special Conference to hear details of the scheme and then to submit it to a ballot vote of the members without having a recommendation from either the Executive or the Special Conference. The result of the ballot was announced on 20th November, 1974 showing that 61.53 per cent of the members rejected the incentive scheme.

This ballot vote decision was a considerable achievement for the left-wing Areas because they had campaigned against incentives on principle, explaining that they would be divisive, pitting man against man, and pit against pit in a struggle which would increase risks and penalize the old and the weak. The majorities against incentives in the left-wing Areas were substantial. In Yorkshire 40,958 miners out of 49,194 voted against as did 11,958 miners out of 15,626 in Scotland and 19,941 miners out of 24,040 miners in South Wales. The overall result was conclusive. The N.E.C. accepted it and the president, in the December 1974 edition of the *Miner,* stated that "the N.U.M. membership have had their say at the ballot box and the productivity deal is not on."

273

The issue, however, was not allowed to drop. Joe Gromley had consistently said that he was in favour of the re-introduction of an incentive scheme and maintained this view despite the ballot. the president of the Nottingham Miners, Mr. Len Clarke, who had moved the acceptance of the draft agreement on the N.E.C. continued to campaign for it along with officials of the North Western Area. Indeed the North Western Area submitted a motion in 1976 to persuade the Union to allow Areas to negotiate their own local agreements but withdrew it from the Conference. The same motion was re-submitted but withdrawn again the following year.

Two motions dealing with incentives were debated at the 1977 Tynemouth Conference. First, the South Derbyshire Area attempted to overcome the result of the ballot vote with a motion which demanded "the immediate implementation of a meaningful Incentive Scheme to improve both coal production and wage levels. If such an incentive Scheme cannot be agreed on a national basis, the individual Areas of the National Union of Mineworkers to negotiate their own Area schemes." There was much exitement amongst the delegates about the motion because a rough count indicated that it might be successful. The Cokemen's Area with its six votes was vascillating. It was said that a lunchtime discussion between Emlyn Williams, the president of the South Wales Area and a convinced opponent of incentive schemes, and the Cokemen's delegation clinched the issue and the motion was defeated. After this a South Wales motion opposing incentive schemes, confirming the result of the 1974 ballot vote and adding that "the reintroduction of the piecework system would destroy the unity in the union which the day wage system has created," was passed as a formality. The opponents of piecework were jubilant for they had both a national ballot vote and a Conference decision to back them. The issue was stone dead they thought as they went away for their summer holidays.

The issue, however, was not dead. Although the wages resolution of 1977 aiming for £135 a week was a badly worded one the national leadership still felt that some action was necessary to take the heat out of it and what better for this purpose than a cash bonus. Moreover, the officials of nine Areas had written to the Executive asking for productivity negotiations to be re-opened and seeking permission to conclude local agreements. When the National Executive Committee met on 1st September 1977, the National officials had already met the N.C.B. over the future of incentives and the Coal Board had responded by sending revised proposals for a scheme. There were claims at this Executive meeting that the Tyneside Conference decisions did not reflect the views of the membership so the Executive decided to continue with the negotiations.

The revised incentive scheme was accepted by the National Executive Committee after some amendments and was submitted

274

to the membership for its approval by ballot vote. The key to success of a ballot proposal usually depended on whether or not it had the support of the Executive. The 1974 proposal for an incentive scheme went out without any comment by the Executive and this was seen as an important contributory factor leading to its rejection. The ballot had been preceded, moreover, by an intensive left-wing campaign against the incentive scheme. But in July, 1977, just after the Annual Conference the National Executive Committee was given a salutory reminder that even a recommended proposal could be defeated. A contentious National Concessionary Coal Scheme was recommended to miners by the Executive through a ballot vote in July. Four Areas, including Nottingham and Yorkshire, had threatened to call strikes if the Scheme was signed. The Scheme was rejected by a 55 per cent majority, even though 91 per cent of the South Wales miners and 97 per cent of the Scottish miners had favoured it.

Nonetheless the Executive went ahead with its ballot vote over the incentive scheme clearly confident that it would be accepted. The balance of votes at the recent Annual Conference had been close. Miners, like other groups of workers in Britain, had suffered a lowering of their living standards since 1974 and, it was thought, would welcome a boost to their earnings. In addition, the ballot was timed so that there was little opportunity for campaigning. A special edition of *The Miner* was distributed to explain and advocate the scheme but the left-wing Areas were caught unprepared for after the vote against incentives at the Annual Conference their officials never contemplated that there would be such rapid developments. Most of these officials gloomily anticipated that the Executive recommendation would be endorsed. They were deeply concerned by the way in which the Union constitution was being misused but could see no way within the rules of redressing the situation.

Judicial Views

It appeared that the only option open was to seek an injunction in law to restrain the National Executive Committee from holding another ballot when the union policy was so clearly against incentives. Some of the left-wing officials, such as Michael McGahey, were opposed to seeking a legal solution to an internal union problem because they recognised that the judiciary had never shown sympathy to the working class and believed, in any case, that the trade union movement should resolve its own disputes. Others, including Arthur Scargill and Jack Dunn, were convinced that their case was so watertight that it could not fail to win. Jack Dunn, on behalf of the Kent miners, took the matter to court after mass meetings at each of the three pits in his Area had endorsed the proposal. Only one miner at these meetings opposed the decision to go to court.

The Kent Area's case aimed to stop the National Executive Committee from calling a ballot of the membership over the question of incentives because the National Executive Committee had no right to do so under the rules. It was not opposed to national ballots but was opposed to their misuse. The Kent miners insisted that according to Rule 23 a ballot could only be called by a Special Conference and that, in any case, a ballot over a national incentive scheme was inadmissible because the Annual Conference had already decided the issue and Rule 8 stipulated that the National Executive Committee could not act "contrary to or in defiance of, any resolution of Conference."

The case was heard in the Chancery Division of the High Court and the decision was given against the Kent Area by the Vice-Chancellor on 19th October, 1977, one week before the ballot was due to be held. It was another illustration in a long history of judicial decisions where the rules were interpreted in a manner which was contrary to the spirit and intentions of those who made them. There is no doubt that these union rules were framed in order to control the exercise of authority and to place the ultimate power in the hands of elected representatives of the miners, not in the hands of miners themselves through ballot votes. The High Court confronted the rules as a series of related guides, looking for what they did not say just as much as for what they did say, looking for shortcomings and loopholes, examining them for logical consistency, even taking notice of the structure of the sentences. It was essentially an upper middle class intellectual activity.

The judgement of the Vice-Chancellor of the Chancery Division mentioned that apart from Rule 8 the rules were silent about the general duties of the N.E.C. On the other hand there were many specific provisions in the rules. The implication was that the rules were intended to give scope to the N.E.C. otherwise they would have contained specific provisions. But for miners the statement in Rule 8 that "In the periods between Conferences the National Executive Committee shall administer the business and affairs of the Union and perform all duties laid down for it by resolution of Conference, and it shall not at any time act contrary to, or in defiance of, any resolution of the Conference" meant one thing which covered all contingencies, namely that the National Executive was subordinate to delegate Conferences. This was made clear at many Conferences. In the same way it was an abuse of the miners' intention to concentrate power with rank and file delegates to interpret Rule 23, which stipulated that ballot votes should be called by Conference decisions, as dealing with nothing "except the mode of voting at a special conference." Union rules which are read literally and out of the context of struggle can provide any number of contrasting meanings.

The judicial view of democratic processes was contained in the conclusion to the judgement. "What the N.E.C. is proposing to do," it stated, "is to hold a secret ballot of all members. This is the very essence of the democratic process. There will be no block votes in which the voice of a majority of a group, however small, was treated as the voice of the whole group; no question arising as to whether a delegate has voted in accordance with the wishes of those he represents. Every member is free to vote; every vote counts; no-one is shut out or left unheard." This view was endorsed by the Court of Appeal, to which the Kent Area took its case immediately after the High Court had rejected it. Lord Denning, the Master of the Rolls stated that it "was a sensible and reasonable proposal by the N.E.C. to take the views by the democratic method of a secret ballot of all the workers affected. It was a far more satisfactory and democratic method than leaving it to the delegates of a conference who might not be truly representative in their individual capacities of views of the various men they represent."

This view of democracy as decision-making by referenda conflicted with the British Parliamentary system and with the way in which the majority of trade unions conducted their business. But it suited this occasion. Indeed Judges have always been able to produce interpretations to suit the occasion, no matter what legal or ethical contortions were involved, so long as they protected the dominant power group. On this occasion the Government's pay policy was at issue. The majority of members of the National Executive Committee supported the Government's pay policy and wanted an incentive scheme as a means of protecting it. Their power to act as they wished for this purpose was endorsed by the Courts. Indeed the unwritten powers of the N.E.C. were made explicit by the Appeal Court and, in a sense, were written into the rules. "Though the rules do not give the N.E.C. an express power to do so," Denning stated, "it is entrusted with such wide powers and duties that such a power can be implied." This was a licence for the N.E.C. to do whatever it wished. On this occasion it wished for a ballot vote.

Miners in their various Areas met and made recommendations about the suggested national incentive scheme. The left-wing Areas urged their members to vote against it; Nottingham, South Derbyshire and the Midlands Areas advocated acceptance. The brief campaign before the ballot engendered much invective and ill-feeling between officials in the different Areas. It had always been a contentious matter when Areas decided to use their considerable financial resources to campaign against National Executive Committee decisions. On this occasion leaflets opposing incentives were distributed and advertisements appeared in the press advising miners to reject the N.E.C. recommendation.

The result of the ballot vote surprised the left-wing officials as much as it distressed the right-wing ones for 55.75 per cent of the miners voted to reject the incentive scheme. As many as 83 per cent of the miners in Scotland and South Wales rejected incentives while in Yorkshire the figure was nearly 77 per cent. Substantial minorities in the right-wing Areas also opposed incentives. The percentage against in the North Western Area was 45.5, in the Nottingham Area 39.75, in the Midlands Area 46.0. These large minorities in Areas where there was no vocal opposition to the incentive scheme ensured a majority vote against it.

The judicially endorsed democratic process had produced a wholly unexpected result. Most of the press and the right wing Union leaders reacted to it in such a way as to confirm the view that in essence democracy is measured by achievements and not the quality of the means used to reach them. Those newspapers which had applauded the judges' decision were not particularly concerned about democratic decision-making when they saw that it operated against what they regarded as the "national interest." The result of the ballot was greeted by *The Times* with the headline "On collision course now as the miners plunge the pay policy into darkness;" the *Daily Telegraph* proclaimed "Confrontation looming for Callaghan." Confrontation, collision, precipice, disaster became favourite terms. Those newspapers did not say 'the democratic voice of the miners has been heard; they do not want to return to a piecework system and that is that.'

The majority of the Union's National Executive Committee were unwilling to accept the ballot result as the last word. When they heard it in November, 1977 they called for the ballot "to be declared null and void," for action to be taken against Executive members who were disloyal to Executive decisions, and for Areas which had supported the incentive scheme to be given the authority to negotiate local ones. Those on the losing side were not at all sure now that the judicial interpretation of democracy was as useful as it had seemed at first. What they could do about it, however, apart from making vocal protests, depended upon the behaviour of the Union president, Mr. Gormley. If Mr. Gormley ruled that the decision of the ballot was final and binding in respect of incentive schemes until such time as the issue could be raised again legitimately at an Annual Conference, the matter would have had to rest there despite pleas to the contrary. But Mr. Gormley did not do this. He opened the way for the majority on the National Executive Committee to assert itself by permitting the question of separate Area schemes to be raised at the same time as the result of the ballot was accepted.

The left wing members of the Executive felt that Mr. Gormley was under pressure from the Prime Minister to get some kind of incentive scheme introduced in order both to devalue the miners' wage claim and to break the solidarity around wages which the day-wage system created. It was believed that the Government wanted to take the miners out of the annual wages struggle as a way of preserving its incomes policy. Having unpublicized backdoor meetings with Prime Ministers had virtually become a way of life for Mr. Gormley since the 1972 miners strike. Whenever crises arose involving the miners there was always a submerged background of political intrigue against which the public debates and the constitutional decision-making took place. The ordinary miners learned about such activities only through rumour or speculation or revelation after the event. In 1977 the basis was rumour. Mr. Gormley, of course, had been consistently in favour of re-introducing incentives. The difference between this occasion and others, however, lay in the lengths he was prepared to go to to get them as he illustrated at the meeting of the National Executive Committee on 8th December, 1977.

It was claimed during the acrimony surrounding the national ballot that incentive payments and bonuses were already being paid out in the Areas opposing incentive schemes. This was elaborated when the National Executive Committee met in December and was informed that "Research has revealed that payments to workmen outside the provisions of the daywage system existed on a large scale . . . the Board's representatives accepted that overtime payments, short shifts and allowances were devices which were being used to conceal extra payment . . ." This explanation was used by the supporters of incentives to justify giving Areas permission "to enter into self-financing production incentive schemes on uniform lines." The National Executive Committee, on a majority vote, agreed to permit local arrangements and rejected accusations that it was acting unconstitutionally because, it claimed, the ballot result referred only to a national incentive scheme.

So each Area was given the right to enter into a local agreement if it wished. There was no compulsion from the Executive to do one thing or the other. Nottingham, Leicester and South Derbyshire began negotiations with the Coal Board and their members were given bonuses on approval, before any scheme was introduced. Local Coal Board officials began what amounted to a propaganda campaign for the re-introduction of incentives. Gossip about earnings, about money for nothing, flowed from pit to pit and from Area to Area. The resistance of the miners opposed to incentives collapsed once some Areas began to operate them. The left wing Areas hung on for a time but they took no concerted action and eventually gave way, first Scotland and Kent and then South Wales and Yorkshire. Incentive payments returned as a fact of life for the miners. By finding a circuitous way around the Union rules the National Executive Committee had achieved its objective.

Before the struggle was over, however, the South Derbyshire

Area, the two national full-time officials, Joe Gormley and Lawrence Daly, and the National Executive Committee were taken to court again, this time by the Yorkshire, South Wales and Kent Areas which sought an injunction to prevent the conclusion of any incentive payments agreement and requiring the N.E.C. to revoke its decision to allow local agreements on the grounds that it was *ultra vires* and, therefore, null and void. Logic, it seemed, had to be on the side of the plaintiffs. Having glorified the national ballot what could the judges but do re-affirm their belief?

Judgement was given by Mr. Justice Watkins in the Queen's Bench Division on 21st December, 1977, and went in favour of the national officials, the Executive and South Derbyshire. The suspicion of the legal system as an instrument for solving Labour Movement problems was confirmed, for the Judgement looked very much like a decision to support the National Executive Committee rather than as an examination of facts leading to a conclusion. There was little logic in it and even less sense in terms of the way miners collectively perceive their business.

Mr. Justice Watkins quite correctly warned against treating union rule books as if they were pieces of Parliamentary legislation though Judges have never been inhibited from reshaping the most thoroughly drafted Acts of Parliament. He quoted from a speech by Lord Wilberforce during an appeal case involving Heaton's Transport and the Transport and General Workers' Union in 1973. "But Trade Union rule books," Lord Wilberforce stated, "are not drafted by Parliamentary draughtsmen. Courts of Law must resist the temptation to construe them as if they were; for that is not how they would be understood by the members who are the parties to the argument . . ." But he proceeded to ignore his own advice and to dissect the rules, the wording of Conference decisions and the question on the ballot paper in a way which had no relevance for miners.

Judges epitomize the values of the system they interpret for if they did not then their positions would be untenable; they would have an undermining effect instead of a protective one. They are the embodiment of upper middle class values, with no experience and understanding of working class life, either of an individual or a collective kind. Their skill is essentially a technical one of interpreting rules but in the process they communicate their own values. They can be objective in their interpretation but never impartial.

The Judgement elaborated and confirmed the National Executive Committee in its power position. Although previously it had been stated that the national secret ballot was the essence of the democratic process, Mr. Justice Watkins now stated that "The result of a ballot, nationally conducted is not binding upon the National Executive Committee in using its powers in between conferences. It may serve to persuade the Committee to take one action or another, or to refrain from action, but it has no great force or significance." This second judicial ruling showed that the Executive could justify virtually whatever it liked before the courts because in legal terms the rule book was so loose. "In my considered view," Mr. Justice Watkins added, "the National Executive Committee are not, and cannot rightly be said to have been acting in contravention of any rule in the rule book or of any resolution of the immediately previous conference or of any conference before that in doing what has been done." It is not surprising that judiciaries have been able to accommodate themselves to transitions from democracy to fascism for the definition of right and wrong so often depends upon who is involved and not upon what is done.

Blocked Avenues

There was much discussion amongst miners around this time about their disillusionment with their Union processes. They saw voting and the passing of resolutions at conferences as futile acts. This response was emphasized during the election campaign in the Scottish Area to find a successor as general secretary to Bill McLean who had died suddenly in September, 1978, when working miners retorted 'what is the use of voting anyway.' It was also reported to be prevalent in Yorkshire and South Wales. The two court rulings seriously depressed those miners concerned about democratic processes.

This depression was all the more warranted because successive attempts to democratize the structure of the Union by constitutional means had failed. The South Wales Area at the 1971 Annual Conference had agreed to remit to the National Executive Committee a motion asking for the progressive integration of "the various existing Groups with the several major Areas of the coalfield" because it "would strengthen and modernise the Union and bring about a more equitable representation from the Areas on the National Executive Committee." At the same Conference a Yorkshire demand for a block voting system on the National Executive Committee was excluded from the agenda because it was not framed as a rule or an amendment to rule. The next year the Yorkshire Area came back with a proposed rule alteration suggesting that each Executive member should have one vote for each 1000 members he represented. The motion was defeated because it did not obtain the two-thirds majority required for a change of rule.

Meanwhile the National Executive Committee did nothing about the South Wales Resolution. In 1973 the Yorkshire Area submitted a detailed plan for re-organization, creating 10 Areas out of the existing 26. It was an equitable plan but if it had been applied it would have swung the balance of power on the N.E.C. to the left.

The proposal was excluded because, inadvertently, it had not mentioned all the Constituent Associations. So, taking the exclusion of their motion seriously the Yorkshire Area officials took legal advice about their motion, dotted the i's and crossed the t's, made good the defects in the motion, and resubmitted it for the 1974 Annual Conference. This time it was kept off the agenda because it excluded "a Constituent Association contrary to rule." In fact it referred to Power Group workers instead of mentioning their formal title, namely Power Group No. 2.

The left wing members of the N.E.C. began to feel that the constitutional avenue was blocked. If the president had wanted to have even a discussion about re-organization at the Conference, the draft of the Yorkshire motion could have been improved after a telephone call to Arthur Scargill. But he made no such call. Nonetheless attempts to improve the Union organization continued to be made. The National Executive Committee had the opportunity of altering the status of small Areas when their respective sole full-time officials retired and permission was sought to re-appoint. An Area without a full-time official would necessarily come under the tutelage of a bigger neighbourhood Area and would cease to have separate Executive representation. Both Cumberland and North Wales with their tiny memberships successfully applied for permission for each to re-appoint a full-time official late in 1974 and so were able to continue as before. The Yorkshire and South Wales Areas appealed against the Executive decision which allowed the anachronism of these Areas to continue but the appeals were rejected. Then the Derbyshire and Yorkshire Areas tried to introduce a block voting system on the National Executive Committee so that each member voted according to the number of members he represented. Such attempts, made right up to the 1981 Annual Conference, also failed.

The National Executive Committee was reprimanded by Annual Conferences, sometimes with its own support, but this had no effect on its behaviour. A resolution from the Scottish Area was passed in 1976 declaring that Rule 8, referring to the powers of the Annual Conference, was "binding and inflexible." The Kent Area successfully moved a resolution in 1978 expressing "deep concern about the failure of the National Executive Committee to honour the Rules of the Union that have led to a diminution of democracy within the Union . . ." The next year the Kent Area had Executive support for a resolution demanding "that the National Executive Committee takes immediate action to recognize and implement policies of the Union determined by Annual Conference each year."

The National Executive Committee had everything its own way. It piously supported the sanctity of the rules whilst flouting them with impunity. There was no possibility of changing this situation

282

without altering the left/right representation on the N.E.C., and this could only be done by the miners in those Areas which possessed a disproportionate amount of power in the Union.

The Contradiction

The cause of the democratic problem in the N.U.M. lies in its structure as a *de facto* federation of semi-autonomous county unions disguised as Areas of a national union. Each of the Areas of the N.U.M. is a trade union in its own right. Each one collects its own finance and sends an allocation to the central office so that Areas have accumulated funds which they control. Each Area meets and formulates its own policy. This situation has its contradiction. Areas can resist changes to make control more democratic in the Union as a whole. By their grip on their historical identities they can prevent the creation of a truly unified, centralized Union in which executive representation throughout the Union is determined solely by a simple arithmetic test. There would be no question of one person representing 16,373 members while another, with the same voting power, represented only 914 members if the Union had a centralized constitution. But, on the other hand, the existence of separate financially independent Areas with their own policies has allowed an expression of contrary, competing views supported by meetings, leaflets and pamphlets, which would be impossible in a centralized union. The big debates about policies in the N.U.M. occur mainly because of its federal character. It is the most open, politically divided union of any in Britain but in action it is the most unified.

The arguments about democratic processes do not always refer to the issue of power. They are often conducted, particularly by the right-wing Areas, in terms of historical identity, of autonomy, of the rights of small groups to exist. Much anger is generated when the question of merging small Areas is raised. But the anger, the talk about identity, camouflage the real issue of power. No right-wing Area, no matter what its size is, is willing to accept changes in Union organization which will tip the balance of power to the left, regardless of how sensible, logical and principled the change might be. Only left-wing Kent amongst the small Areas has expressed a willingness to merge. The point is that the Union does not operate in a vacuum. It is a crucial political weapon in the class struggle. The magnificent solidarity of the miners is fought for both by those who wish to keep capitalism and those who wish to change it. This occurs through the medium of struggles between the Areas of the Union to win the allegiance of miners, to dominate Annual Conference deliberations and to achieve consistent majorities on the National Executive. The issue of democracy in the National Union of Mineworkers, then, is not an internal Union one but has wide political implications.

CHAPTER 20

STRUGGLE

The Charters

During the course of the 1974 miners' strike, Bill McLean stated that the Scottish Area executive committee had decided to publish a Miners' Charter which would be presented to the next Union Annual Conference. The intention was to draw together into one document the conditions which had to be improved in order to raise the standard of mining to a socially acceptable level. It was to deal with all the main facets of the work environment.

The idea of arousing support amongst miners around a Charter had historical precedents. *The Miners' Next Step* had been published in 1912 by the Unofficial Reform Committee in South Wales. It arose out of a deep discontent with worsening coal-getting conditions and disillusionment with the ability of the South Wales Miners' Federation to deal with them. It generated enthusiasm from ordinary miners and hostility from the leadership. Much of *The Miners' Next Step* was concerned with organization and methods; with attacking the authoritarianism of the South Wales Miners' Federation and its conciliatory policies. It projected proposals to democratize union action in a class struggle with the coal owners. Its long-term aim was syndicalism through which employers were eliminated and industrial democracy was secured. Its shorter term aims included a minimum wage for miners and a 7 hour day achieved by a single, centrally organized, compact mining union. Almost all of its proposals remain unfulfilled though as a document it secured a place in the history of mining trade unionism.

The next Charter was drafted for entirely different reasons. In the period between the election of the Labour Government in 1945 and the nationalization of the coal industry in 1947 the Minister of Fuel and Power, Mr. Emanuel Shinwell, asked for the assistance of the N.U.M. in tackling the problem of recruitment into the mines. The Union's National Executive Committee responded by listing the changes in conditions which it thought were needed in order to attract new recruits and presented them as a Charter of Demands in January, 1946.

Some of the demands were met though they did not cease to be relevant because of the changing levels of expectations of miners. Issues concerning improvements in conditions of work, of welfare and of housing are in a sense timeless. The demand for two consecutive weeks' holiday was eventually satisfied but was overtaken by improvements in holiday provisions outside of mining. New safety laws were introduced but the conditions of modern mining altered making it necessary to affect further changes. The Mines and Quarries Act of 1954 could not have anticipated the rapid mechanization of mining which followed that date. New mining towns and villages were built after the Second World War but were transformed in their industrial composition by the closure of pits in the 1960s. The breakdown of segregation between mineworkers and others occurred through the dispersion of miners as pits closed rather than through social policy decisions.

In important aspects concerning wages, the protection of earnings, hours of work and the provision of health and safety measures, the Charter's demands were still not met when the Scottish Area of the N.U.M. decided in 1974 to present another one. *The Miners' New Charter* aimed at these issues, emphasizing the rejection of dirty, dangerous work and low wages. But this time the miners did not just submit a shopping list. They presented a philosophy within which the demands logically slotted. In its introduction it stated that:

"We miners reject the old popular image of the miner as a person apart, conditioned by harsh, deadly conditions, living in closed communities, to be both feared and pitied, capable of hard living in work and leisure. We have had much public sympathy on this score and in our struggles we have welcomed it. But we do not intend to live by it. We intend to change the conditions which have given rise to the truths and half-truths about mining . . .

"We miners refuse to accept the values which place the lowest rewards on the dirtiest and most dangerous jobs and the highest rewards on the lightest, most comfortable, least dangerous work . . . We want to be rewarded for our respective contributions to the welfare of society, for our skills and for the risks we undertake . . .

"We miners reject the idea that bad conditions can be compensated for by paltry increases in earnings. Miners in the past have always been bought off when working conditions have been bad . . . What we are saying now is that coal must be mined in acceptable conditions. The era of financial compensation for discomfort, disease, injury and death is over. If water is excessive then it must be controlled; if temperatures are high they must be lowered; if dust is excessive it must be contained."

The Miners New Charter, though formally initiated and then published by the Scottish Area resulted from collaboration between miners in a number of Areas and reflected in its demands emphases from those Areas. Miners know that some Areas have long-standing interests in particular issues, such as the Nottingham concern about protecting the earnings of miners who are compelled to switch jobs because of injury or disease.

Nineteen demands were listed. Some attempted to establish guiding principles, such as the one rejecting the "sharp differentiation between management and miners in the mining industry in terms of pay and conditions of work." Others were specific, demanding £5,000 a year at 1974 values, a four day working week between Monday and Friday and guaranteed wages during sickness and injury. The third category was concerned with providing medical and social protection to miners and their families in the event of injury, disease or death. It must "no longer be the gruesome case," the seventh demand declared, "that when a dead miner enters the front door, poverty moves in through the back door." And as a vital precautionary, preventative measure the *Charter* insisted on the introduction of an extensive industrial health service with panels of full-time doctors with specialisms in industrial medicine to be available on demand and a qualified nurse to be located at every pit. It wanted frequent compulsory medical checks and the recognition of emphysema and bronchitis as mining industrial diseases.

The Coal Market

The *Miners' New Charter* was launched from a position of strength. The 1974 strike was over and the Government had lost; the fuel crisis was intensifying and a Labour Government had been elected which aimed to tackle it by exploiting indigenous coal resources. As soon as the strike was settled tripartite talks between the National Union of Mineworkers, the National Coal Board and the Government were held to ensure the future of the industry. The talks were conducted around the National Coal Board's *"Plan for Coal"* which was accepted as a broad strategy for the development of the industry. Everyone was optimistic. The mood was reminiscent of that in the immediate post-war period. The optimism was reflected in the preliminary results of the talks published in the *Coal Industry Examination Interim Report* in June, 1974.

The National Coal Board intended to reverse the trend in which the total output of deep mined coal had fallen from 210 million tons in the 1950s to 120 million tons in 1973 and the number of miners had fallen from more than 700,000 to less than 270,000. It planned to raise an extra 42 million tons of coal a year by extending the lives of pits which in different circumstances would have been closed, developing major schemes at existing pits and sinking new collieries. Ten million tons of coal a year were to come from the new Selby coalfield in Yorkshire.

The major consumers gave comforting reassurances about future demand. The Central Electricity Generating Board which accounted for 58 per cent of coal consumption in 1973, amounting to 76 million tons, believed it would be able to burn 90 million tons or more in 1985. The National Coal Board anticipated that the C.E.G.B. would take all the coal it could get up to that date but some new coal-fired generating plant would need to be installed. The second largest consumer, the British Steel Corporation, estimated that its total consumption of coking coal would rise from 16 to 18 million tons a year by 1981 and that it would "continue to depend heavily on indigenous supplies." All in all the National Coal Board believed that the demand for coal up to the mid-1980s was likely to exceed current levels of output and could reach an annual amount of 150 million tons. The industry's emphasis was on production and, in consequence, on obtaining an adequate supply of miners.

The Government agreed to back the Report's proposals for increasing output by 42 million tons and to assist the N.C.B. to meet their estimated £600 million cost. The leaders of the left wing coalfields, however, believed that this figure was inadequate, as was the production target which the N.C.B. had set itself. *The Miners' New Charter* had demanded a level of output of 200 million tons which had been the figure discussed at a meeting of left-wing miners in Chesterfield eight years earlier. The N.U.M. had asked for a yearly output of 150 million tons in its evidence to the Tripartite Committee but this level was seen as a holding operation. If the fuel crisis had taught real lessons then the level of 200 million tons had to be reached. The proposals, moreover, were just about coal. There was no mention of the planned production and use of other energy sources. The Report assumed that the relationship between alternative sources of energy would continue to be determined by the hazardous play of market forces and this was a major defect in its proposals. The Government, however, did give an assurance "that short-term fluctuations in the price and availability of competing fuels will not be allowed to interfere with steady progress in the implementation of the Plan" but it added the rider that "coal must remain competitive in the light of long-term trends."

The plans laid for the coal industry by the Coal Industry Tripartite Committee envisaged the development of large centralized centres of coal production through sinking new pits, linking up existing pits and rationalizing and expanding existing pits. The programme was similar to that launched at the inception of nationalization in 1947. It will be recalled that there were pit closures in that period but they were kept to a minimum by the buoyant market for coal. When plans were introduced in 1974 it was assumed that at least the country's total energy requirements would be maintained and that coal would increase its share of the energy market because of difficulties over the supply of oil. For this reason it was anticipated that the issue of pit closures would be peripheral and determined mainly by the exhaustion of coal reserves. The principal problem, from the National Coal Board's point of view, was to maintain production levels.

Britain's energy requirements in 1974 compelled the Government to be serious about the expansion of the coal industry. This was emphasized by Mr. Tony Benn, who was appointed Secretary of State for Energy from June, 1975, for he was acutely sympathetic towards the miners' interests and reflected this in his policy-making. It was of practical importance that the miners' welfare should have been given priority for the question of uplifting the earnings of miners within conditions of stable employment and satisfactory working conditions was inextricably linked with the future of the coal industry. The expansion of the industry was not simply about finance. It was also about human investment. The demands of the 1974 Charter and the needs of the Government re-inforced each other.

The leaders of the left wing Areas recognised the interlocking character of the interests of miners and the industry in the expansion period after 1974 and, indeed, made it a part of their case. Yet Scargill, McGahey, Williams, Heathfield and Dunn never forgot that they were involved in a class struggle in which every incremental improvement had to be fought for. But because of past successes and the impact of the fuel crisis they were optimistic about winning at least some of the Charter's demands. This optimism did not last long for the conditions on which it was based were seriously eroded during the second half of the decade.

Fractured Unity

Firstly, the unity which had characterized Union activity between 1971 and 1974 was fractured. The left-wing leaders were not able to mobilize the Union on any issue which was at variance with Government policy. I have described in the previous chapter how the Union president, Joe Gormley, used his authority to manipulate the rules in the Government's interest. On every important issue the left wing leaders were confronted by opposition from the two full-time national officials and a majority on the National Executive Committee before having to deal with either the National Coal Board or the Government. They made no progress at all on the issue of wages between 1974 and 1981. Moreover, because the Labour Government's incomes policies after 1974 generally included fringe benefit impovements under the heading of wage advances, no progress was made on any issue in the Charter which would have increased labour costs. Left wing initiatives, including those which were directed against the Conservative Government led by Mrs. Thatcher, were firmly and promptly defused until the issue of pit closures was raised in February, 1981.

Secondly, the ideological struggle became more intense after 1974. Governments framed and timed policies to take account of the miners' power, as, for instance, when the Government's incomes policy was announced on the eve of the Miners' Conference in July, 1975. Public attention was focussed on every miners' demand which was likely to ruffle the National Coal Board or upset the Government. Left wing demands largely had to prove themselves through their relevance to mining conditions in the face of much hostile public comment. Miners frequently had their minds made up by accusations that they were intensifying inflation, increasing unemployment, threatening the Government, jeopardizing the future of the coal industry, before alternative explanations could influence them. Miners, no more than other workers, did not want to be seen as disruptive.

The left wing Areas had scanty resources in relation to the mass media in the campaign of explanations though what they did have were important. In times of crisis they published leaflets on a national and local scale, convened delegate conferences and held mass meetings. The practice was continued in the Scottish Area of holding pit-head meetings for each shift to give miners first-hand reports of negotiations and confrontations. Other Areas used different methods. In Yorkshire, for example, the traditional means of activating ordinary members was to hold mass meetings of branch officials. There was virtually no support for left wing initiatives from the national daily press except from the *Morning Star*. There was the same unsympathetic response in the provincial daily and weekly press. *Coal News* retained a wide circulation for managerial ideas though it had to contend with increasing competition from Union journals. The National Union of Mineworkers published *The Miner* but this was always regarded as the mouthpiece of the official Union, reflecting the views of the president and with a marked bias towards conformity with the management. Until January 1977 when the Yorkshire Area published the *Yorkshire Miner* through the initiative of Arthur Scargill, the *Scottish Miner* was the only miners' journal which consistently challenged the legitimacy of the mass media. Both of these journals were distributed in other Areas and played an important part in moulding miners' views. The Derbyshire Area added its voice in January, 1981 when it began publishing the *Derbyshire Miner*. The leading officials in the left wing Areas appeared more frequently on television and radio after 1974 to give snippets of counter-information. Some of them became household names in non-mining homes. But all of this was insufficient to contradict the images created by the mass media and to undermine those political attitudes which protected Governments from extra-parliamentary action by trade unions.

Thirdly, the unity of the left-wing Areas was weakened by the combination of pressures against them. As old tactics failed there were disagreements about which new ones to pursue. The officials continued to meet periodically to discuss both policies and tactics but inclined to carry their differences into practice rather than resolve or submerge them. The people who had so successfully raised the consciousness of the miners up till 1974 found it difficult to live with the changes which that success had created. Chauvinism amongst the Areas became more pronounced, due mainly to the mistaken belief that their unity had become less important for directing the course of the Union.

289

There were personality differences. Arthur Scargill had intruded as an official leader with national importance with the speed of a projectile and had disturbed the fairly settled leadership relations which had been established during the struggles in opposition. Some left wing Area officials were disturbed by the speed of the intrusion. The mantle of unofficial leader which had been borne by Michael McGahey was carried less securely after Scargill became the president of the Yorkshire Area. There were rival left wing contenders for whatever crown in the Union became vacant who were reluctant to resolve their competition in a quiet, informal manner. There were discussions about styles of leadership, contrasting Scargill with McGahey, with rival camps emerging.

Personality differences existed but they were less significant than the ones projected in the media. Virtually all problems in the N.U.M. were explained in terms of a rivalry between Arthur Scargill and Michael McGahey. Their relatively minor differences over policies were transformed by the press into mutual hostility. Unfortunatley, however, betweem 1975 and 1979, the main persons in this scenario tended to act out the imagery which was created by the media. They subordinated analyses of policies to a pre-occupation with leadership styles. Both Scargill and McGahey felt under attack from each other. They virtually lost the ability to communicate with each other and re-inforced the emergence of opposing factions. None of the left wing leaders was unaffected by the undercurrent of hostility stimulated by the circulation of rumours. McGahey began to perceive Scargill's activities as a form of adventurism while Scargill felt isolated and shunned. The quality of his contributions was overshadowed by a suspicion about his motives. He felt impelled to act independantly.

The president of the Union made his substantial contribution to the difficulties of the left wing by periodically hinting that he intended to retire early. This encouraged speculation about the contenders for his position and gave ammunition to the press to be divisive. Michael McGahey had been choosen in 1971 to stand as the left wing candidate in the election for president and no subsequent meeting had decided that he should be displaced. There was no open debate within the left wing Areas, therefore, about the situation in which Arthur Scargill was a contender. Moreover, as Joe Gormley's hints about retirement became recognized as a provocation these Areas refused to intensify their differences by engaging in a debate about the relative merits of McGahey and Scargill. Gradually the superficiality of the personality differences began to emerge in 1978 as pressures on miners, along with other members of the working class, intensified and their attachment to the Labour Government began to weaken.

Time made a decision for them for once McGahey reached the

age of 55 years in 1980 he became ineligible according to the rules of the Union to stand for national office. Then, early in 1980, the left wing Areas united behind Scargill. Michael McGahey publicly came out in support of Scargill as the sole candidate of the left wing in a contest for the presidency of the Union and threw his considerable influence behind him, providing fresh avenues for Scargill to expound his views. Without fuel to fire the personality contest it was entirely extinguished. The left wing began again to talk and agree about policies.

The Degradation of Labour

Many issues out of the totality of treatment of mining labour were raised after the 1974 strike. Three of them, claims for compensation, the provision of medical and general health facilities in pits and early retirement were especially important. Progress was made on only two of these but even there much remained to be done. None of the issues had finite boundaries; they were all subject to rising horizons so at no stage was a satisfactory end even in sight.

(i) *Claims for Compensation*

The Labour Government introduced a new Pneumoconiosis Compensation Scheme in October 1974 as a mark of its rekindled interest in mining conditions through the strike and oil crisis. The Scheme gave automatic financial relief to all pneumoconiotics or their dependents who were entitled to weekly disablement benefit for pneumoconiosis contracted as a result of 10 years' employment in the coal mining industry. It removed uncertainty by making it unnecessary for miners or their dependants to use litigation in order to get compensation. In return for the new provisions the Union agreed to withdraw approximately 4,000 cases from litigation.

The scheme applied to all living certified pneumoconiotics and the dependents of those who had died after 26th January, 1970. The incidence of pneumoconiosis can be gauged from the fact that by 31st March, 1980, 63,477 cases which had been outstanding at the inception of the Scheme in 1974 had been settled and that 2,614 cases had arisen between 1974 and 1980. There was dissatisfaction with the Scheme because of the paucity of the amounts paid and because it excluded from benefit so many widows of pneumoconiotics who had died before 1970 but it was a significant advance. The improvement it brought, however, focussed attention on other facets of the incidence and assessment of industrial diseases which penalized miners and their dependants.

There is much concern about the refusal of Governments to recognize emphysema and bronchitis as industrial diseases. Emphysema is common amongst miners. It can only be diagnosed during life when it is in an advanced state. It so frequently accompanies pneumoconiosis that it is possible that it is caused by it. Yet only pneumoconiosis is recognized. There is no problem about separating chronic bronchitis, which is common amongst miners, from the other diseases even though it may accompany pneumoconiosis. There is neither logic nor serious medical evidence to support the decision to recognize only pneumoconiosis. The Union has raised the issue with both the Trades Union Congress and Governments but it has made no progress because emphysema and bronchitis are common outside of mining and a decision in favour of miners would have repercussions amongst other groups of workers.

Then there is the question of the diagnosis and certification of pneumoconiosis.* Pneumoconiosis is described as being of two kinds: simple and complicated. As it does not produce specific symptoms it is diagnosed only through chest X-Rays. The official Government view is that the simple form does not lead to the complicated one and that, in general, it does not cause disability or reduced life expectancy. A miner with simple pneumoconiosis, whatever his disability, cannot get a disability assessment. He is in fact forgotten and is allowed to work under ordinary mining conditions even though these may result in complicated pneumoconiosis. If a miner has complicated pneumoconiosis he is eligible for assessment for disability and for loss of faculty, namely whether he should be transferred to less dusty work usually entailing a reduction in earnings. He has to apply to a Pneumoconiosis Medical Panel for examination if he believes he is suffering from the disease. The Panel determines whether pneumoconiosis is present and in what degree. If an X-Ray does not reveal pneumoconiosis, no matter what physical disabilities may be present, then no assessment is made. A miner may re-apply more than once or he may appeal against a Panel's decision though a period of one year must elapse before an appeal can be heard by the Pneumoconiosis Medical Appeal Tribunal. The effect of the system is to treat miners as possible malingerers. They are accorded no generosity for working under dangerous conditions.

The diagnosis of pneumoconiosis depends entirely upon radiological evidence about the condition of the lungs. There has, however, to be a considerable progression before a worsening is reflected through X-Rays and before, therefore, a miner can move from one disability assessment to another. In consequence, the disease often gets worse before preventative action is taken. For this reason, once the disease has been diagnosed, it seems sensible from the miners' point of view that respiratory disabilities should be considered as evidence for reassessment purposes. X-Ray evidence, however, is of primary significance in tracking changes and is especially important for revealing the onset of pneumoconiosis, which is the time when action should be taken.

---

* See *Coalworkers' Pneumoconiosis, Emphysema and Bronchitis.* A Report to the National Union of Mineworkers. By John Crow, Dewis Davies, Julian Tudor Hart, Stephen Jones and Michael C. S. Kennedy, 1977. I have drawn on this Report in this section.

Under the prevailing system of diagnosis a National Coal Board X-Ray Unit visits each pit in every coalfield once every 3 to 5 years with the result that about 90 per cent of all miners are now X-Rayed every four years. The X-Rays are undertaken voluntarily and the response rate varies between age groups and, to some extent, between coalfields, depending upon the prevalence of dust. In 1980 there was a general tendency for young miners to be reluctant to volunteer for X-Rays though this was not the case in South Wales where an increasing number of miners within the 20 to 40 years age group had been having as many as one X-Ray a year outside of the N.C.B. scheme. The practice of the National Coal Board in Yorkshire has been to give all miners possessing a disability assessment and young miners in dust exposed jobs an X-Ray every two years. But there are still miners whose first X-Rays occur only after they have lodged an application for a disability assessment due to breathlessness or pains in the chest. The climate of control does not encourage miners moving into their peak earning capacity to cooperate fully with early diagnosis procedures for, no matter how distasteful the prospect of contracting pneumoconiosis might be, they are reluctant to take action which might result in permanently damaging their earning power. This climate can only be altered by the introduction of a number of related simple and humane measures.

First, because a prompt diagnosis of the disease is necessary and in order to catalogue all changes in it, miners should be obliged to have yearly X-Rays. The National Coal Board opposes this innovation because it claims it would entail unnecessary radiation risks. This view was put to the Scottish Area of the Union by the medical adviser to the N.C.B. when it requested yearly X-Ray tests. It was also expressed by the Senior Medical Officer of the Pneumoconiosis Panel in 1979 when he informed the South Wales Area that those miners who were having relatively frequent X-Rays, in addition to the N.C.B. ones, were taking unnecessary risks. When Michael McGahey sought a second medical opinion about radiation risks from yearly X-Rays he was told that there were none. This state of contrasting opinions clearly expresses the state of knowledge about radiation from X-Rays. It is known that X-Rays do transmit radiation and that the less radiation a person receives the better for her or him. X-Rays may create damage to people in particular conditions, such as pregnant women, but their effect in general cannot be calculated because there are certain places in the body where radiation doses cannot be measured. There is no known threshold, therefore, over which X-Rays may carry radiation risks. The position, however, is not entirely inconclusive for miners in the Soviet Union are subjected to annual X-Rays and there have been no ill-effects. Moreover, there are reasons why individual miners should prefer annual X-Rays. Miners have to balance the unsure risks of radiation against the much surer risk of contracting pneumoconiosis. There is also the risk of worry about becoming a pneumoconiotic.

The N.C.B.'s opposition to annual X-Rays has not rested entirely on medical opinion. The officials of the Scottish Area were told by the Board that it had insufficient X-Ray units to carry out annual checks, that there were not enough qualified staff available and that the exercise would be too costly in any case.

Secondly, miners should be certified at the first sign of either simple or complicated pneumoconiosis. The link between these two types is too problematical for simple pneumoconiosis to be dismissed as of little consequence. As soon as a miner has been certified he should be transferred to a non-dusty job. Usually this means a move away from face or development work. There is no surer way of eliminating pneumoconiosis than by meeting this second condition. The N.C.B. would have to pursue a constant policy of recruiting and training young miners to fill the gaps in face work teams which a policy of early detection and transfer would create.

Third, the earnings of workers transferred to lower-paid jobs because of illness or injury caused by work have to be fully protected so that financial penalties are not added to other disabilities suffered by miners. This could be done either through a special wage protection scheme administered by the National Coal Board or through an arrangement whereby a disability pension could be adjusted to make up the pay of a transferred worker to the level it was before the transfer took place. The 1978 Annual Conference of the N.U.M. demanded that the earnings of workers compelled to take up lower paid work "by reason of accident, ill-health, physical disability or old age" should be maintained at a level comparable to their highest rates of pay. The resolution was specifically designed to assist those who had to leave underground work for surface jobs. At the end of 1979 the N.C.B. conceded the principle of a rate protection scheme and allocated £1 million to cover its cost in the first year. A Joint Working Party was set up to devise a scheme. The N.C.B. wanted a limited one to cover new cases of men over the age of 60 years and providing only a proportion of the pay necessary to protect earnings. The Union, on the other hand wanted a comprehensive scheme based on the 1978 resolution and applied retrospectively. No agreement was reached by the time of the Annual Conference of the Union in 1981. The difficulties arose out of differences of conception but also because a limited form of compensation, called a Hardship Allowance, was already available for miners who had been assessed for a disability allowance and who had lost earnings in consequence of the disability. A Hardship Allowance is a tax free weekly sum which is carried on after retirement. It is subject to review as the relevant circumstances of the miner vary. Though it does not satisfy the requirements of the Union policy it possesses features which some miners do not want to lose.

Last, the National Coal Board must continue with its stringent attention to dust control techniques. The problem of suppressing dust has been aggravated by the use of larger, more technically efficient coal-cutting machines and by the fact that with the increased speed in coal-cutting, production is taking place at longer distances from the air intake so that dust particles are circulated for longer periods. The dust from machine cutting is finer than with hand production methods and it includes stone dust. The consequences of intensive mechanization in terms of dust diseases have still to be calculated.

The National Coal Board has been influenced in its attitude to pneumoconiosis by cost factors. It has tended to treat it as a collective bargaining matter. Admittedly both it and the Union have been constrained in their capacity to deal with the protection of earnings question by Government incomes policies but that has not always been the case. To argue in any sense against measures which would enable miners to work with less risk of incurring crippling disabilities is symptomatic of the historical neglect of human resources in coal mining. The National Coal Board carries an enormous liability from the private ownership period which it has not yet discharged.

The ultimate obscenity is reserved for the widows and dependents of miners. A miner's wife must, in most cases, be willing to submit her dead husband for a post-mortem examination in order to qualify for a death benefit. The examination is done by a Coroner's Pathologist who sends the heart and lungs to the Panel. The Panel in turn tells an Insurance Officer whether pneumoconiosis was a material factor in causing death or not. There is much room for a conflict of medical opinion at this stage, particularly when emphysema or bronchitis is present. Some miners' widows have preferred to suffer deprivation rather than go through this humiliating ritual. Those who have done this have seen poverty follow quickly in behind the coffin.

These are but examples of the humiliation of people in the contemporary coalmining industry. It also occurs whenever a miner suffers an injury and claims compensation. Then the National Union of Mineworkers, on behalf of the miners, employs medical consultants and legal counsel to argue with similar experts hired by the National Coal Board over the precise disabling and loss of faculty effects. The person suffering the injury becomes a name on a file. Cases sometimes take years to settle. The expert witnesses argue and thus present the spectacle of medical specialists competing with their evidence to serve their respective employers. This reveals the nature and extent of the margin of discrepancy in medical diagnosis which are normally hidden from patients but it also emphasizes how people are treated as cost factors in production rather than as persons with emotions, aspirations, social rights and kinship obligations.

(ii) *Medical and Health Facilities*

The degradation of contemporary mining labour occurs in the totality of the work situation and not only in the manner in which its depreciation is assessed. It is expressed through the conditions under which it is compelled to work both underground and on the mine surface and through the provisions made for its care whilst at work. I have already mentioned how financial cost has always determined the conditions under which coal has been extracted and how social and human costs have always had to be forced to the attention of employers. The National Coal Board has been more sensitive to social and human costs than the private coal owners were but it has not necessarily been more responsive. The market constraints which made the private coal owners treat labour power as an inanimate factor of production requiring less care and attention than machinery continued for the National Coal Board.

Conditions underground may seem brutal to the outside observer but most miners become inured to them and even legitimize them as necessary for efficient production. They adopt an attitude of fatalism about injury, disease and actual working conditions which permeates their Union. Left wing miners have tried to undermine this attitude by changing Union policy. In 1975 the Union Annual Conference accepted a Scottish Area motion that there should be "a complete review of the health services provided in the mining Industry with the aim of establishing full-time doctors on each shift at all collieries; qualified nursing staff; fully equipped first-aid rooms incorporating emergency operating theatres; and a six-monthly medical check for all employed in the industry." Two years' later the Yorkshire and Derbyshire Areas demanded that the 1975 resolution should be implemented and that, in addition, adequate eating and toilet facilities underground as well as on the surface should be provided.

The issues which these resolutions raised were not new. Shortly after the election of the Labour Government in 1945 the Parliamentary Secretary to the new Minister of Fuel and Power met the Safety Sub-Committee of the N.U.M. Executive to discuss improving conditions in the pits. He declared that an outline scheme had been prepared to provide for "(a) the erection of modern Ambulance and Treatment Centres on the exit sides of Pithead Baths: (b) Doctors in attendance at mines or groups of mines; and (c) Nurses to be employed at the Treatment Centres."* The Parliamentary Secretary added, however, that the scheme had to be placed in the category of long-term planning because of the lack of resources and personnel. He did not believe, moreover, that it would be necessary for the Government to legislate for improved

* National Union of Mineworkers, Annual Report and Proceedings, 1945, p.621.

conditions because after nationalization the 'Coal Corporation' would voluntarily take on the task.

The long-term became exceedingly long and the Government did after all legislate. It introduced minimum standards in Regulations made under the Mines and Quarries Acts of 1954 and 1969. These Regulations stipulated that a room should be allocated for first aid purposes at every pit employing more than fifty persons and that it should be clearly recognizable from the outside by a notice stating "First Aid" or "Medical Centre." The room should have separate, convenient waiting accommodation; it should be used exclusively for medical work and should be kept clean, ventilated, lit, warm and should possess a supply of hot and cold water, a stretcher, a couch and essential first-aid equipment. Every such room had to be controlled by a person with recognized medical, nursing or first-aid qualifications. The Regulations also specified that underground there should be one person with first-aid qualifications for roughly every fifty miners though colliery managers could alter this if they found it difficult to obtain or persuade sufficient people with the requisite qualifications to work underground. First-aid stations, in effect storage places for first-aid equipment, had to be provided at specified locations underground.

When the position was reviewed in the 1970s it was clear that in many cases the minimum standards had become the actual ones. Information about medical and first-aid facilities was collected in 1978 which showed that only those collieries employing more than 750 workers had the services of a full-time State Registered nurse. 20 of these had full-time cover on the day shift only. At other collieries part-time Medical Centre Attendants, usually Bath Attendants with first-aid training, were used though in a very uneven fashion. Some collieries had no Medical Centre Attendants at all, others had part-time provisions on night shifts or on afternoon shifts. There was no provision for doctors to attend Medical Centres at pits.

The National Coal Board employs a small number of doctors for its own purposes but the Union uses the services of outside consultants. Miners who suffer from injuries or diseases depend upon the general provisions of the National Health Service. The position is that nothing exists in the mines which even resembles the services envisaged by the delegates who changed the Union policy in 1975 and 1977.

The provision of sanitation facilities is also covered by legislation. The Sanitary Conveniences Regulation of 1956 specified the location and quality of toilets above and below ground. There had to be one at or near the winding engine house and at other places on the mine surface which were convenient for miners at work. Underground there had to be a sanitary convenience near to every entrance to every shaft or outlet used as an access to working places and at suitable places along any length of road. Colliery managers were instructed to provide disinfectant or dry coal dust and to empty waste in a "hygienic manner." Miners were told not to relieve their "bowels . . . on a road below ground other than in a sanitary convenience" but if they did so they had to "cover the faeces with disinfectant, dry coal dust, or other suitable substance."

The legal standards were primitive yet even these were not always satisfied. When the Union and management representatives discussed sanitation in July, 1979, there were eighty pits without water or chemical toilets. In the remaining pits there were 660 chemical toilets but only 27 flush ones. One special type of flush toilet, manufactured in the U.S.A. and used on ocean-going liners, was on trial at one pit but its installation and maintenance were considered to be too expensive. No fresh water for drinking or washing is provided underground in any pit either through pipes or in containers. The National Coal Board claims that this is because of the risks of contamination. But the provision of contamination-free water is not technically impossible. It is simply expensive in management terms.

(iii) *Early Retirement*

Requests for retirement at 60 years of age had been made frequently in the mining industry. It was understandable that because miners aged prematurely and rarely lived long in retirement, they should want to lower the age of retirement. Moreover, they had the examples of retirement at 50 years for underground miners in France and the Soviet Union and at 55 years in Belgium and West Germany. As British mining conditions were similar to those in these other countries there seemed to be no sense or humanity in making British miners work until they were 65 years old. Between 1962 and 1975 early retirement was sought on six occasions but each time the National Coal Board found financial or manpower reasons for rejecting the claim. Then in 1975 a resolution from the Nottingham Area became the policy of the Union and the basis for an actual retirement scheme.

The Nottingham miners have been the most persistent in pressing for early retirement measures. They have the reputation of being compliant towards management but they have frequently been oddly militant about non-wage issues. In 1976 they proposed that the retirement age should be 60 years by January, 1977 and then lowered by a year every six months until retirement at 55 years was reached in June, 1980. They insisted that no loss of income should be involved until the State retirement age was reached. Then, in a manner quite out of character for the Nottingham miners, they added as the tail of the resolution an instruction to the National

298

Executive Committee to "consult the membership by way of ballot vote in order to determine which course of industrial action shall be taken to bring this matter to a successful conclusion," if neither the National Coal Board nor the Government granted their demand by January, 1977. The resolution was framed in the style of a left wing wages one which left the N.E.C. with little scope for compromise.

The resolution was promptly rejected by the National Coal Board because of its "astronomical cost" and the effect it would have on production by reducing the labour force underground. Then followed a phase in which a variety of alternative schemes were examined by a Joint Steering Group. The officials of the Trades Union Congress were consulted to ensure that the Social Contract was not breached by such a scheme. The T.U.C. view was that the Union could go forward with any scheme provided it was contained within the Government's wages policy. Then on 23rd November, 1976 the National Coal Board submitted its own proposals which the Union Executive rejected. These suggested a reduction in the age of retirement from 64 to 62 years in annual stages on a purely voluntarily basis and to be confined to miners with 25 years' experience underground. Members of the Union were consulted about the Coal Board's offer through a ballot vote in December and 78 per cent endorsed its rejection and gave the National Executive Committee permission to call a national strike in support of their demand if necessary.

The Union then sought to extract concessions from the National Coal Board. Early in the New Year the N.E.C. accepted a revised scheme which was voluntary for one year in the first instance, placed the retirement age at 62 years at the commencement of the scheme and reduced it to 60 years after two years. It was to apply to miners with 20 years aggregated service underground but allowed for the possibility of including workers who had been forced through injury or disease to leave underground work and take jobs on the surface after less than 20 years' experience underground. Surface workers without underground experience were excluded from the scheme for neither the N.C.B., the Trades Union Congress nor the Government was willing to accept their inclusion. The Trades Union Congress believed that if the scheme were extended to surface workers other unions would be aggrieved and would seek the same kind of provisions for their own members. It wanted an orderly progression to early retirement for all workers.

The revised proposals were accepted by a 55 per cent majority of the Union members about six weeks after they had voted down the original offer. In Yorkshire, Scotland and Kent, however, there were substantial majorities against them. Even 51 per cent of the Durham miners were opposed to them. The exclusion of surface workers without underground experience was regarded as the major reason for wanting to turn the proposals down.

Early retirement became possible on a voluntary basis from 1st August, 1977. The scheme entered its final phase on 1st August, 1979 with the provision for miners with less than 20 years underground service to retire early provided they had between 25 and 35 years' total employment in coal mining. For example, men with five but less than ten years' service underground and 35 years in the industry could retire at 63 years. By March 1981, 29,896 miners had taken early retirement.

Protests continued to be made about some features of the scheme, such as the indignity of compelling early-retired miners to sign on at Employment Exchanges as if they were unemployed, the continued exclusion of surface workers without underground experience and the low level of benefits. But overall it was a significant benefit. It was not won by reason and understanding for if these qualities had been dominant miners would have achieved their aim at the first time of asking. It was won by the miners' display of intolerance over at least 13 years' prevarication by the National Coal Board. It was confirmation of the perpetual experience of miners that improvements in their working conditions have been extracted and never presented as gifts out of the goodness of the employer's heart.

CHAPTER 21

CONSCIOUSNESS

The mundane details about compensation payments for pneumo-coniotics and injured miners, widows' benefits, early retirement provisions and many other matters can only be seen in their proper context if set against the dominance of uncertainty in mining life, expressed through disease, injury, disability and death. There is no other industrial activity where these elements have such a complex, interacting and overwhelming presence. Their importance in the detail of the everyday life of mining families is presented through the activities of officials at all levels of the Union. These people spend their time, not in strike confrontations with management, but mostly arguing, pleading, conniving with managers, solicitors, doctors, politicians and their own members to cushion hardship, relieve suffering and provide compensation in a variety and multi-plicity of ways.

The features of mining life which protect people in so many diverse ways are important not only for what they do to people's lives but also because they represent the imprint which miners make on their own environment. They show that miners are not passive recipients of managerial decisions or market forces but continually interact with them - responding, interpreting, negating, elaborating and improving them so that their experiences become partly of their own making. Miners thus participate in shaping their own history.* They do so, however, only insofar as they act collectively through their trade union and to a lessor extent through their cooperative societies, miners' clubs and political parties. Sometimes their imprint is blurred because they are dissuaded from using their collective strength. But the most important blurring factor is collective weakness caused by unemployment. Miners, as is the case with all workers, have a collective strength only when they have jobs.

Attitudes to Closures
The provision of mining jobs after 1974 seemed secure. Nonetheless, following the experiences of the 1960s, miners were both sensitive and apprehensive about pit closures. They recognized that there would be pit closures but harboured the feeling that the next one might be the thin end of a wedge. The National Union of Mineworkers had adopted a policy in 1972 of rejecting all pit closures except when they were caused by the exhaustion of reserves. The Union argued against closures for economic reasons in part because this insulated technically exploitable reserves. The National Coal Board estimated that there were about 500 million tonnes of technically exploitable

* Karl Marx stated in *The Eighteenth Brumaire of Louis Napolean* that "Man makes his own history, but he does not make it out of the whole cloth; he does not make it out of conditions chosen by himself, but out of such as he finds close at hand."

coal in pits which had been closed between 1959 and 1979. If the loss-making pits in 1979 alone had been closed a further 350 million tonnes of coal would have been sterilized. Nonetheless each year after 1974 pits were closed, sometimes through exhaustion, at other times because the financial cost of continuing production was too great and, occasionally, simply to release labour for other pits. So in practice the term 'exhaustion of reserves' came to mean 'uneconomic' and the only serious objection the Union offered arose from its concern to protect jobs.

The Union and the National Coal Board had an agreed Colliery Review Procedure whereby decisions made by the Board to close pits could be contested by the Union. The initiative to oppose the closure of a pit came from the Area in which it was located and the strength of the opposition depended upon the feeling in the Area. The Area officials were responsible for collecting technical and economic reports in support of a case. If they failed to convince the Board then they called for assistance from the National Executive Committee and if this failed then the Union appealed to the Secretary of State for Energy. The Colliery Review Procedure seemed always to be in use though most pits which were closed through it ended their lives without protest.

The attitudes of miners towards pit closures in the 1960s had been clear. Miners had believed then that closures were caused by market forces over which they had no control. They had been advised, moreover, that if they struck against closures they would exacerbate the position of the industry. It so happened that, until the late 1960s, there were alternative jobs available for most miners who were made redundant. Miners' attitudes after 1974 were ambiguous. There was increasing unemployment in general so they had a greater need to protect mining jobs. Proposals to close pits were invariably initially accompanied by local protests. But as the protests were processed through the Review Procedure the affected miners who wanted work tended to find it in nearby pits and this influenced their attitude to the Coal Board's arguments for closure. Where the protests were sustained to the point of considering strike action the ambivalence remained for in the last resort, although they wanted their pits to remain open, even the affected miners in general were not prepared to strike. Left wing officials, who were the most vociferous opponents of pit closures, realized from experience the difficulty of getting unified action over individual closures. Michael McGahey, for instance, frequently stated that constitutional strike action over closures was impossible because of the divisive character of closures: those with jobs were not keen to jeopardize them while those who had experienced closures in the past resented being called on to strike for pits which had not supported them when their pits had closed.

302

There were some outstanding examples after 1974 of the problems associated with protests against pit closures. The first occurred in 1975 when the National Coal Board decided to close Langwith colliery in the Derbyshire Area because its reserves had become thin, dirty and expensive to mine. There was much inconclusive argument about the nature of the seams and the possibility of extracting coal profitably from them. The Coal Board refused a Union request to test the workability of the seams so the National Executive Committee applied a complete overtime ban for all N.U.M. members from 15th February, 1976. Strong opposition to the ban came immediately from many Areas, branches and individual members. As a result a special meeting of the N.E.C. was summoned only four days after the ban was enforced and called it off. This decision divided left wing members of the N.E.C. and caused much unpleasantness between some who were personal friends. A national ballot over the issue showed that 61 per cent of the miners favoured lifting the overtime ban. Even in Derbyshire a majority of the members were opposed to taking industrial action to save Langwith colliery. There were majorities for banning overtime only in Yorkshire, Scotland, South Wales and Kent. The 880 workers employed at the Langwith pit were offered jobs in nearby pits.

Other protests had similar endings. The Nottingham Area raised the N.C.B. decision to close Teversal colliery with the Union N.E.C. late in 1977. The issue here was again about the nature of the reserves and the cost of developing them and, as in the case of Langwith, there was a suspicion that the Board's intention was to release labour for other pits. When the National Coal Board finally rejected the Union's case early in 1979 the Nottingham Area was given permission by the N.E.C. to ballot its own members on the question of taking industrial action to support Terversal. It did so but 72 per cent of the Nottingham miners voted against industrial action.

Just as the Teversal case was drawing to a close interest began to be focused on the Deep Duffryn pit in South Wales. The South Wales miners became particularly apprehensive about the future of their coalfield during 1978 when coal stocks began to accumulate in great heaps in their villages. So when the National Coal Board announced its intention to close Deep Duffryn the pit served as a focus for the underlying fear about widespread closures. The branch at the pit organized opposition both in the local community and throughout the South Wales coalfield which served as a backcloth to the formal procedural review involving the Union and the N.C.B. The National Coal Board had made its decision because the economically workable reserves were reaching exhaustion and because Deep Duffryn had made heavy losses over the previous six years. The arguments in the review meetings were largely about these factors. Outside, however, the talk was about strike action. Both Michael McGahey and Arthur Scargill made public statements supporting the Deep Duffryn miners in their fight against closure. When the South Wales president, Emlyn Williams, made an impassioned plea to save the Deep Duffryn pit at the Union's Annual Conference in 1979 he was given many promises of support from delegates.

The South Wales officials took no constitutional steps to test the feelings of their members. They realized that the divisive elements generated by pit closures would predominate in South Wales, as they had done in Derbyshire and Nottingham, if miners were asked to assess the closure in a detached, rational manner and in relation to their own interests. A protest about pit closures, they knew, had to be an emotional thing, generated by sympathy and anger, during which formal decisions were avoided whenever possible. The solidarity which was expressed on this occasion, however, was never tested for the Deep Duffryn pit was reprieved in the week following the Annual Conference. The 440 miners were allowed a six week period to develop one coal-face but within that time they met such dangerous conditions that the development was stopped. Everyone concerned, the South Wales Area and the N.C.B. officials and those from the pit branch then agreed that Deep Duffryn had to close.

The anxiety which was generated throughout the British coal-fields over the decision to close Deep Duffryn reflected an increasing uncertainty about the coal industry in general. The demand for coal was still subject to the vagaries of the energy market and the capricious behaviour of oil prices. An element of long-overdue stability was introduced in November 1979 when the Central Electricity Generating Board, the largest consumer of coal in Britain, agreed to take 75 million tonnes of N.C.B. coal a year for the next five years, which was 5 million tonnes more than it had ever taken before, provided pit prices increased by no more than the rate of inflation in Britain. But at the same time the C.E.G.B., which had made secret coal import contracts which were hidden even from the Secretary of State for Energy, increased its coal imports. The British Steel Corporation also increased its coal imports from Australia. Imported coal came to Britain from Australia, South Africa, the U.S.A., Poland and China. Natural gas had become more freely available and was encroaching on the demand for domestic coal. The total demand for energy, moreover, was falling because of the deepening world recession. The medium term prospects for the coal industry were bleak. In January, 1979, in a meeting between the N.U.M., the N.C.B. and the Government it was stated that the Government would have to double its subsidy to the industry in each of the next five years in order to maintain the production

304

targets set in the 1974 *Plan for Coal*. Outside the coal industry the prospects were also bleak with unemployment in July, 1979 reaching 1½ million and inflation running at an annual rate of 15.6 per cent.

By the time the protests about Deep Duffryn were at their peak a Conservative Government was in office intent on reducing public expenditure and, hence, Government support for nationalized industries. The Government made no direct threat to the coal industry but by pursuing its monetarist policy and insisting that the industry should be self-financing it generated powerful pressures for contraction which had not been present when the Labour Government was in office. In 1980 it passed the Coal Industry Act which aimed to remove all social grants from the coal industry by the end of the 1982/83 financial year, thus exposing the industry still further to unfair foreign competition. The British Steel Corporation was compelled to make substantial cuts in steel production, resulting in the dismissal of more than a third of its total labour force in 1980. This caused a fall in the consumption of coking coal from 10.5 million tonnes to 9 million tonnes. The British Steel Corporation, moreover, sought to reduce its production costs by increasing its imports of cheap coal. It claimed that it could import coal from Australia, Poland and the United States at about £10 per tonne less than British coal. By the end of 1979 it imported 24 per cent of its coking coal compared with 14 per cent in 1978.

The price disadvantage which British coal suffered was not due to inefficiency in the British mining industry. Australian coal came from thick seam, short-life opencast mines; that from South Africa was produced by oppressed, under-paid black workers employed under virtual slave conditions while the United States had relatively easily mined coal produced largely by non-union labour. The coal from Poland was subsidized by the Government. The British coal industry had not been able to gain compensation by making inroads into the energy markets of other members of the European Economic Community because the Governments in those countries heavily subsidized their own coal industries. This fact was illustrated by E.E.C. figures for 1979.

Country	Coal Production Costs £ per tonne	Direct Aid to Coal Production £m	£ per tonne
Belgium	58	207.7	34.05
France	45	334.1	17.96
West Germany	41	1385.7	14.85
U.K.	29	195.4	1.62

The West German coal industry was particulary favoured because the level of subsidy there covered the difference in price between domestic and imported coal. All in all West German coking coal received a subsidy of more than £35 a tonne in 1979. With this

305

support it could undercut coal in the U.S.A. from where American coal was shipped to Britain where it threatened the existence of pits.

The Government Recoils

The issue of coal imports was an obvious injustice. Late in 1979 it received much publicity as the British Steel Corporation faced a world slump in steel sales and endeavoured to cut its costs by importing cheap coal. During 1979 its coal imports rose from 1.7 million to 2.9 million tons. The National Coal Board held discussions with the British Steel Corporation for it had invested heavily in coke production to meet the anticipated increase in coke consumption by the B.S.C. Miners in South Wales claimed that if the British Steel Corporation went ahead with its plans to increase coal imports there then six pits, employing 4,500 miners, might have to close. The situation became increasingly uncertain as plans for a substantial reduction in steel production were announced which would, it was estimated in December, 1979, cause between 7,000 and 20,000 South Wales miners to lose their jobs, depending upon how the contraction was applied. 21 out of 37 South Wales pits could be closed.

It was no longer a case of processing occasional closures through the Review Procedure but of confronting the possibility of the destruction of whole coalfields or parts of coalfields. The position seemed more ominous than in the 1960s. The South Wales miners reacted promptly for their coalfield was under greatest threat. They persuaded dockers at Newport in South Wales to refuse to handle foreign coal and then joined with steel workers in the Wales Trades Union Congress in pressing for a national strike in the Welsh steel and coal industries from 21st January, 1980 unless the steel contraction plans were suspended for 2 years. Then the constraints began to appear. When the national steel strike for a wage increase began on 2nd January the South Wales miners and steel workers tried to get its demands widened to cover the closure of steel plants but they were unsuccessful. The National Executive Committee of the N.U.M. also refused to consider a national strike. The British Trades Union Congress urged its Welsh offshoot to postpone the strike called for 21st January which it did by organizing instead a Welsh 'day of action' on 28th January. Then when the Wales T.U.C. laid plans for an indefinite strike by the coal, steel and transport unions on 10th March the General Secretary of the British Trades Union Congress asked it to temper its militancy and to take into account the national co-ordinated action which was being organized to persuade the Government to alter its plans. The Wales T.U.C. again accepted advice from London and called off its strike. It then arranged a recall conference for 27th February to reconsider strike action but postponed it. The Welsh miners' leaders, in opposition to the

T.U.C. decisions, were isolated but they continued with their efforts to call a strike as the only effective means of challenging Government policy. Eventually a miners' delegate conference decided on Wednesday, 20th February, 1980, to call a coalfield strike from the following Monday, 25th February. The strike call, supported by the Area Executive and the Area delegate conference went to branch meetings over the next 3 days.

It is difficult for workers collectively to maintain a high level of consciousness with a vacillating leadership. The experiences of miners in the unofficial strikes of 1969 and 1970 illustrated this point but there are many other examples. Leadership has to be consistent and clear. The South Wales miners' leaders, Emlyn Williams and George Rees, were consistent from the time of the banning of coal imports in November, 1979, but they were only a part of the leadership for they had agreed to act under the aegis of the Wales Trades Union Congress. At first the Wales T.U.C. breathed fire and brimstone then, as the British Trades Union Congress intervened, it vacillated and eventually retreated.

Nonetheless, when Emlyn Williams and George Rees advised a strike from 25th February they had some reason to be confident. The South Wales miners had behind them a history of militancy. From November the reports from pits had consistently revealed a determination to strike. Moreover, Emlyn Williams knew that if a strike started in South Wales, even though it was strictly unconstitutional, it would quickly spread to Kent, Derbyshire, Yorkshire, Scotland and then perhaps further. The strike simply had to start and it could only start in South Wales for no other coalfield at that time had justification for it.

The confidence which Emlyn Williams and George Rees possessed in their members' commitment to militant action resulted in them taking that commitment for granted. In the week before the strike was due to start they did little campaigning in the pits. Even the pit delegates appeared to assume that no persuasion was necessary in their own pits. Because they had little contact with working miners they were unaware of the effects which the vacillating leadership of the Wales Trades Union Congress had had on them. Nor did they anticipate the intense campaign conducted by the National Coal Board and the press to dissuade the miners from striking. The miners leaders accused the National Coal Board of "gross interference" in Union affairs by trying to influence the ballot but by then it was too late. The result of the ballot was an almost overwhelming rejection of the call to strike as about 22,000 miners out of a labour force of 27,000 turned down the leaders' recommendation. It was a humiliating experience for Emlyn Williams and a lesson in campaigning which he did not forget.

The state of the British economy deteriorated rapidly during

307

1980. Production fell and unemployment rose by 1 million to the official Government estimate of 2½ million. Unofficial estimates, which included people who for a variety of reasons do not register when unemployed, put the total at 3½ million. The incidence of unemployment was heaviest in the traditional depressed areas which, except for Northern Ireland, contained coalfields and steel plants. The decline in production particularly affected coal using industries with the consequence that the domestic market for coal virtually collapsed. Coal imports had increased fourfold over the previous two years. There was a sharp rise in coal stocks from 30 million tonnes to 39 million tonnes during the year. All the indices pointed to the need for the National Coal Board to contract production.

Many miners expected a pit closure programme to be announced after the scare in February, 1980 and the refusal of the South Wales miners to strike over the issue but no such announcement was made. Arthur Scargill frequently charged the National Coal Board with having a secret closure list but each time the accusation was denied. Eight pits were closed during the year but in the normal haphazard way which characterised pit closures in the 1970s. Altogether the miners seemed to be insulated from the worst of the economic crisis but in an unreal way. The Government had refused to restrict imports or to subsidize coking coal in order to block imports. The question in the minds of many miners' leaders was, therefore, at what stage would the coal industry be compelled to adjust to the economic depression around it.

Arthur Scargill maintained his insistence that there would be large scale pit closures, despite the N.C.B. denials. He initiated a campaign against pit closures in Yorkshire in the belief that as many as 18 pits in his Area were scheduled to be closed and then, at the end of January, 1981, sought to test the opinion of the Yorkshire miners through a ballot vote about the principle of striking against pit closures. 85.6 per cent of the Yorkshire miners who voted favoured strike action. This was an exceptional result in the light of previous ballots about pit closures but it was only a decision in principle whereas previous ballots had been about action over actual closures. The real test of attitude was still to come.

On 10th February, 1981, little more than a week after the result of the Yorkshire ballot, conjecture about pit closures ended. The National Coal Board made a statement about the condition of the industry to the executive committees of the three mining unions which described the problem of over production in detail. It did not suggest pit closures as a possible solution but simply stated that "We shall, therefore, have to reduce output, but to do so in a way that does not prejudice the future of the industry . . ." During the course of the discussion pit closures were discussed. Union officials came away from the meeting believing that as many as 50 out of a total of

219 pits were at risk.

The immediate reaction of members of the N.U.M. Executive was one of alarm and hostility. They were given no details at the meeting. These were to be provided by each of the 12 N.C.B. Area Boards at intervals from Friday, 13th February. Nonetheless on Thursday, 12th February, the N.E.C. of the Union decided to call a national strike if necessary to stop the closures but to request a meeting with Government Ministers before proceeding formally to ballot for a strike. Miners from various coalfields lobbied their Executive and then held a mass meeting addressed by leaders of the left wing Areas. Both Arthur Scargill and Michael McGahey were given standing ovations as they urged miners to fight for their jobs. Feelings amongst miners were running high.

The timing of events was of great importance in the sequence which followed the special N.E.C. meeting. First, the Government failed to recognize the urgency of the situation for itself. Ministers agreed to meet with the N.U.M. Executive and the National Coal Board but only on Monday, 23rd February, 1981, that is almost two weeks after the miners had decided to strike and four days after they had agreed to start the strike ballot proceedings. The Prime Minister, Mrs. Thatcher, refused to expedite a meeting with the Union and the N.C.B. even though the National Executive Committee had expressed its anger about the proposed closures. She was influenced in her judgement, perhaps, by the high degree of compliance which had been shown by workers in the steel and car industries and even by the miners themselves up till that point.

Secondly, as the N.C.B. Area Boards spread their meetings with the Union Area officials between Friday, 13th February and Wednesday, 18th February a spontaneous but unified reaction to the complete closure programme was not possible. The left wing Areas decided therefore to hold special delegate conferences during the week beginning 15th February in the expectation of having strike decisions which they could operate in unison on Monday, 23rd February, the day of the meeting with the Government. The South Wales Area, which was to receive information about closures on Friday, 13th February, decided to hold its delegate conference on the following Wednesday. Both Scotland and Yorkshire were to be amongst the last to receive pit closure information and intended to hold delegate meetings on Friday, 20th February. Although the Yorkshire Area had voted in principle to strike it still had to hold an Area Council meeting before it could act. The ballot vote had not given Arthur Scargill the right to call a strike. Indeed, none of these Areas had the right to call a strike within the rules of the Union. Their actions were unofficial but they were not inhibited by this. The left wing leaders knew that an official national strike was possible because tension was high amongst miners in all of the coal fields but they also recognized that there would be an intense media campaign to dissuade miners from striking before a national ballot could be held.

Each coalfield in Britain has industrial and political character-istics which become particularly marked during a crisis. The militant coalfields stand out in marked contrast to the non-militant ones. No coalfield, however, is an organic unit. In each one there are contra-dictory tendencies. Within the conservative coalfields there are militant segments. The conservative North Yorkshire coalfield, for example, has to tolerate the militant Kellingley pit. The militant coalfields comprise pits representing shades of militancy which in the main coincide with district geographical areas. Thus in Scotland the Ayr coalfield, physically separated from Fife and the Lothians, has a conservative reputation. The Doncaster cluster of pits has traditionally been more militant than either North or South York-shire. These distinctions are important for they are reflected in the images which miners have of themselves and which they expect others to recognize. The pits with reputations for militant action guard them jealously and take on the function of providing industrial and political leadership in their respective Areas. They frequently resent initiatives coming from other pits. In order to understand the industrial and political behaviour of any Area in the National Union of Mineworkers, therefore, it is necessary to be aware of the relation-ships within it. Whether a movement for strike action spreads or is confined will depend very much upon these relationships.

The South Wales Area has its contrasting tendencies. The pits in the anthracite coalfield of West Wales have tended to be conservative whereas those in and around the Rhondda Valley have provided leadership. Even amongst the militant pits in the Rhondda there was a gradation of militancy with Mardy colliery assuming the leadership mantle. Mardy has provided the Labour Movement with Arthur Horner and Emlyn Williams. Now it stands as the solitary pit in the Rhondda Valley but it retains its image and influence. Similarly, Penrhiwceiber colliery in the Cynon Valley, adjoining the Rhondda, regards itself as having a leadership function. When disputes occur these pits are characterized by both the speed of their reactions and the intensity of their solidarity.

Coegnant colliery, near Maesteg, has never been recognized as a militant pit. Its Union officials define themselves as being the 'middle of the road' sort. When their pit was put on the 'jeopardy' list for possible closure in 1980 they agreed to trim down the labour force and accept reduced earnings in an attempt to increase the pit's profitability. The N.C.B. invested about £500,000 in developing a new face but gave the miners only two months in which to do it. The new face was opened within the time limit. The National Coal Board responded by sending two senior executives to Coegnant on

Thursday, 12th February to congratulate the miners for their effort in saving the pit.

It is customery for Union lodge officials to be informed in advance of a visit by N.C.B. executives. On this occasion no advance warning was given so instead of meeting the executives the lodge officials went to London to lobby the National Executive Committee to oppose pit closures. The officials were annoyed at this apparent snub. Their annoyance turned to anger, however, when they learned from the N.C.B. Area Director on the following morning that Coegnant, despite passing its survival test, was one of the seven pits scheduled to be closed in South Wales. A mass meeting was called at Coegnant on Saturday which, with only one dissenting voice, voted for an immediate strike and a resolution to picket other pits.

The Coegnant decision had immediate repercussions. It was wholly unexpected and, in the words of Dai Francis, the former general secretary of the South Wales Area, went through the coalfield like an electric shock.* The militant pits objected to being picketed by the moderate Coegnant miners and immediately built up pressure for a strike in the whole of the coalfield. By Monday morning nearly half of the South Wales miners were already on strike, a week before the intended time for striking.

Emlyn Williams was sensitive about the need to keep in step with his members. He did not want an untidy divisive strike or a repeat of the previous year when his advice to strike in support of the steel-workers was rejected. Since that rejection he had worked hard and successfully to re-establish his authority in the coalfield and he did not intend to destroy it by a lack of leadership on this occasion. So Emlyn Williams brought forward the coalfield conference from Wednesday to Monday. It called an immediate, indefinite coalfield strike.

Events moved quickly from that moment. The Associated Society of Locomotive Engineers and Firemen and the National Union of Railwaymen pledged their support. The Kent miners who had been told that Snowdown, one of their three pits, was to be closed, struck on Tuesday, 17th February, six days before they had intended to strike. The next day the Scottish Area came out on strike after hearing that three of their pits, including the large Lanarkshire pit, Cardowan, were to be closed. The Derbyshire miners agreed to strike in support of the Welsh miners from Monday, 23rd February, even though no Derbyshire pits were listed to be closed. The strike spread into the Midlands and Durham Areas. The Yorkshire miners were told the names of three of their pits to be closed at a meeting with the Area N.C.B. on Wednesday. One of these pits, Park Hill, struck immediately. By Thursday morning about 10,000 Yorkshire miners were on strike though the Area Council had not yet met to give its formal endorsement.

* Dai Francis died shortly afterwards, at the end of March, 1981.

311

Miners' pickets had begun to operate and were beginning to stop the movement of coal by road and rail. Some had moved into other Areas. It was apparent by Wednesday that a national ballot would be a ritual and that there would be a complete stoppage within a few days. The full list of closures was now known to the miners. Only 23 pits were to be closed but the precise number and their location had ceased to be a relevant indicator of the mood of the miners.

In an increadibly uncanny fashion the miners again acted as the focus of working class resistance, evoking support from other unions and sympathy from the public. Their actions were impatient and aggressive. They did not stop to consider the legality of their actions for these derived their own legitimacy from the exigencies of the miners' situation. They behaved as other groups of workers would have liked to behave. For the last year or more it had been commonly said that only the miners could halt the Government for only they had both the power to harm the Government and the determination to use it. This forecast seemed to be valid on Tuesday, 17th February when the picture suddenly became familiar to the Prime Minister.

Once it realised that a crisis was unfolding around it, the Government brought forward its talks with the mining unions and the National Coal Board to Wednesday and made substantial concessions to the strikers. The Minister for Energy, Mr. David Howell, emphasized that the Government was committed to the *Plan for Coal*, that it accepted the need to reduce coal imports to the "irreducible minimum" and to relax the financial restrictions imposed on the National Coal Board. After these assurances had been given the Chairman of the N.C.B. agreed to withdraw the closure proposals. The news was flashed on to television screens that the miners had won. It was wholly unexpected.

The dramatic presentation of the Government's retreat had an immediate and divisive impact on the strike. Some pits on strike did not wait to get confirmation from their Area officials but returned to work on Thursday morning in the belief that everything was settled. Pits in Yorkshire which had been intending to strike from Thursday morning altered their decisions. The strike lost its momentum though this was not obvious at first. Most left wing officials received the news with some scepticism. The details of a settlement had not been worked out nor had an agreement been signed to bind the Government. They had only promises and they knew that these, particularly when made by Governments, could easily be broken. Their scepticism was made clear at the meeting of the Union N.E.C. on 19th February which received the details of the Tripartite talks. The left wing officials opposed a resolution which proclaimed the Government's concessions "as a victory for the N.U.M. policy and commonsense" and which then instructed

"members who are now on strike to return to work immediately."
As they left the meeting they expressed their determination to carry
on with the strike.

London, on this occasion, was not where the real decisions were
being made. The strike had been created by pressure from branches
and whether it continued or not depended upon their reactions.
Moreover, each coalfield on strike had to be of like mind. The strike
could only continue if it spread to Yorkshire, at least, and this would
occur only if those Areas already on strike continued with their
action. If one striking Area weakened the strike was in jeopardy.

There was some confusion in the coalfields. The National Coal Board
had created divisions by staggering the announcements of closures
in different Areas, thus preventing a unified reaction. Many miners
on strike by the Wednesday were angry with the Yorkshire miners
because, as far as they knew, they were still at work. The national
press emphasized the divisions by neglecting to publicize the
spreading strike in Yorkshire and ignoring press statements by
Arthur Scargill. The distorted impression was created that Scargill
was unwilling to lead the Yorkshire miners out on strike despite the
mandate which the ballot vote had given him.

On the other hand, there were weaknesses in the striking Areas.
In all of them some miners had returned to work after the news
flashes had appeared on television on Wednesday evening. It is
difficult to maintain morale in a strike when cracks appear in its
solidarity for whatever reason. There was moreover, some hesitancy
about the strike in sections of the coalfields which had conservative
traditions. Unofficial strikes suffer from the inherent defect that
they lack constitutional union legitimacy. This is significant on all
occasions for a union derives strength from the uniform acceptance
of a common set of governing procedures. Action which is not
processed through these procedures can be a threat to the union
itself. Miners have a dual set of procedures to contend with at
national and Area level and the strongest action is that which is
legitimized through both. Miners who are unwilling to engage in
unofficial strike action invariably accept a national strike decision
without hesitation. But there are others whose primary loyalty is
with their Area procedures. For example, because Park Hill colliery
in North Yorkshire called a strike as soon as it heard it was destined
to be closed, the North Yorkshire panel censured it for acting
before the Yorkshire Area Council had made its decision. The
sections of coalfields which have conservative traditions tend to be
more constitutional-minded than the rest. They are willing to strike
whole-heartedly provided it is done through what they regard as the
proper procedures. They might strike, nonetheless, but in a hesitant,
grudging manner, looking for a way out. This was the case in the
West Wales coalfield of the South Wales Area.

313

When the left wing officials returned from the insulated environment of the Union's London office to their respective coalfields they were confronted with the task of pursuing the strike and maintaining the solidarity of their Areas. This was a specially sensitive task for Emlyn Williams. His Area had started the strike with a great expression of solidarity but after the news flashes there were signs of strain in it. He was reluctant to provoke divisions by prolonging the strike. On the other hand, he knew that if South Wales withdrew from the strike it would collapse nationally. His mind was made up eventually by the considerations which had dominated his thoughts the previous weekend, namely the desire to preserve the unity of his Area and prevent a repeat of last year's experience. Therefore, when his Area delegate conference was held the morning after the N.E.C. meeting he recommended a return to work. Only one member of his Area executive opposed him.

While the South Wales miners were making their decision to call off their strike, delegates were gathering in Scotland to maintain it and in Yorkshire to join it. Neither Arthur Scargill nor Michael McGahey knew of the South Wales decision until their respective conferences were due to meet. Both of them recognized that they would have to reverse their intentions and recommend a return to work. McGahey, indeed, had to reason out the case for cancelling the strike while he was actually chairing a meeting called to continue it. The Yorkshire Area Council refrained from striking after receiving an additional assurance that Orgreave colliery, one of the three pits under threat, would be saved. The Derbyshire miners also revoked their decision to strike from Monday. Only in Kent did the miners decide to continue though it became quickly obvious to them that their action too would have to end.

The Sequel

The sequel to the strike has not ended as I write. The Union's National Executive Committee did not cancel its decision to strike but put it aside to be acted on if the negotiations with the Government failed. Each left wing Area stated its intention to resume strike action if necessary. Against this background the search for a detailed solution to the problems of the coal industry began.

Little progress was made in a succession of Tripartite talks over the substantive issue of formulating new financial arrangements for the coal industry to provide for investment, a way of substituting domestic coal for imports and the creation of a larger domestic market. There was, in the first instance, a wide discrepancy between the £600 million the N.U.M. estimated to be necessary for the task and the £100 to £200 million calculated by the National Coal Board. The N.C.B. obviously saw the problem differently from the Union

314

and this made a settlement of specific issues more difficult. Capital was required both to cover the losses of the reprieved pits in the short run and to improve their efficiency in the longer run. There was much disquiet in most of the affected Areas because there was no provision for investment in these pits thus keeping them as targets for closure when the dust had settled after the strike. There were other unsettled questions concerning financial help to the N.C.B. for increased stockpiling during periods of slack demand, subsidies for private firms which wanted to convert from oil to coal and the creation of coal-fired electricity generating stations either through conversion or new construction. Then, apart from finance, the N.U.M. raised the issue of genuine involvement with the National Coal Board in the formulation of its finance and investment policies.

During the months following the strike it became increasingly clear to the Area and branch officials who were directly concerned with the threatened pits that the strike had not brought a solution. The package of closures which had been collectively rejected was being processed at local levels in a fragmented way through the Review Procedure without the focus of publicity on it. This is as it would have been before the strike. The Government had announced improvements in the mineworkers' redundancy benefits and in transfer payments to miners moved to other pits near their homes but these were seen as devices to defuse the situation still further by encouraging miners to accept closures. Many miners believed that they had been outwitted and they could do little about it because the mood for unified action which had characterized the strike had been dissipated. Such moods are not easily recreated. In their earlier successful strikes the miners had refused to return to work until the details of the settlements were worked out, written out and signed. On this occasion they broke their strike for the sake of promises. It seemed a dramatic mistake. Indeed the Yorkshire Area had to threaten strike action a second time, in July 1981, in order to keep open two of the three pits which had been threatened with closure but reprieved in February.

The promises, however, even if fulfilled, are little more than palliatives for the sequel can only end satisfactorily for miners through a substantial, continuing expansion and development of the coal industry within the overall context of full employment. The long-run solution cannot result from subsidies. There have to be expanding uses for coal. But within the present capitalist market context none of these conditions can be fulfilled.

All the ingredients for a further contraction in the coal industry are present. Firstly, Britain's total energy needs are falling as production declines and coal's share is falling at a greater rate because of the high incidence of decline in the major coal-using industries. It needs much more than expediencies extracted through a strike to reverse this process. Secondly, the older electricity generating stations are largely coal-fired ones and these will become vulnerable as the Central Electricity Generating Board struggles for its own exisitence. Thirdly, the Government's nuclear power programme, though unlikely to be fulfilled, will cause some further displacement of coal-burning capacity. Fourthly, as the National Coal Board is forced to become more competitive it will endeavour to accelerate the process of modernization and centralization by concentrating production in the thick-seamed Nottingham, Midlands and Yorkshire Areas and discarding the bulk of the remainder.

This prospect for miners is compounded by the character of mechanization being devised for the new and long-life pits. Miners may again be caught in the pincer movement of pit closures and mechanization which was their experience in the early 1960s. But this time they may be displaced altogether from underground work, not to escape to more congenial employment in light industries as they did previously but to join the army of unemployed.

Micro-processor technology has made completely automated control systems possible for underground mining. Hitherto, control engineering was highly developed theoretically but had not been successfully applied. Difficulties of application were encountered when the National Coal Board attempted to introduce the Remotely Operated Longwall Face in the 1960s. Most pits were not sufficiently mechanized, in any case, for a control system to operate. Moreover, there was not a convenient, relatively cheap means of achieving an electronic co-ordination of functions even where the pits were mechanized. This situation was altered by the appearance of the silicon chip, a small, reliable, cheap and adaptable microprocessor, from the middle of the 1970s. The National Coal Board invested in the new technology and by 1979 it had developed an electronic system of mine control called MINOS. MINOS involves control over the whole mining operation. It comprises control equipment on the mine surface, a data transmission system linking the control equipment to outstations underground and transducers and control equipment on the plant itself. It monitors production, coal clearance, environmental hazards, coal preparation and provides management with information to enable it to measure performances, compare results, take corrective action and set new targets. The operations associated with MINOS are simple and can be performed by relatively unskilled labour.

One of the most difficult tasks has been to subject coal cutting operations involving the large Anderton Shearer to automatic control and then to coordinate this with the automatic control of the other production activities. But with the new electronic system there are no insuperable technical problems. It is envisaged that even roofing and repair work will be covered by it. The real problems will be confronted by miners. The new technology will displace faceworkers altogether and generally reduce the need for manpower: it will dilute skills and place all the operations firmly within the control of management. It could transform the nature of the mining labour force into one comprising a small elite of technicians, computer operators, machine-minders, maintenance workers and a base of general service workers. There would be no comparison between the work situation changes which were caused by the introduction of power-loading and automatic roof supports in the early 1960s and those which micro-processors would create.

The Consciousness of Miners

Just how the British miners tackle their unresolved problems will rest on the way in which they analyze the issues and, as a consequence, to whom or what they attribute causal significance. Ultimately, the character and force of their policies will be determined by the depth of their political understanding. At the one extreme they might resume their attitude of fatalism which was dominant in the 1960s or at the other extreme locate their problems firmly in the structure of capitalism where in fact they lie. Their consciousness is more complex than this, however, for miners might be fatalistic about some things and not about others, progressive about some aspects of their lives but not about others. A miner might believe in democracy for himself at work but authoritarianism for his wife and family; he might struggle for equality yet practice sexism. This is a general phenomenon. Individuals comprise differing combinations of attitudes towards themselves at work, others at work, themselves on strike, others on strike, women and men, other ethnic groups, black people and white people, old and young people and those in other social classes. Some people support politically reactionary ideas yet oppose them in their own work situations. They see nothing wrong or illogical in espousing contradictory attitudes. It is accepted as a fact of life.

The matter is complicated further because attitudes are a process which is moulded by changing pressures. They result from the interaction between ideas about experiences which produce perception and the experiences themselves. If either ideas or experiences, or both, alter radically then so will attitudes. The contradictions in the configurations of attitudes, therefore, change over time. They can alter, in reality, quite suddenly and dramatically. No persons, are ever likely to have simple, general and logically consistent attitudes which embrace the totality of their lives. Thus a consistent pattern of behaviour between individuals over a range of issues may rarely be achieved.

There is not, moreover, a direct correlation between attitudes and action. Miners may have an attitude towards a problem which

317

they do not practice because institutional factors stand in their way. This has been illustrated many times during the recent history of the National Union of Mineworkers. What any group of workers is prepared to accept or reject, ignore or be angry about, how it is prepared to react and how it actually reacts are perplexing matters.

In the period of pit closures after 1956 miners generally agreed with the Government and the National Coal Board that the problem affecting the coal industry was caused by immutable market forces. They were advised that their industry was inevitably, irreversibly declining, that there was nothing anyone could do about it and that, by implication, they should leave and get jobs elsewhere. The Government and National Coal Board gave the impression that they were sitting helplessly on the side-line. There were alternative jobs available during this period so many miners took the advice and left coal-mining. They adopted individualistic solutions. Each miner did what he thought best for himself and his family. There were no serious collective protests about pit closures or about related matters such as falling real wages and worsening working conditions. The National Union of Mineworkers busied itself with the task of making the contraction as painless as possible. Its attitude effectively depoliticized miners and facilitated the process of contraction.

The conditions in the coal industry during most of the 1960s were not propitious for collective protests. Miners refused to listen to alternative explanations to those offered by the Government and the N.C.B. Then, from the late 1960s material conditions began to change. Unemployment in general and amongst miners began to increase. Miners were not able to leave their industry and get jobs elsewhere so easily. If they wanted to improve their living standards they had to find ways of doing it as miners. Then, there was a switch from traditional piecework to day-wages. The wages issue changed from being a divisive factor to become a single, unifying issue.

Many factors in the environment of miners as well as unemployment and the day wage system, influenced their responses. From the late 1960s there was a heightened political consciousness in the working class as a whole due to the Government's attempts to penalize strikers and impose legal controls over trade unions. The world energy crisis focussed attention on coal and brought in its wake both unemployment and inflation. There was the National Coal Board which was unaccustomed to dealing with miners who refused to be compliant and which was clumsy in its industrial relations. And there existed a group of politically articulate miners who argued for the emancipation of their fellow miners from the conditions which made them compliant, vulnerable and dispensible wage labour. They worked to make miners conscious of their strengths and weaknesses, their rights as well as their responsibilities.

318

If any one of these elements had been absent or present in a different degree then the events involving miners such as the 1972 and 1974 strikes would either not have taken place or would have taken a different course. Their particular relationships produced the conditions where the two major successful strikes were possible. But they did not all possess the same causal priority. Some were more important than others. The factor with the greatest significance at that time was undoubtidly the coterie of Communists and left wing Labour Party members which arose out of the meeting in Sheffield in 1967. These men did not create the achievements but without them things would have been different and less successful for miners.

There is not a simple mechanistic relationship between environmental changes and consciousness. There is, therefore, no coalition of elements which can produce spontaneity of action by workers. The belief in action by workers without leadership and organization is a myth. It is equally mythical to suggest that leaders with formal union positions inevitably obstruct this quality of spontaneity and prevent the emergence of progressive movements by the 'rank and file.' The trade union movement is not compartmentalized into bureaucratized officials and the ordinary members. It is impossible to define a union official in a meaningful sense. Is, for example, a branch official who spends all of his time on union work but is paid by the N.C.B. less of an official than an Area organizer who is paid by the Union? Moreover it is not realistic to assume that 'the rank and file' is immune from the socializing influences which create compliance and which purportedly handicap union officials. The primary division in the trade union movement is ideological and relates to the understanding of the causes of union organizations, methods and purposes and, therefore, to policies and strategies to achieve these. This division cuts through the 'rank and file' and 'officials.' It divides those who believe that union problems can be solved within capitalism from those who believe they cannot; it divides those who believe in consensus in society from those who believe in class struggle; it divides those who believe that reason can prevail in industrial relations from those who believe that force dominates.

In the early 1970s miners in their tens of thousands did not suddenly say 'as we cannot leave the industry, except to be unemployed, we shall stay and fight' or 'what a marvellous thing the day-wage system is because it unites us all.' They did not suddenly see warts on the faces of those friendly politicians who had been urging moderation to cope with immoderate conditions. Nor was the facade of benevolent paternalism which Lord Robens had constructed around the National Coal Board suddenly exposed and penetrated. And it was clearly not the case that the ordinary miners rose spontaneously against the influence of the right wing officials who dominated the Union to enforce collaboration with the N.C.B.

The miners had to be persuaded about the nature and extent of the deterioration in their work situations and convinced that they had the industrial power to halt it. Before a wages struggle was possible or a campaign against pit closures could emerge information had to be distributed; there had to be arguments in the pits. The National Union of Mineworkers had to be democratized and, through this, politicized. These tasks were undertaken by Jock Kane, Sammy Taylor, Arthur Scargill, Owen Briscoe, Jack Dunn, Jack Collins, Dai Francis, Emlyn Williams, Peter Heathfield, Michael McGahey, Bill McLean, Joe Whelan and many others, some of whom later became Area officials such as George Rees and Eric Clarke, and those who did not, such as Jimmy Dowd, the secretary of Bold colliery in Lancashire, who struggled almost in isolation against a hostile Area leadership. Some were full-time Union officials but most held union jobs of one kind or another. These miners used whatever resources they controlled in Union branches and Areas, as well as their own considerable campaigning and histrionic skills in order to conduct a classic, successful exercise in consciousness-raising. They focussed attention on injustices and created the organization for action. They consistently provided flows of information and arguments which related to the changing circumstances of miners and made sense to them. Their actions were dialectically related to mining conditions. They were not an elite but an integral part of the total situation. That was the pre-condition for any of the successes they achieved.

What in practice did this heightened consciousness entail? For miners who had been told continually for more than a decade that they did not have the strength to strike and that a strike would both ruin their industry and penalize themselves, it meant a willingness to fight despite the costs. It entailed a readiness to strike against the Government and a determination to win. This was a new phenomenon though at the same time other groups of workers, such as those in the Upper-Clyde Shipbuilding industry and the dockers and engineers in their struggle against the Industrial Relations Act, behaved similarly. Until 1969 there had never been such an open, avowed determination to use industrial action to change Government policy since the abortive attempts in 1919 and 1920. The British Government was exposed to a power struggle from which the ethics of trade unionism had hitherto protected it.

The quality of the consciousness of miners made the 1972 and 1974 strikes historic ones but it would be mistaken to see revolutionary implications in them. The miners wanted only wage increases on both occasions. They did not aim to threaten the Government, nor did they blame the institution of Government. Indeed they adopted a negative attitude, one of cynicism and irreverence, towards the Government. It was this which was new. Its significance was that it was a first step towards disillusionment with the system of Government itself. But it ended as soon as the miners' wage demands were met. The miners' consciousness did not rise to a consistently higher permanent political plane. Consciousness does not work like that. It goes up and down with circumstances. Some things, however, were learned. The miners knew afterwards that they could strike and survive; that they could take on a Government and win and that striking on a grand scale can generate pride and dignity and restore confidence.

After the 1974 strike the British miners were no longer subdued and disillusioned and they set about the business of transforming their work situation with great confidence. The left wing forces were stronger than at any other time in the history of mining trade unionism. The substantial resources of South Wales, Yorkshire, Kent, Scotland and Derbyshire were harnessed for campaigning. Left wing officials increasingly traversed the coalfields, whatever their political complexion. Some of them were allowed access to the mass media. Yet their achievements were meagre. They made annual wage demands but fulfilled none; they sought a shortening of the working week but failed to get it; they tried to achieve a transformation in health provisions for miners but with no success; they failed to prevent the re-introduction of piecework. The only advances were in compensation for pneumoconiotics and early retirement and neither of these was the consequence of left wing initiatives.

What hapened then to the consciousness of the miners after the great strikes? It was always clear that the path from individual consciousness to collective action passed through institutions. That is why the Miners' Forum concentrated on changing Union policy. But it was believed that the path though difficult to traverse was not complicated. It just entailed hard campaigning work. Experience in the National Union of Mineworkers after 1974 showed, however, that the path was an institutional maze containing obstacles and diversions and very few warning signs.

A firm conference decision or a clear referendum verdict was not, it appeared, a guarantee of action. It was not sufficient for working miners just to make clear their intentions for the Union administration could thwart them, force them to reconsider under different conditions or simply sit on the policies. The Union president discovered that he had exceptional powers. He was able to rule motions out of order, obstruct debate, remake rules through his interpretations, alter custom and practice or simply ignore instructions. Moreover, he was able to do this largely without effective recrimination for his rulings could only be challenged successfully by the N.E.C. which he dominated anyway or a two-thirds majority in Conference. In addition, because his position is a symbol of the unity and prestige of the Union, miners were loathe to discredit him in public. And so long as he acted in order to smother militant action, to protect the Government or the National Coal Board, he was supported by the mass media. If his actions were seen to coincide with the "national interest" then the courts also protected him.

But neither the president of the Union, the National Executive Committee, nor even the Union constitution is in any sense immutable, no matter what protection the wider society provides. The Union is the collective expression of the aspirations, intentions and decisions of miners in their branches. If miners decide collectively in sufficient numbers on a particular course of action then all the institutional obstacles crumble and the manipulations appear as futile abuses of the authority vested in people. Sensible leadership learns how to detect such movements and joins in, otherwise it is rejected. This was illustrated during the 1981 dispute over pit closures. In that issue the Union president and the National Executive Committee were largely instruments for communications and not custodians of power. Sensibly, from their point of view, they joined in but it would have had little bearing on the result if they had done so. The dispute showed that the institutional maze of obstacles and diversions can be avoided by being side-tracked. The Government was confronted starkly by miners organized in their Areas and branches.

But why did miners suddenly become so conscious about the importance of pit closures in 1981? In the past pit closures had been accepted either because the explanation for them was plausible and could not be contradicted, as in the 1960s, or becuse they acted divisively by causing miners to concentrate on their own subsistence, as in the 1970s. All attempts to oppose closures in recent years, up to but not including the Deep Duffryn dispute in 1979, had been frustrated by the divisive qualities of the labour market. When there is a jobs crisis it seems logical for workers to concentrate on individual survival even though this disrupts solidarity. But for workers to react in this way there has to be no single common recognizable injustice in what is happening. If there is such an injustice and workers feel commonly aggrieved about it then organized collective protests can be expected.

The conventional explanation for pit closures in February, 1981 was roughly similar to that given in the 1960s. It was a market explanation. Coal was not being demanded therefore the supply had to be cut back. But whereas this explanation made sense in the 1960s it did not do so in 1981. Firstly, the material conditions were different. In 1981 there was a high level of unemployment. Redundant miners would become unemployed miners. Secondly, the argument itself was defective. Pits were to be closed largely because of cheap imports. British coal was produced more efficiently than in most other countries but it still could not compete with imports because they were highly subsidized whereas British coal was not. No finely wrought phrases about the laws of the market could hide the injustice here. The situation was obviously, visibly offensive to British miners, hence their angry collective reaction.

The miners have not adopted a negative stance over pit closures. They know that there is an alternative strategy for the industry which does not involve contraction. Many of the campaigns, with leaflets, speeches and Union newspapers, have been about strategies. This is the essence of consciousness raising. It has to open up options and pose alternative courses of action. It has to provide supporting data and arguments. This in the main is what has happened. No matter how miners have responded they have learned that there is an alternative to every decision, to every course of action, to every situation even including the capitalist system itself. Nothing is so accurate and relevant that it cannot be challenged. Even in the case of the introduction and application of automatic control, decisions have to be made about design, scale and priorities between technical and social needs. These decisions influence who controls what process and in whose interests. The concentration of production in particular coalfields with large automatic pits is not the ultimate, inevitable way of organizing coal-getting. It is one way. There are others. Decisions have frequently to be made about the scale of the coal industry, its location, the number and size of pits as well as about the treatment of miners. Because of the intervention of left wing miners such matters are no longer taken for granted. In a society which claims to be democratic this must surely be regarded as a substantial achievement.

INDEX OF NAMES

Wood, Richard, 59
Woods, W., 170
Wyatt, Woodrow, 207
Wynn, Bert, 6, 119, 126, 127

Y

Young, Jimmy, 174

INDEX OF SUBJECTS

Coal imports, 104, 304, 305, 306, 308, 323
Coal industry, 1, 13, 34, 42, 172, 286
Coal Industry Act (1971), 116
Coal Industry Act (1973), 255
Coal Industry Act (1980), 305
Coal Industry Examination Interim Report, (1974), 286
Coal Industry Nationalization Act, (1946), 102, 103, 110, 214
Coal Mines Act (1930), 36
Coal News, 58, 66, 67, 68, 175, 177, 230, 289
Coal output, 13, 40, 50, 286, 287
Coal owners, 23, 30-1, 32, 36, 56, 74, 104, 108, 296
Coal stocks, 191, 192, 237, 303
Coal subsidies, 304-6
Coalworkers' Pneumoconiosis, Emphysema and Bronchitis, (Crow et al), 292n,
Cockenzie Power Station, 190, 191
Coegnant colliery, 310, 311
Cokemen's Area, 268, 274
Collaboration, 62-6, 106, 125, 127, 164, 269
Colliery Office Staffs Association (C.O.S.A.), 239, 266, 267, 268, 269
Colliery Review Procedure, 302, 306, 315
Combs colliery, 94
Communications, 5
Communist miners, 17, 121, 127, 130, 133, 139, 158n, 187, 209, 238, 239, 246, 319
Compensation to coal-owners, 104; to miners and widows, 291-6
Consciousness, 6, 12, 125, 135, 173, 317-323
Conservative Government, 10, 57, 171, 238, 241, 243, 244
Conservative Party, 247, 256
Consensus, 56, 124
County unions, 22, 23, 24, 260, 283
Cumberland Area, 267, 268, 282

D

Daily Express, 207
Daily Mail, 207
Daily Mirror, 207
Daily Telegraph, 208, 278
Darfield Main colliery, 21
Dawdon colliery, 232
Day-wage system, 87-9
Deep Duffryn colliery, 303-4, 305, 322
Democracy, 259-263, 277, 278, 283, 323
Denby colliery, 45, 47, 150, 151, 262

Deparment of Energy, 255
Depoliticization, 65-6
Derbyshire Area, 57, 118, 126, 127, 133, 144, 152, 166, 227, 228, 231, 268, 282, 289, 296, 303, 311
Derbyshire Miner, The, 289·
Devon colliery, 40, 68
Disasters, 93, 94
Dockers, 222
Domestic labour, 74-84
Doncaster Panel, 134-5, 140, 154, 155, 158, 162
Dowty Group, 112
Durham Area, 179, 268, 269, 311
Dust control, 295
Dust diseases, 94, 254, 285-6

E

Early retirement, 298-300
Easington colliery, 252
Eighteenth Brumaire of Louis Napoleon (Marx), 301n
Election for N.U.M. general secretaryship, 118, 124-5, 136, 140, 141, 160, 167
Election for N.U.M. presidency; in 1960, 119; 160; in 1971, 166-8; and Union rules, 166
Elections, 118-9
Electoral Reform Society, 265n
Emergency Powers Act, 235
Emphysema, 291
European Coal and Steel Community, 36, 236

F

Facts, meaning of, 67-8
Financial Times, 199, 207
French miners' strike of 1948, 121-2
Fuel policy, Command Paper on, 1965 (Cmnd. 3438), 60-1

G

General election in 1974, 240-7, 251, 256; results, 256n
General Strike, 17, 25, 156, 197
Glasgow Herald, 207, 238n
Glencraig colliery, 124
Glenochil colliery, 40, 41, 48
Grimethorpe colliery, 191, 252
Group No. 1, 268

Group No. 2, 268
Guardian, The, 207, 233n
Gullick Ltd., 111, 112

H

Hardship Allowance, 294-5
Hartley colliery, 94
Harworth colliery, 18-19
Hemsworth colliery, 225
Hours of work; for surface workers, 148-159; 170, 222
Hulton colliery, 94
Human capital, 71, 74, 79, 84
Hydraulic roof supports, 111-113, 115

I

Idealogical apparatus, 57
Incentive scheme, 257, 272-5
Incomes policy, 11, 208, 210, 219, 223-4, 228, 235, 236, 271, 277, 279, 288
Incorrigible Rebel (Horner), 121
Industrial Relations Act, (1971), 10, 171, 176, 221, 222, 224, 230, 244, 247, 249-250, 320
Industrial Re-Organization Corporation, 114
In Place of Strife, (H.M.S.O.), 10
Investing in Coal (1956), 36

K

Keadby Power Station, 197
Kellingley colliery, 71, 140, 251, 310
Kent Area, 8, 11, 118, 133, 163, 185, 222, 268, 276, 279, 280, 282, 283
Kent miners, 186, 192, 219, 275, 311, 314
Kincardine Power Station, 191

L

Labour costs, 30, 74, 103, 179, 230, 288
Labour Government, 10, 29, 32, 40, 41, 56, 57, 58, 60, 62, 64, 65, 66, 108, 122, 136, 221, 269, 270, 272, 286, 288, 290, 291, 296, 305
Labour Party, 161, 241, 243, 247, 256
Labour Research, 200
Labour turnover, 69-70, 85
Langwith colliery, 303

U

Underground, conditions, 38, 44-8; relationships, 90, 92
Uneconomic pits, 60
Unemployment, 13, 15, 172, 221, 305, 308
Union journals, 57, 289
Unofficial strikes; in 1969, 155-9; in 1970, 163-5
Upper Clyde Shipbuilders, 10, 171, 221, 320

V

Vesting-day, 28, 29

W

Wages, 100-101, 158-9, 170, 230, 254
Wages negotiations, 144, 158, 161, 179-180, 218, 223
Wages resolutions, 142, 144; in 1971, 174-5; 222, 270-2
Wales Trades Union Congress, 306, 307
Warsop Main colliery, 3, 198
West Midland Gas Board, 198
Wilberforce Award, 217, 254
Wilberforce Inquiry, 211-7
Wilberforce Report, 92, 217, 254, 272-3
Woolley colliery, 92, 189, 196
Women, 5, 74-5, 79
Women workers; pit brow, 72, 73; on the pit surface, 147

Y

Yorkshire Area, 41, 118, 134-5, 137-140, 144, 145, 154-5, 156, 158,
 163, 185, 189, 191, 222, 224, 226, 267, 268, 269, 272, 278, 279,
 280, 281, 282, 289, 293, 296, 308, 309, 315
Yorkshire Area Council, 134, 154-5, 226, 309, 314
Yorkshire coalfield, 38, 134, 139, 140, 156
Yorkshire Miner, The, 289
Yorkshire miners, 8, 171, 192, 252, 273, 311